YARn WORks
How to Spin, Dye, and Knit Your Own Yarn

W. J. Johnson

Creative Publishing
international

First published in the United States of America by
Creative Publishing international, Inc., a member of
Quayside Publishing Group
400 First Avenue North
Suite 400
Minneapolis, MN 55401
1-800-328-3895
www.creativepub.com
Visit www.Craftside.Typepad.com for a behind-the-scenes peek at our crafty world!

ISBN: 978-1-58923-788-9

Digital edition published in 2014
eISBN: 978-1-61058-928-4

10 9 8 7 6 5 4 3 2 1

Library of Congress Cataloging-in-Publication Data available

Edited by Kari Cornell
Proofreader: Kathy Dragolich
Illustrations: W. J. Johnson
Photographs: W. J. Johnson, James V. Gambone

Printed in China

DEDICATION

*I dedicate this book to my Swedish ancestors,
who spun for necessity so I may spin for joy.*

Contents

71

part 3 Dye Workshop

115

part 4 Knit Workshop

Introduction

Why spin and dye our own yarn? The most obvious answer is, to make the yarn we want in the fiber and colors we desire. The less obvious answer is, to give balance to life. If we value our time as much as materials, it's not a cost savings to create yarn by spinning and dyeing it ourselves. But it can be a "life" savings. For some, it's a way to connect our modern lives with a far-off past that seems simpler and more balanced. Spinning, and all the activities associated with making yarn, force us to slow down and consider the act of creating. To actually make something completely from the original source is so rare. I equate it to gardening in an age of warehouse supermarkets. We may not need to grow our own food to survive, but we may want to do it to feel closer to the source of life. Being a spinner, dyer, and knitter of your own yarn is like growing a garden from seeds—you will be growing your knitted project from its true beginnings. Best of all, the fruits of your labor contain the story of your experience.

Knitting from yarn that was spun and dyed by your own hands is the ultimate experience for fiber lovers. The memories of how the fiber was acquired, where you did the spinning and dyeing—all of these thoughts and emotions unfold as the knitting proceeds. It's impossible to knit anonymously when the fiber carries such strong memories. The spinning and dyeing experience becomes part of your history. The only danger in creating your own yarn from scratch is that you may wish to work only with the yarns you've spun and dyed from now on. Never fear. Continuing to spin, dye, and knit your own yarn will bring you full circle in your love of fibers and yarn.

WHY THIS BOOK?

Yarn Works is indeed a guide for knitters who wish to try spinning and dyeing. But this book will also appeal to current spinners and dyers who want to gain further background and increase creative inspiration in their work. I've written this book from the perspective of the "why" or the science behind the subject, since I believe that a more fulfilling and freeing experience results when someone knows why something does or doesn't work. This book will help answer questions such as these:

- What is the best spin method for a chunky yarn?
- How can I dye this fiber to the color I want?
- Why doesn't this yarn hold its shape when knit?

HOW TO USE THIS BOOK

Yarn Works can be read from front to back, or by individual section. The book is divided into four main sections—Fiber Workshop, Spin Workshop, Dye Workshop, and Knit Workshop—and each main workshop section includes a brief history of the subject. The workshop sections are structured with short, informational workshops that take you through the most essential learning activities for spinning, dyeing, and knitting.

In Fiber Workshop, you learn the specific attributes of various fibers; Spin Workshop examines how to spin them; Dye Workshop discusses how to dye the spun yarn with natural and synthetic dyes; and Knit Workshop continues the exploration of fiber with actual knitted projects from each of the fiber groups (protein, cellulose, synthetic blends), using the actual yarn created and dyed with techniques from the preceding workshops. At the end of each pattern, be sure to read the "Details from Spinning and Dyeing" section. It's here that you'll find the specifics on how the yarn for each project was made. Each of the main workshop sections has a separate appendix containing supporting material for that section. At the very end of the Fiber and Dye Workshop sections is a Creative Workshop in which experimentation is the rule!

So, roll up your sleeves and enter the creative and limitless world of *Yarn Works*. Once you've tried the techniques shown on these pages, I encourage you to go on and create your own workshops based on the knowledge you've gained.

part 1 Fiber Workshop

This section gives an overview of the various fibers available to spinners and knitters today, with an emphasis on the fibers used in the *Yarn Works* projects. Fiber Workshop provides a strong foundation in the fundamentals of appropriate fiber selection so spinners, dyers, and knitters may progress in their work, confident that they've picked the right fiber for the project.

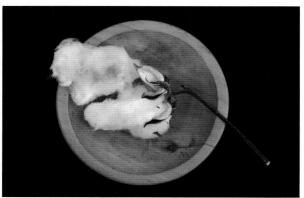

Gandhi saw the rich culture of Indian fiber spinning as a means to celebrate the peasant class and bring India away from British industrial oppression. In the 1920s, he founded a spinning movement in India that raised money to give peasants spinning wheels so they could make yarn for cloth that they could sell to help support their families and raise them up from squalor. Saying, "The act of spinning is the symbol of nonviolence," Gandhi even placed the wheel of a spinning wheel at the center of his party's flag—where it remains part of the national flag of India to this day. But beyond the political and economic applications of spinning, Gandhi also spun every evening for its "rhythm, music, poetry, romance ... and spiritual solace."
Pictorial Press Ltd/Alamy

"There is no yajna (sacrifice) greater than spinning calculated to bring peace to the troubled spirit ..."

—Gandhi

A BRIEF HISTORY OF FIBER

Since fiber is a material that disintegrates relatively quickly, little is known of the earliest fibers used by people. We assume that these early fibers were derived from local plants and animals. Wool is known as one of the first spun fibers, along with plants such as flax and nettle.

The origin of silk (before 2600 BC) is linked to a Chinese legend about an empress who, while sitting under a mulberry tree, had a silkworm cocoon unexpectedly drop into her cup of tea. She noticed how the fiber that floated from the dissolving cocoon made a very fine thread—and so began the silk industry. Although it's uncertain whether this tale is true, we do know that silk was a greatly guarded secret in China for centuries before it was carried along the Silk Road (a trading route that reached from Asia to Europe and Africa from 200 BC to AD 200) and subsequently spread around the world.

Flax is an ancient plant with a history that stretches back before recorded time. Flax has had a tremendous impact on human life, not only as a fiber source for sturdy clothing, but also as a food source that is extraordinarily nutritious. Every garden of preindustrial times contained a patch of flax just for household use—the seeds for food and the stalks as fiber to spin. It is because of flax that flyer spinning wheels (sometimes called "flax" wheels) exist. These wheels were developed just for spinning flax more efficiently.

Cotton has also been in our spinning baskets since before written history. Archaeological evidence shows that cotton was grown in the Middle East and Americas since about 5000 BC, but there is no clear historical record of its origin. It may have been indigenous to the Americas, India, Asia, and Africa. Nevertheless, prior to 1793, flax remained the most sought-after fiber for warm-weather clothing because, even with flax's multiple processing steps, it was still produced for less cost than handpicked and teased cotton. When the cotton gin was patented in 1794 as a means to expediently gin (remove the seeds of) the North American variety of upland cotton, flax was quickly shown the back door and cotton came raging in, making comfortable clothing more affordable for the average person.

Sheep's wool was also a part of the prehistorical fiber record, but it became more common during the Roman era, when the wool industry was born. As the Roman Empire spread into today's Europe, more sheep became domesticated and bred, further advancing the influence of wool. The popularity of wool continued beyond the age of the Romans until today—as wool arguably has become the most sought-after fiber in the world. As the demand for wool grows, more is learned every day about breeding for the best wool fiber qualities. It's fairly certain that we haven't seen the end of how this fiber can enrich our lives.

By the 1900s, test tubes became the incubators for new fibers. From nylon to polyester, modern-day fibers bear the mark of the scientist, sometimes with their very own trademark—the modern attempt to guard our new fiber "silks." But in the end, these new fibers are mostly mimics and wannabe's of the real thing— natural protein and cellulose fibers.

SELECTING THE BEST FIBER FOR A PROJECT

We live in a time of phenomenal worldwide fiber access. With such access comes wonderful opportunities—and challenges. This section walks you through what you need to know to pick the perfect fiber for your project.

Step One: Choose a Project

Of course, you may jump right in and start working with any fiber that suits your fancy, but if you want to have the most success in your spinning, dyeing, and knitting, it's smart to decide what you want to make before you select the fiber. For instance, garments that are worn next to the skin are best created with fibers that are gentle to the skin. And those meant for hard use are best created with fibers that can stand up to the rigors of their final purpose.

Detail of yarn, showing twist

Can Your Fiber Do the Twist?

To be spun, a fiber needs to be able to retain a twist when the force that has been turning it (the wheel or whorl pulley) has been removed. For some fibers, like wool, the twist is naturally held. Other fibers, such as flax and hemp, hold their twist best when moistened. The twist in cotton needs to be set under tension or it won't stay in the yarn. Synthetic fibers have been scientifically designed to enhance the twist for a particular yarn or end use, so their twist qualities vary depending on the fiber.

Hint for Beginning Spinners: Try Wool!

The best fiber for beginning spinners is wool. It's the most forgiving of novice pulling and tearing, and the least cantankerous to control. Of all the wool options for beginners, a medium wool (such as Corriedale) is the best since it's easily spun into soft, balanced yarn. After a medium wool, move on to a fine wool like Merino. After Merino, consider a blend of silk and wool, followed by silk alone. At this point, try short fibers, as your ability to control the spin will be well tested. Start with short protein fibers, like angora and cashmere. Then experience even shorter cellulose fibers, like cotton. Before you know it, you'll be ready for the unique spin process of flax and hemp (which is often spun wet), and you'll be spinning like a master!

Step Two: Determine What You're After in a Yarn

First determine the characteristics you're looking for in a yarn (softness, durability, dyeability, etc.), then determine which fibers most closely match the characteristics you've listed and will spin, dye, and knit to the qualities you want in the yarn.

CHARACTERISTICS TO CONSIDER IN FIBER SELECTION

- staple length—the total measurement of a fully grown lock of fiber when stretched.
- crimp—the natural wave formation of the fiber. In a sheep's wool, the crimp helps to determine the best way to spin a fiber. Not all fibers have crimp.
- fiber diameter—the width of any given strand of fiber. This is measured as a micron count or a Bradford count. The finer the diameter of a fiber, the shorter the staple length tends to be.
- strength—the tensile strength of a fiber. A fiber's strength determines the ability of a fiber to hold together when being pulled in different directions.
- elasticity—the ability of a fiber (and knitted material) to return to its original state after being stretched.
- durability—the ability of a fiber to resist abrasion.
- comfort—whether a given fiber produces a warming effect (heat retaining) or cooling effect (heat/moisture wicking).
- natural color—a fiber with a light natural color like white or cream can be dyed to a truer color than a fiber with a darker natural color like gray or brown.
- dyeability—ability of the fiber to accept dye particles, mainly determined by the molecular structure of the particular fiber.
- stability—the ability of a fiber to hold a twist. A stable yarn is less likely to stretch out and "grow" between washings than an unstable yarn.

MEET THE FIBERS

Now that you have guidelines for what to look for in selecting a fiber, it's time to explore the specific fiber choices.

Protein Fibers

Protein fibers are chemically composed of protein compounds. Most originate from animals, such as wool, alpaca, silk (worm), and cashmere (goat), but some manufactured fibers are also composed of protein compounds such as soy and casein (milk).

Note: See Beginning to Spin (page 51), Spin Methods (page 57) and The Finishing Act: Wrapping Up the Spin (page 65) for more on the prep, spinning, and finishing techniques mentioned in this section.

WOOL

Wool is sheep fiber. It's not rabbit, yak, alpaca, or goat. It's just the fiber from sheep. Despite all of the advancements in textile science over the past century, there isn't a fiber that can compare to wool—the fiber of the gods.

Wool Qualities

Let's break down the wool fiber to see how it's truly unique. First of all, wool is a protein fiber with growth scales. That alone is not unique. All fibers grown by animals are protein fibers, and some of these also have scales on their hair shaft. But sheep have the most—literally thousands of epithelial cells (scales) that swell and open when exposed to water and heat. If these scaly hair shafts are agitated while wet and hot, the scales grab each other, and felting results. Felting qualities vary among different sheep breeds because of differences in hair shaft/scale structures.

Wool also has a high grease factor compared with other protein fibers. The grease is caused by sebaceous glands, which secrete a greasy substance onto the hair follicles as they grow. This substance protects the sheep's skin and hair, giving it waterproofing qualities and protection from the environment. Chemically, the substance is a wax.

1. **Softness.** The feeling of softness is mainly due to scales on the hair shaft of the particular sheep breed. Fine wool sheep, like Merino, have many very small scales. Coarse wool sheep, like Lincoln, have fewer scales that are much larger.

   The softness or coarseness of the wool from different breeds is not only related to the number and size of the scales, but also to the structure of the hair shaft itself. In coarse wool fleece, a canal called the medulla runs the length of the fiber within the hair shaft. While this canal is common in sheep with coarse fleece, Merino sheep have been bred to eliminate the medulla. The lack of this stiff, structural piece is one of the reasons why Merino wool is so soft and delicate.

2. **Elasticity.** When dry, a wool fiber can stretch up to 30 percent of its length, and when wet it can stretch up to 70 percent, yet it returns to its original shape when dry. This same elasticity can be seen when wool is compressed. The property of crimp in the fiber and the structure of the hair shaft are the reasons wool has great elasticity. This quality gives resiliency to garments, allowing them to stretch or be packed tightly and yet hold their shape well when normal conditions return.

3. **Absorbency.** The chemical structure of wool attracts water molecules that the wool cells subsequently absorb.

4. **Warmth.** Air pockets formed within the crimps of wool help to create a feeling of warmth. Another factor of warmth is due to the prickly hair shafts that stick up out of the wool mass. When a wool garment is worn, the shafts poke us and create action in our nerve endings, resulting in more blood flow and a warming sensation. In addition, wool can actually *create* heat when it's wet, due to the heat that's produced when water molecules and the wool fiber microscopically collide.

A sheep, source of the most popular fiber among spinners and knitters alike.

Allergic to wool?

Maybe not. You may just have skin or nerve sensitivity from the prickly wool hair shafts. Some people have allergic reactions to the vegetation and/or pesticides that may be in the wool but an actual allergy to wool is quite rare.

Angora

5. **Fire resistance.** Wool only smolders, it doesn't burn. Again, water is the reason. Because water molecules are continuously held to the cellular structure of the fiber, when exposed to an open flame, wool responds by producing steam.

6. **Dyeability.** Wool accepts dyes very well, partially due to its exceptional absorbency. Dyes that best respond to wool are the high pH acid dyes. Natural dyes, which use mordants that raise the pH of the dye bath, also work well on wool.

7. **Spinnability.** Spinners favor wool due to its crimp, fiber length, and all of the factors listed above. It's just so darn easy to spin! Plus, with the great variety just within the 200-plus wool breeds, you can sample nearly every type of spinning method without ever leaving the sheep.

Follow the processing and spinning of Hanna's fleece—a part Corriedale, Romney, Lincoln, and Border Leicester sheep—our subject in the Knit Workshop projects: Vallkulla, Hanna, and Sami (pages 120–134); and follow the processing and spinning of wool roving in the Gabriel Knit Workshop (pages 135–138). Learn how to dye wool in the Natural Dye Workshops and Acid Dye Workshop (pages 92–102).

OTHER PROTEIN FIBERS

This book could have easily been just about spinning, dyeing, and knitting wool, but then you would miss out on the rest of the vast menu of protein fiber options. So let's see what else is out there and explore their unique qualities for spinning, dyeing, and knitting.

Note: Protein fibers dye best with either acid synthetic dyes or natural dyes using an acid pH mordant and dye bath.

Angora

Angora is the fiber from Angora rabbits. Plucked angora is considered premium for hand spinning since it is the complete long fiber, from base to tip. Angora fiber has three components: bristles (long and stiff guard hairs), down (fine, lightweight, and the highest percentage of the coat hairs), and awn (another guard hair that is between the bristles and down in size).

The fibers have a core consisting of hollow chambers that enhance warmth, making angora eight times warmer than wool. The hair surface has a tight scale pattern, creating softness and a slippery surface that produces a halo effect when the fiber is spun and knit.

Angora doesn't have good elasticity or memory (memory is a fiber's ability to return to its original shape after being stretched or compressed), so choose knitting projects that won't suffer from stretching or sagging—or blend angora with an elastic fiber such as wool to encourage more elasticity. It dyes well, but because of the variety of fiber types in the coat, angora doesn't take dye evenly. Angora blends well with other fine fibers and felts well. It often doesn't need cleaning or carding and is best spun as an even yarn with a high twist that is softened and strengthened by fulling after spinning. (See page 67 for fulling process.)

ABOVE It's really no wonder that the Swedish Bohus garments were so popular in northern regions during the 1940s–1960s, since many were knit with angora. The lightweight fiber was a welcome and elegant alternative to traditional heavy Nordic wools. We are rediscovering the beauty of angora fiber today, with the resurgence of interest in Bohus knitting.

Bison/Buffalo

This fiber is sheared from slaughtered buffalo or plucked from fence lines and bushes. (Shearing a live buffalo is not advised!) Often it's not necessary to wash the fiber, but if you do, wash it gently. The fiber used for spinning is the downy undercoat—strong, soft, elastic, and warm. Because of its great elasticity, this fiber is harder to block in knitting. It has a dark natural color (rarely white) that can be overdyed to rich tones. Buffalo blends well with other fine fibers. The down, being a short fiber, is often spun with a high-twist woolen technique. It should be fulled after spinning to strengthen the yarn.

Camelid Family

All camelids have a number of nonmedullated (hollow) fibers, providing light-weight warmth. If purchased as a raw fleece, these fibers have no grease but may have vegetative matter that needs to be shaken or perhaps washed out.

Alpaca. There are two types of alpaca: Huacaya (a dense fiber with a wave crimp and elasticity) and Suri (no crimp, long, soft, and lustrous with a beautiful drape). Alpaca fiber is strong and durable, and it creates a warm garment—warmer than wool. It blends well with other fibers and is bred in a wide variety of natural colors—some of which overdye beautifully. Although Huacaya is often spun with a woolen technique and Suri with a worsted technique, the fiber preparation determines the best spin method. Follow the processing and spinning of alpaca in the Knit Workshop Project Róisín (page 139).

Camel. The Bactrian (two-humped) camel is the one that provides fiber for spinning. The best spinning fibers are found in the undercoat, which is soft and fine, with great thermal properties. The camel's coat is shed in the spring in large tufts, and the fibers are hand gathered. The fiber has little elasticity. Camel overdyes to rich hues and blends well with other fine fibers, including wool. Card it with fine cotton carders, but instead of making a typical rolag (a rolag is a carded fiber preparation, see page 28) for spinning, roll the fiber across the horizontal width of the carder so the fibers remain more parallel for a semi-worsted spin.

Llama. Llamas have a hair that is similar to alpaca, but weaker. The llama has a dual coat of soft down and long guard hair. The overall coat lacks crimp and elasticity, but has a beautiful drape. The down is a warm, lustrous fiber and has the best dyeability of all the hairs in the llama's coat. Llama blends well with other fine fibers. The two types of fibers in the coat are often separated and the woolen down is spun with a woolen spin and the guard hairs as worsted.

Guanaco and Vicuña. The guanaco is an ancestor of the llama, and the vicuña is an ancestor of the alpaca. Both have soft, lightweight, warm fibers with great strength. Vicuña has been measured as the softest fiber on earth. Both guanaco and vicuña are wild animals and are classified as endangered species, as a result of being killed for their fiber. Recently, an ancient Incan method of vicuña fiber harvesting has been encouraged, in which the harvesters round up the animals and shear them, releasing them again to the wild. Since these animals are endangered, the fibers are not readily available to spinners, although this is changing as vicuña are starting to be bred in the United States. Guanaco and vicuña

Alpaca

Camel

Llama

Guanaco

Vicuña

Cashmere

don't have natural white coats, but their fiber can be overdyed to create rich colors. Both fibers blend well with other fine fibers, and because of their high cost, they are often spun in a blend. The fiber preparation (carded or combed) determines the spin method for both of these fibers, but they are most often spun from a puni preparation (see page 166) with a high-twist, woolen spin.

Cashmere (Cashmere Goat)

This is a luxuriously soft, fine fiber with a matte appearance that comes from the downy undercoat of the cashmere goat, which originates from the Kashmir region. The best cashmere comes from combings made during the spring molting season. The nonmedullated (hollow) hairs in cashmere provide air pockets that add to its lightweight warmth. The raw fleece should be cleaned very gently. Cashmere blends well with other fibers and dyes well, although dyeing it can affect the softness. It should be fulled after spinning to strengthen the yarn. The fiber preparation determines the spin method. It's most often spun woolen to enhance the softness and warmth.

There are two main blends of cashmere. Protein fiber blends created by cross-breeding have fiber characteristics corresponding to the animals from which they were bred:

- Cashgora—from the cashmere and angora goats, cashgora is typically a longer fiber and not as fine as pure cashmere.
- Pygora—from a pygmy and angora goat cross-breeding, pygora has a fine, cashmerelike down from the pygmy goat and long locks from the angora goat.

Mohair

Mohair comes from the angora goat, named after the province of Ankara, Turkey. Mohair grows quickly, so goats are sheared twice a year. The wool is lustrous, strong, and elastic, with the youngest fibers (also called "kid mohair") being the softest. Mohair has some nonmedullated fibers that add to its fineness. The raw fleece has grease, so it's advisable to wash it prior to spinning. Mohair is notable for its great dyeability. It blends well with wool. Mohair may be spun woolen or worsted, but its fiber qualities are enhanced by a worsted spin.

Mohair

Qiviut

Yak

Qiviut (Muskox)

Qiviut is a seasonal shedder, blowing its coat in large pieces in the spring. The downy undercoat of domesticated qiviut is harvested by combing during the shedding season. It often doesn't need washing prior to spinning, but needs to be well prepared to separate the coarse guard hairs from the favored down. Qiviut is elastic, eight times warmer than wool, and softer than cashmere. It blends well with other fibers. Fulling after spinning is recommended. The natural coat is typically dark in color and often not dyed, but it does take dye well and overdyes to dark, rich colors—although dyeing may affect the softness of the fiber. The fiber preparation determines the spin method, but the down, being a short fiber, it is often spun with a high-twist, woolen technique.

Yak

As a member of the bovine (cattle) family, yak fibers are rather short, but yaks have longer hair than most bovine, averaging 1.2 in. (3 cm). The spinning fiber is the downy undercoat that is shed in the spring and collected by combing. It doesn't need to be washed before spinning, but it should be fulled after spinning. Natural white/cream yak fibers dye well, and other natural colors overdye to rich tones. Yak combines well with other fine fibers. The fiber preparation (carded or combed) determines the spin method, but because it is a short fiber, a high-twist, woolen technique is often used.

Cat/Dog (Chatgora and Chiengora)

Now we're talking about local fiber—maybe right in your own house. Certain breeds of cat and dog have a downy undercoat that is wonderful for spinning. The fiber can be gathered by plucking or combing while the animal is shedding. It can be washed prior to spinning, but often spins best if not washed. (The dog/cat smell should come out of the fiber/yarn after a thorough washing.) The fibers dye fairly well, depending on the breed and natural color. They're often blended with wool and make a fabric with a fiber bloom similar to angora. The fiber preparation determines the spin method, but a woolen spin is usually the most appropriate.

Silk cocoons, before
degumming process

SILK: THE OTHER NATURAL PROTEIN FIBER

Silk doesn't come from a coat that's sheared or combed off an animal, but it is instead spun by a silkworm and boiled to release the fiber from the silkworm's cocoon. The silkworm is created by one of two primary types of silk moths:

The Bombyx Mori produces silk that is called "bombyx" or "cultivated." This moth is fed only mulberry leaves, which give its silk a bright white color and a fine micron count. The Tussah moth produces what is called is called "wild" silk, since it's fed a diet of oak, mulberry, and other tree leaves from the wild. This moth creates a fiber that ranges from off-white to brown, depending on the amount of tannin in its leaf diet. Tussah silk is about twice the diameter of bombyx/cultivated silk.

Silk fiber is actually a construction of two silk filaments in a fibroin solution encased by a protein called sericin. The silkworm shoots the fibroin solution from two glands on either side of its mouth and simultaneously twists its head in a figure eight formation, to create a single, continuous strand of fiber from the two filaments. The strands of fiber eventually encase the silkworm and form a silk cocoon. Silk fiber is extremely fine and translucent, triangular in cross section and slightly twisted, enhancing the reflection of light on its surface.

Silk Qualities

1. **Strength.** Silk is the strongest natural protein fiber, rivaling steel in tensile strength. But water is to silk like Kryptonite is to Superman. Silk loses its strength when wet because of weakened hydrogen bonds in the filaments. Although it has great tensile strength when dry, the smooth-sided fibers don't have a very strong abrasion resistance.

2. **Elasticity/plasticity.** Silk is more plastic than elastic. This is felt when spinning with silk. The fibers slide and stretch past each other like a crazy elastic silly putty.

3. **Absorbency.** Silk can absorb 30 percent of its weight in water before it feels wet, making it a very comfortable fiber to wear in all seasons.

4. **Durable.** Even though silk has a very delicate feel, it's resistant to mold and mildew, and it's usually not bothered by clothes moths.

5. **Resilience.** When silk fiber is forced into a tight wad, it will quickly spring open. Parachutes have been made out of silk due to this resilience and great tensile strength.

6. **Warm/cool.** Silk is a poor conductor of heat, making it more comfortable in both summer and winter. It repells heat in the summer and contains heat to the body in the winter.

7. **Dyeability.** Silk is a fantastic fiber to dye, but it is easily damaged by acids, so care must be taken when working with acid dyes to be sure the acid fixer (vinegar or citric acid) doesn't sit on the fiber for very long. It also dyes well with natural dyes and is the only protein fiber that can be effectively dyed in an alkaline fiber-reactive dye bath.

Silk is a good fiber for spinners who have learned some control of the wheel and their spin. Tussah is the best silk to start spinning since it has a larger diameter and a less slippery surface than cultivated silk. Spinning with a hard twist brings out the luster of silk. The wheel tension needs to be lightened and a smaller whorl used. Learn more about spinning different silk preparations in FA-5 (page 165). Follow the preparation and spinning of silk hankies (a bundle of silk cocoons stretched into a square formation) in the Knitting Workshop project Sylph (page 146). Follow the process of dyeing silk in the Acid Dye Workshop (page 100).

AZLON FIBERS

Azlon fibers are manufactured fibers derived from regenerated, naturally occurring protein, casein (milk) or soy. Like silk, both casein and soy can be dyed with acid, natural, or fiber-reactive dyes, but the colors will be not as rich as they are on silk.

Casein (Milk)

Casein, sometimes called "milk fiber," is chemically processed from milk protein and extruded through spinnerets into fiber form. It may seem to be part of the recent eco movement, but casein was first created in the 1930s as an alternative fiber to wool. It has many properties similar to wool and has the feel of silk, but it mildews easily. Care must be taken when dyeing casein since it is quite weak when wet. The fiber preparation determines the spin method, although its qualities lend themselves to a semi-worsted spin.

Soy

Developed in the 1930s as an alternative fiber to silk, soy fiber is made with oil from the processed protein of the soy cake. The oil is combined with other solutions to make a material that is extruded through spinnerets into fiber. It contains the softness and luster of silk and blends nicely with silk. Soy is often blended with more elastic fibers to create lightweight knits with elasticity. The fiber preparation determines the spin method, but the fiber qualities suggest it be spun worsted.

Cellulose (Plant) Fibers

Cellulose fibers are usually not the first fiber choice for beginning spinners, since their structure and fiber length can be a challenge to spin. But they are great fibers to help develop spinning expertise. When you have the command of a cellulose fiber, you will truly be awarded the title of Spinster! There are two main types of cellulose fibers: seed hair and bast.

CELLULOSE/SEED HAIR FIBER

Cotton

Cotton grows on 3- to 6-ft-high (1 m to 2 m) bushes. The spinning fiber comes from hairs in the seedpod of the plant's flower. When the flower dies back and the seed pod (also called "cotton boll") ripens, the pod splits open to reveal the cotton fibers attached to between five and eleven seeds, depending on the cotton variety. When safe inside the cotton boll, the fiber structure is essentially a tube filled with a sap material. When the cotton boll bursts open from the growing pressure of the fibers, the walls of the tubes collapse and become ribbonlike and twisted as the seed hairs dry out. It's this convoluted shape of the fiber that gives friction and spinnability to cotton.

Note: Pima (long-staple) cotton is more easily removed from the seeds than upland (short, hairy) cotton. Being able to more easily remove the seeds was one reason the cotton gin was a wonderful invention for the U.S. cotton industry. The United States was (and still is) a primary grower of the upland variety.

Depending on the variety of cotton, the fiber varies in staple length from about ½ in. (1.3 cm) to as much as 2½ in. (6.3 cm), and is fine with little variation in diameter. There are three major types of cotton for hand spinners to choose between: Pima, with the longest staple, up to 2½ in. (6.3 cm), is also called Egyptian cotton, although there is an American variety, too. Upland, with medium staples of ⅞ to 1⁵⁄₁₆ in. (2 cm to 3 cm), is considered to be American cotton. Colored cotton (available in brown/red, green, and cream) has a short staple of ½ in. (1.3 cm). (A recently created organic colored cotton [FoxFiber®] has a longer staple and comes in a wide range of colors.)

Note: Colored cotton isn't a new fiber. It's been in the Americas (Peru, Central America, Mexico) since at least 5000 BC. Before the Civil War, slaves in the United States could only grow brown and green cotton in their gardens because the plantation owners feared the slaves might sell white cotton if they grew it. The last laugh is on the plantation owners, since colored cotton has become a highly sought-after variety!

ABOVE Cotton boll, detail. Cotton has been called "white gold" in the southeastern United States, where cotton was an important part of the economy beginning in the late 1700s. And like the flax seed, cotton seed is of note for more than just textile reasons. It's also greatly valued for its significant nutritional qualities.

Cotton Qualities

1. **Strong.** Cotton is a resilient fiber. It even gains strength when wet (up to 120 percent of its dry strength) due to the water-bonding structure of the fiber.

2. **Absorbent and wicking.** Cotton likes water and absorbs it quickly, making the wearer more comfortable in hot weather.

3. **Good heat conductor.** Cotton conducts heat energy away from the fiber, making it a great hot-weather fiber.

4. **Inelastic.** Cotton will not return to its original state after being stretched unless exposed to the right conditions for shrinking, namely moisture and heat.

5. **Comfortable.** Because of cotton's twisted shape, it makes only random contact with the skin, and that type of contact is more compatible with the nerve endings and general physiology of human skin, making cotton more comfortable to wear.

Colored cotton bundles
(left: green cotton; center:
red cotton; right: white cotton)

Acids, mold, bacteria, and mildew destroy cotton, but it's fairly resistant to alkaline conditions. It dyes well with fiber-reactive and natural dyes with alkaline mordants/baths. Acid dyes damage the fiber. A good cotton yarn should be smooth and even in spin and ply. Cotton blends well with man-made fibers. Due to its short length, cotton is often spun woolen with a high twist.

Hand spinners have many different types of cotton preparations to choose from, including

- tufts of cotton taken directly from the cotton boll
- ginned cotton
- puni preparations
- prepared top

Follow the processing and spinning of cotton top in the Knit Workshop project Bene (page 149). Follow the dyeing process in the Natural Dye Workshop (page 92) and the Fiber-Reactive Dye Workshop: Cellulose/Bast Fibers (page 103).

OTHER CELLULOSE/SEED HAIR FIBERS

Other fibers derived from the seed hair of plants are butterfly weed, milkweed, cattail, and cottonwood. These fibers have very short staple lengths of ¼ to ½ in. (6 mm to 1.3 cm), depending on the plant, making them very difficult to hand spin.

CELLULOSE/BAST FIBERS

Bast fibers are the actual fibers of plant stalks. The fibers are typically very long, often the length of the stalk, and fairly complicated physical processing is required to extract the fibers.

Flax (Linen)

There are two types of flax. One type of flax is grown for its seed, which is used to make linseed oil and has many nutritional uses. This flax has multiple branches to encourage more flower heads. Linen flax, the second type of flax, has fewer branches and is planted closer together to promote long, straight stalks that

A flax flower in bloom

The Fabulous Language of Flax Processing

When flax is ready to be harvested, the plant is pulled out of the ground with its roots intact. The stems are tied into bundles called "beets" and set upright in "chapels" to dry outdoors. Next, the seed pods are "rippled" off (pulled off with a flax hackle) and the fiber is "retted" (laid out in the weather for the stems to slightly rot—*ret* means "rot.") When the retting is done, the fiber is dried again in flat "stooks" and is now ready to process for spinning. Spinning processing involves: "breaking" the dried fiber to break the woody stems (the "boon") from the fiber strands; "scutching" (scraping the strands with a wooden knife to clean off more boon); then "hackling" the strands (combing them with a hackle comb into separated spinnable strands); and finally the strands are wrapped into a "strick" (a tied bundle) for later spinning.

mature to a height of 2 to 3 ft (61 cm to 1 m). Both plants have delicate, light blue flowers and seeds that are edible. Linen flax enters the spinning wheel as "flax," and as soon as it hits the bobbin, it's called "linen."

The actual spinning fiber of the flax plant lies within a ring that is inside the outer bark and outside the woody core of the stem and extends continuously along the entire length of the plant—from root to tip. Microscopically, the cells of this long fiber have large overlapping pieces that are held together with a gummy substance. The fiber is thick, with bumps where the cells overlap. The bumps catch each other and help to hold the fiber together in spinning. The staple length ranges from 4 in. to 3 ft (10 cm to 1 m). Its color is typically light brown to a grayish blond, depending on the growing and retting conditions (see The Fabulous Language of Flax Processing sidebar). Flax can be bleached to a bright white.

There are two different kinds of processed flax lengths:

1. Line—fibers that are as long as the plant was tall. They are bundled into "stricks" (long hanks of flax fiber) and placed on distaffs for spinning.
2. Tow—the shorter fibers that broke away from the long line preparation.

Much of homegrown flax ends up as tow, and most flax fiber for sale in shops is line. Flax available as top is made from cut lengths of line flax.

Flax Qualities

1. **Strong.** The long polymers of the flax fiber give it great tensile strength. Flax is stronger when wet—about 20 percent stronger than when dry.
2. **Absorbent and wicking.** Flax readily absorbs moisture and quickly wicks it out of the fiber.
3. **Good heat conductor.** Flax fiber has better heat resistance and conductivity (ability to transfer heat out of the fiber) than any other fiber. This is why linen is the ideal summer textile.
4. **Comfortable.** Because of its heat conductivity and smooth surface, linen is extraordinarily comfortable. But the yarn or cloth must first undergo a boiling treatment to bring out the softness. The more linen is washed in hot water, the softer it gets.
5. **Inelastic.** If flax is stretched too much, the fiber is damaged and can break.
6. **Luster.** Because of its gummy wax coating, flax has a natural luster.

Due to the heavy weight of the fiber, flax is usually spun fine, with a slight twist—making a smooth, even surface. Line is spun directly from the strick, often as a singles yarn. Because the fiber has a slight left-handed spiral and a tendency to lie in a left-handed direction, it's best to spin singles with an S-twist. (See Spin Methods [page 57] for more information on twist direction.) Tow is carded, spun semi-woolen, and plied. Flax is spun best wet since that spreads the fiber's gummy coating like glue along the entire surface of the yarn and strengthens it. If spun dry, the yarn will have a hairy appearance.

Since it's damaged by acid, linen must only be dyed with fiber-reactive or an alkaline-based natural dye process. It resists mildew, but isn't safe if stored in a humid environment, so be sure to wind your yarn off the bobbin as soon as you are done spinning if you spun with a wet method. Even though the seeds are yummy, few pests bother to eat the fiber. Flax is a remarkable but often-ignored fiber in our spinning baskets and a unique fiber to spin.

Follow the processing and spinning of flax top in The Knit Workshop project Liv (page 152). Follow the process of dyeing flax in the Fiber-Reactive Dye Workshop: Cellulose/Bast Fibers (page 103).

OTHER COMMON CELLULOSE/BAST FIBERS

All of the following fibers must only be dyed with a fiber-reactive or alkaline-based natural dye process.

Bamboo

The bast version is processed like flax and available as top. It is considered to be more ecologically friendly than extruded bamboo (see Cellulosic Fibers on page 25). Bamboo makes a soft knit. Spin it like flax.

Burning for the Truth:
How to Test Yarn for General Fiber Content

Select a safe location, close to a sink or water source, and take safety precautions, such as wearing goggles, controlling the flame, and using tweezers to hold the fiber, so you and others aren't hurt in the experiment. Do the test in a small bowl lined with aluminum foil so you can throw out the mess after the test. You only need to test 1 to 2 in. (2.5 cm to 5.0 cm) of the yarn. Use tweezers to hold the yarn sample and light one end of the yarn on fire. Evaluate the results according to the following characteristics:

1. **Natural protein:** Smells like burning hair and turns to a black ashlike mass. It will also be fairly hard to ignite and keep aflame. Wool is harder to ignite than silk, for example.

2. **Cellulose (seed):** Burns easily, glows as the flame dies, and the fiber turns to ash.

3. **Cellulose (bast):** Takes longer to ignite than cotton and becomes brittle close to the flame.

4. **Cellulosic (manufactured from cellulose material):** Doesn't extinguish as quickly as cotton and bast, also leaves a crusty ash.

5. **Synthetic:** Melts when you try to burn it, so be prepared for oozy, melting plastic and a fairly nasty smell. The final result will be a hard, plastic-looking black mass.

Hemp

Coarser and longer than flax, hemp is processed in a similar manner to flax. The fiber length varies from 3 to 13 ft (1 m to 4 m). Hemp fibers have a right-handed direction and are best spun as Z-twist singles. It's difficult to find unprocessed hemp, but many fiber shops carry it in prepared top form. It's still illegal to grow hemp in the United States unless a huge number of regulations are followed. Most of North American hemp comes from Canada where it's more easily (legally) grown. Hemp is often blended with other fibers for knitting. Spin it wet like flax.

Nettle

This is another ancient fiber that lost its popularity when cotton took over. As a wild plant, it's very difficult to gather enough to actually spin. The sting of the nettle has also been a hindrance to harvesting. (The sting comes from a hollow needlelike hair that actually contains a venomous solution.) Nevertheless, there's a recent movement to reintroduce nettle fiber, also called "puwa," as an ecologically alternative fiber. The nettle fiber is hollow and has natural insulating qualities, depending on the way the fiber is spun (tight spin for summer garments and loose spin for winter). Spin it wet like flax.

Ramie

Ramie is actually a nettle, but of the nonstinging variety. Like flax, ramie is one of the strongest natural fibers and exhibits even greater strength when wet, although it's not as strong as flax. It has little elasticity and, when dry, is quite brittle and stiff. The long, fine, processed ramie fibers are naturally white and lustrous, with a silky appearance. Ramie has a soft feel, and its permeable surface structure dyes better than flax. But there can be variation in the feel of ramie due to variations in the stalk surface: Some stalks produce a silklike fiber and some are coarser— like coarse flax. Because of this variability and its inherent stiffness, ramie is often blended with other fibers (typically cotton) to give an enhanced softness. One-hundred-percent ramie is wet spun like flax or carded with fine carders and spun with a woolen spin.

   Note: Cellulose/bast fibers may also be processed from the leaves of plants such as agave, banana, New Zealand flax, pineapple, raffia, yucca, and sisal. Leaf fibers can have a staple length of 3 to 5 ft (1 m to 1.5 m), depending on the plant. They are processed like bast fibers but are not commonly available to hand spinners.

CELLULOSIC FIBERS

These are fibers derived from plant material and turned into a spinnable state by chemically processing the plant material into a pulp form called "viscose" (chemically resembling cotton), adding some liquid chemical elements, and then extruding the liquid into a fibrous form. Cellulosic fibers are created from plants that either cannot be directly turned into fiber in their natural form, or their natural form doesn't have a fiber that's as useful as an extruded version. They have the real, or perceived, properties of natural fibers, but exist only through a manufacturing process. These cellulosic fibers (and their cellulose sources) are acetate (from cotton or wood pulp), rayon (wood pulp), bamboo, banana leaves, lyocell/Tencel® (wood based), SeaCell® (wood and seaweed based), modal (wood pulp specifically from beech trees), sugar cane, pineapple leaves, and paper (wood) —and more are being created all the time. Since the fiber is manufactured, the staple length is determined by the fiber it is most trying to mimic. They commonly have 50 percent *less* strength when wet, are generally limp fibers, distort easily, and don't hold their shape well in knitted garments. In other qualities, they are similar to cotton and are dyed, spun, and finished like cotton. The spinning preparation depends on the fiber characteristics of crimp, length, and fineness that the scientists have bestowed on them. They are often blended with natural fibers for knitting.

   Note: It's important to know the impact we are making on the world due to our love of fibers. Even though cellulosic fibers are derived from renewable plant material and are seemingly an ecologically smart choice compared with a synthetic fiber, there is some concern about the ecological feasibility of extruded fibers. The main issue is whether the extrusion process creates pollution and/or the misuse of water resources. This is an issue currently undergoing a good deal of investigation. Become knowledgeable and weigh all the factors before deciding what is an acceptable level of ecological intrusion for you. Since the industry is constantly changing (we hope by improving its environmental impact), being an educated user is good practice.

Two synthetic fibers side by side: left: Firestar; right: Angelina. Firestar is a glittery, metallic-fused nylon that can be added to creative spinning as a novelty element. It's sold dyed and undyed. The undyed version can be dyed with protein fibers, creating a fun, sparkly yarn blend. As nylon has Firestar, polyester has Angelina—a mylar material that is actually a thin plastic film with some metallic elements. Like Firestar, Angelina is used in creative spinning as a novelty filler and sparkle agent. But it's best to get Angelina predyed since it has a polyester base that requires toxic disperse dyes.

Synthetic Fibers

Okay. You're probably saying, "Are you nuts? Synthetic fibers to spin and knit? Who in the world would want to work with nasty synthetics?" Well, there are a few spinners who can't work with natural fibers due to allergies or sensitivities, and some spinners who like to incorporate a bit of synthetic fiber in their spinning for yarn strength or sparkly glitz. For the rest, this workshop reveals a bit more about the commercial synthetic knitting yarns we sometimes use.

Note: Synthetic fibers share some similarities to the cellulosic fibers that are creating such a buzz among the eco-conscious these days. The main difference between synthetic and cellulosic fibers is that synthetic fibers have a petrochemical base and cellulosic fibers have a plant pulp base—otherwise, they are both chemically manufactured, extruded fibers with all the inherent concerns regarding waste material and chemical processing.

Even though we may knit with acrylic and polyester yarns, hand-spinning versions of these fibers aren't commonly available. So for now, our synthetic hand-spinning experience is pretty much limited to nylon.

NYLON FIBER

No scientific name here. The origin of the word *nylon* comes from the words *no-run*. The name was derived in the 1940s as a marketing technique to emphasize the durability of nylon for women's stockings. Nylon was created as a substitute for silk fiber. Without getting into the chemical technicalities, nylon is a man-made synthetic polymer polyamide filament—in other words, a staple fiber made from petroleum. The staple length, crimp, and fiber diameter can be anything the scientist orders, but they tend to mimic the natural fiber the nylon is emulating. Under the microscope, the fiber surface is as smooth as a glass rod.

Qualities of Nylon

1. **Strong.** Polymer is a tough, resilient material.
2. **Nonabsorbent.** However, some nylon fibers have been designed to attract water in order to reduce static electricity.

3. **Poor heat conductor.** Nylon becomes limp when warmed and, if exposed to high heat, it actually melts!

4. **Elastic.** Nylon has very good elasticity. After being stretched, the molecules in the fiber immediately return to their previous positions.

5. **Abrasion resistance.** As stated before, it's a tough, resilient fiber, and that includes a resistance to abrasion. This is also why nylon is often added to sock yarns as a supporting fiber.

6. **Dyeability.** Nylon can be dyed with the same acid or natural dyes used with protein fibers, since it has a similar molecular structure. Some insects—such as ants, crickets, and roaches—will eat nylon if they're trapped inside, but otherwise it's not a fiber on any particular insect or microorganism's menu.

Nylon blends well with most fibers and is useful as filler or a strength-adding fiber. It can be spun according to the fiber that the nylon is emulating or, if blended, with the spin method that is recommended for the primary fiber blend. Examples of pure nylon fibers for spinning are 100 percent nylon, imitation cashmere, imitation angora, Firestar, and imitation mohair. Follow the process of spinning and dyeing nylon from fiber to final knitted project in the Knit Workshop project Catherine (page 156).

Other Spinning Fibers

New fibers are continually being developed in labs to suit the demands of the textile industry. Most recently, these new fibers are attempts to combine natural materials with a synthetic process, in an attempt to derive the best aspects of both fiber worlds.

PLA (POLYLACTIC ACID) FIBER: A BRIDGE BETWEEN SYNTHETIC AND NATURAL FIBERS

These are defined as any manufactured fiber in which at least 85 percent of the weight of the fiber is derived from naturally occurring sugars in the source material.

Ingeo (Corn)

This fiber comes from sugar/starch elements in the corn plant that are combined with other solutions to make a polymer-based extruded fiber. Ingeo makes a soft, lustrous knitted garment with drape. Since it has properties similar to polyester, ingeo dyes best with disperse dyes, a more toxic synthetic dye used to dye polyester fibers and not recommended for the home dyer. The fiber preparation determines the spin method, although a worsted spin method would enhance the luster.

Mineral Fibers

Mineral fibers are not found in the average spinner's or knitter's stash: gold, silver, stainless steel, and asbestos. You probably would never want to spin with asbestos, but there are stories of a guy named Rumpelstiltskin who managed to turn straw into gold. Good luck doing that! (And if you do, look me up because I'd like some lessons!)

Hand carders—Top: standard wool carders; middle: flick carder; bottom: cotton carders.

Flick carders help to align fibers for worsted spinning.

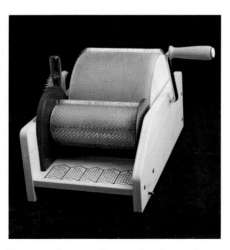

Drum carders greatly expedite the carding of fiber.

FIBER PREPARATION TOOLS

Fiber preparation tools are essential for the spinner working with unprepared fibers and often helpful to ready commercially prepared fibers for specific spinning purposes.

Carders—for Woolen Spin Preparation

The idea of carding fiber may evoke images of early prairie life and "olde tyme" museums. But for contemporary hand spinners, carding is as useful today as it was in the past. The purpose of carding fiber is to open up and align the locks for the woolen spinning method. Carding is also helpful when blending fibers and colors.

Note: Staples longer than 6 in. (15 cm) need to be combed rather than carded. Or, if you can stand to cut a lovely, long lock of fiber, they can be cut and carded—although to most fiber lovers cutting them seems like a sacrilege!

Hand carders. Hand carders are basically the same today as they were in the 1200s: wooden handles that support a "card" of pins of a given length that are arranged in a density that allows for the best carding of fine to coarse fibers. Carders align fibers through a brushing process, transferring and straightening the fiber as it's passed between carding heads. The brushing process ultimately produces a "rolag," which is used for the woolen spinning method (see page 34 on how to use hand carders and page 58 for information on the woolen spinning method). There are different types of carding cloths for different types of fibers. ("Cloths" refer to the material and pins on the carder.)

Note: Carding cloths are identified by ppi numbers (pins or points per inch). For fine fibers like cotton and cashmere, use a card numbered 208 ppi (sometimes called a "cotton" carder); for medium to coarse fibers, use cards with a ppi number of 72 or 108. There are also different carder sizes available: mini, student, and standard.

Flick carders. These small carders align fibers for making worsted spun yarn. They separate the shorter fibers from the longer ones and force the fibers into the very parallel arrangements necessary for a true worsted preparation. Flick carders are also used to prepare slightly matted or thick locks for drum carding.

Drum carders. This is a slightly more "modern" tool. It was originally designed in the 1700s as a power-driven carder and modified with a hand crank for smaller operations. Many spinners consider drum carders essential since they expedite the work of carding to a few revolutions of a crank. Drum carders are also useful in color blending.

Drum carders come in many different styles, depending on the manufacturer, but they all have similar basic parts: a feed-in area or tray (the platform in front of the small roller where the fiber is placed before it is fed into the carder) and two rollers (one large, one small—also called the "licker in"), which are both covered with a carding cloth.

Note: As with the hand carders, you can get different card blankets for drum carders to allow for carding different types of fibers.

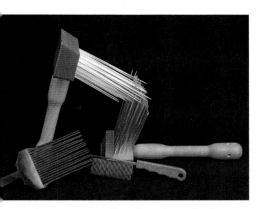

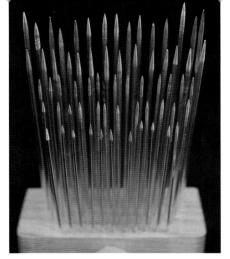

Various types of hand combs—all will assist in preparing fiber for worsted spinning.

The scary tines on an English comb!

A primitive bone comb

Combs—for Worsted Spin Preparation

If you want to create a true worsted yarn, combs are essential. Their history goes back to ancient Greece and Rome. Combs look like tools of torture and, quite honestly, are very dangerous. They must be kept under lock and key so little fingers and unwelcome guests don't get anywhere near them. But they are the most efficient method of preparing fiber for worsted spinning.

There are several different types of combs available, from small, hand-held, curved Russian combs to big, scary English combs. The big combs come in different tine diameters, lengths, and row numbers. The finer and more numerous the tines on the comb, the finer the fibers are prepared. Since combs are quite expensive, a hand carder or hackle with a dog comb, or a flick carder can be adequate substitutes.

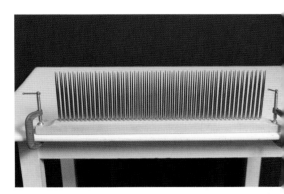

Hackles are useful when blending fibers.

Hackles—for Worsted Spin Preparation

There are two kinds of hackles used in spinning: one that's used in flax processing (also called a "hetchel" or "hatchel") and the more common wide, two-row tined version that is used in worsted prep (instead of combs), fiber blending, and color blending.

Diz—for Worsted Spin Preparation

A diz pulls combed fibers into a roving, and it often has various hole sizes to allow for the preparation of different size roving. Use a small hole for fine-weight yarn and a larger hole for heavier-weight yarn. The size of roving should be based on the final type of yarn to be spun. For more information on using a Diz, see Combing Workshop (page 36).

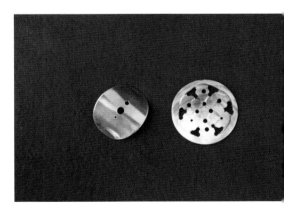

Two diz tools

For more on how to use these tools, see: Hand Carding Workshop (page 34); Flick Carding Workshop (page 35); Drum Carding Workshop (page 35); Combing Workshop (page 36); and DA-6: "Painting" with Fleece (page 184).

Also see SA-2: Fiber Prep and Spinning Tools on a Budget (page 172) for how to create or purchase alternative and inexpensive tools for fiber prep.

THE FIBER PREPARATION WORKSHOPS

You have the option of either choosing a fiber that is already prepared and ready for spinning—such as a batt, roving, sliver, plate, or top (see FA-5: Pre-Prepared Fibers and Their Typical Spinning Methods, page 165)—or getting the fiber directly from the animal or plant source and preparing it yourself. At least once, get a fiber directly from the source. Starting from scratch can be an enjoyable, centering process, bringing you full-circle from the fiber source to final product. And the experience will be a valuable lesson in how fiber prep can affect the outcome of your spinning and knitting. Buying directly from the producer can also save you a substantial amount of money, and there's nothing to equal the personal relationship you'll have with the person (and animal) who provides the fiber.

If preparing all of the fiber yourself is more than you care to take on, check out FA-4: Raw Fiber Preparation Options, page 165, for options in getting it processed. For the rest, read on!

Note: Heed these words! The better a fiber is prepared, the easier it is to spin. There are two basic steps in the preparation of raw fiber for spinning:

1. Cleaning, if there's grease or vegetative matter (VG), like grass and seeds, in the fiber.
2. Arranging the fiber for spinning.

There's Never a "Free" Fleece!

Don't be tempted by a sheep farmer's offer of a free fleece. It's the real meaning of "getting fleeced." First of all, you may be getting a fleece from a sheep that's been bred for meat. That fleece is typically not worth spinning, as the sheep's breeding has been focused on the meat and not on spinnable fleece. Or maybe it's a fleece from the sheep farmer who does raise sheep with adequate fleece for spinning, but usually sends the fleece out for chemical processing so doesn't take extra care to keep the field clean. You will be pulling out burrs and other VG in the wool forever!

Keeping the Grade—or Not

The wool of a complete fleece has zones with different grades of fiber. The best wool is found on the neck, shoulders, and about a quarter of the way down the back. The belly wool may be shorter and is usually fine and soft. The wool from the lower back and sides is less fine and typically has a more open crimp. Some spinners like to separate these zones into different cleaning batches and ultimately use them for different spinning purposes. Potential issues that could arise if you don't separate a fleece with varying zones are uneven spinning due to the different wool qualities; uneven dyeing due to the ways different parts of the fleece accept dye; and uneven knitting tension (affecting the final garment shaping) due to the different crimp measures in the fleece. Quite honestly, I usually can't be bothered with such fussiness, so I often process the entire fleece as one. But for fleece that has different coloring in the different zones or very distinct grade differences between the zones, I might

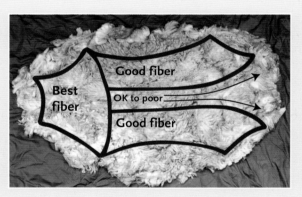

Every fleece can be divided into specific wool zones, as seen here.

consider processing each zone separately. In the end, separating the fleece is entirely up to you. The freedom to make that choice is another wonderful thing about processing your own fiber.

Wool Fleece Selection Workshop

Look for a fleece that has very little VG. The locks should have a well-defined crimp and, when pulled, they should not break. There should be few second cuts and no kemp (chalky-white, brittle fiber). Use a recently shorn fleece. Raw fleece that is more than a year old is tough to clean since the natural grease of the wool and suint hardens over time.

Note: You may see experienced spinners take a lock of wool between their hands and pull and snap the fibers. Like the wine connoisseur who rolls the wine around in a glass and breathes in its "essence," the fleece connoisseur is checking for soundness in the fiber. If the fiber makes a "ping" sound, it's a sound fleece (no pun intended). If it breaks or sounds dead, it's an unhealthy fleece and is to be avoided.

Fiber Cleaning Workshop

A large part of preparing raw fiber for spinning involves making sure it as clean as possible prior to the spin.

WOOL

Wool should be cleaned of VG, manure, and most (if not all) of its grease before it is spun. The first steps in cleaning a fleece occur at the time of shearing. The sheared fleece is immediately placed on a table and "skirted"—meaning the dirty and too-short edges of the fleece are taken off. Next, large bits of manure, straw, and other VG are pulled out by hand, along with short cuts from the shearing. When the fleece is sufficiently clean of these nasty bits, it's rolled up, weighed, and ready for the spinner to purchase and take away.

Just skirting the fleece and removing the VG isn't enough to prepare it for spinning. The grease, suint, and general dirt and dust must also be washed out. See FA-3: How to Clean Raw Fleece (page 164) for detailed washing instructions.

Grease on a Fleece—Do Fine Sheep Sweat or Perspire?

The words *grease* and *lanolin* are often used interchangeably when talking about the greasy substance on a sheep's fleece but, technically, grease is not lanolin. Lanolin is actually purified sheep's grease and comes from a centrifugal process that refines and purifies the grease from shorn fleece.

You may have heard of "spinning in the grease" when the wool is spun with the grease still in it. It's a way of providing superior water-repelling qualities to the spun yarn. But it's also a way of attracting dust, dirt, and bugs to wool—not to mention the cost of future repairs to spinning equipment. And forget about dyeing wool that still has grease. Dye particles will not adhere to greasy wool.

There's another part of the unclean wool fiber that's worth mentioning: suint. Suint is dried perspiration on the sheep's hair shaft. It plays an important role in keeping the sheep's skin clean and healthy by drawing dirt away from the skin and bringing it to the tip of the hair shaft. But if not cleaned out of the fleece soon after shearing, suint, along with remaining grease, hardens and turns the fleece yellow, making it harder to clean.

My Typical Wash Schedule

First soap bath—1 hour or more

Second soap bath (with half the original soap)—30 minutes or more

First rinse (clear water)—20 minutes

Second rinse (with 1 cup vinegar)—20 minutes

Third and final rinse (clear water)—20 minutes

See FA-3: How to Clean Raw Fleece (page 164) for detailed washing instructions.

Hint: Don't Be an Agitator!

Hot water opens the fiber scales, and they gradually close as the water gets cooler. The scales need to be opened as far as possible to get the fiber clean. But if the wool is agitated, those open scales will easily grab on to each other and fuse together (felt) as the water cools and the scales close. Trying to open the scales again with hot water won't work. So avoid the problem and don't move the wool around in the water. Push it down gently—just once—and leave it!

Angora can be spun directly from the rabbit. The rabbits enjoy the attention and may even fall asleep during the process.

Spin Directly from the Cotton Boll!

Although time-consuming, spinning from the boll really connects you to the source of your fiber. Just pull a fiber bundle out of the boll, separate the seed from the lint, gently tease the lint to achieve some uniform direction—and spin!

OTHER PROTEIN FIBERS

Most nonwool protein (animal) fibers don't require any cleaning prior to preparing them for spinning unless they are very dirty or their coats contain natural grease.

PROTEIN FIBER: SILK

Silk is a fiber that has often been processed a bit by the silk grower to make it ready for sale and doesn't require any cleaning prior to the spin. The exceptions are silk cocoons or other raw silk products. Raw silk needs to be "degummed" to remove the sericin (a gluelike substance that the silkworm produces to keep the cocoon intact).

CELLULOSE/SEED HAIR FIBER: COTTON

Raw cotton should not need washing, but it may need to be teased and carded with fine cotton carders. Cotton can also be spun directly from the seeds in a cotton boll with no prep. (See sidebar.) Really short, clean cotton fibers (less than 1 in., or 2.5 cm) can be whipped with a stick and spun directly from the whipped mass. Most cotton is sold as top, requiring only predrafting prior to spinning.

   Note: Be careful to not squeeze cotton. Cotton is very sensitive to pressure and will draft out in lumps if compressed. The key is to *relax* when spinning it.

CELLULOSE/BAST FIBER

Bast fiber does not need to be washed. If purchased as a strick (a tied bundle of long line fibers), you will need to prepare the fibers for distaff spinning. (A distaff is a tool that holds the strick for spinning.) If purchased as top, you can spin directly from that by just opening up and loosening the fibers.

SYNTHETIC FIBER PREPARATION

Synthetic fibers need no preparation since they are already prepared in top or roving form when they leave the manufacturing facility. The only preparation needed is predrafting the fibers just prior to spinning.

Fine Fibers Need Diva Care!

When washing a fine wool fleece such as Merino, wash it in lingerie bags and use a laundry tub or a square dishpan as the soaking container. This will keep the fine wool fibers in lock order and avoid felting. Excess water can be removed from the fibers in the machine's spin cycle, but beware of overmanipulating them, since they felt extremely easily. Locks can also be washed individually. Even though this method is very fussy, it's the best way to keep the locks in "tip to cut end" order. It's also perfect for fibers that will be worsted spun.

Teasing the fleece. This process can be done either by hand, as shown, or with a special device called a "picker." (Pickers have sharp, dangerous tines and are typically only used by spinners who process very large quantities of fiber.)

Straightening Fibers for Spinning

Even if a fiber doesn't need cleaning, it usually needs to be aligned to be ready for the spinning method chosen.

TEASING/PICKING

Washed and dried wool and other fibers in lock formation are hand "teased" or "picked" (gently pulled apart) to open up the locks prior to preparing them for spinning. Some well-cleaned fibers can be spun directly after picking, but usually the fibers are carded or combed before spinning.

PREPARATION FOR WOOLEN AND WORSTED YARNS

Yarns are spun either with a woolen or worsted method, or a combination of the two. (See Spin Methods, page 57.) Either a carded or combed fiber preparation is needed to put the fiber in a direction to make a well-spun yarn with the selected method.

Woolen Yarn Preparation

Woolen yarns have fibers that are spun in a mix of parallel and nonparallel directions. Hand carders or drum carders are used to prepare the fibers and open them to an airy loft for spinning.

Worsted Yarn Preparation

Worsted yarns are prepared with rakelike combs to remove short staples and to straighten fibers so they can be spun in an even, parallel direction.

(1) Dressing the carder

(2) Gently brushing

(3) Transferring the wool between carders

(4) The final rolag

HAND CARDING WORKSHOP

The goal of carding is to create a rolag of fiber (it looks like a big ol' Cuban cigar) that becomes the fiber supply for woolen spun yarn. There are many different methods of hand carding, from just touching and releasing the fibers between carders to more physically brushing the fibers. All methods are fine as long as the end result is an open, airy preparation. My method involves (1) laying the fibers on the carding bed of one carder—parallel to the carder handle (this is called "dressing" or "charging" the carder)—and (2) gently brushing the fiber on that "holding" carder with the "working" carder so the fibers transfer from the holding carder to the working one. Then I flip the carders around and repeat the brushing steps, transferring the fiber to the empty carder until the fiber appears clean of VG and well brushed. The spinner's cigar—the rolag—is made next by (3) picking up one end of the fiber (from the top or bottom of the carder, not the sides) and rolling it into a loose cigarlike shape. (4) Now it's ready to spin with the woolen method of spinning.

Note: Don't overfill the carder! The pins should still be felt beneath. Don't ram the carders together when brushing. Use a rolling action and pretend you are gently brushing a child's hair. If there's vegetative matter in the pins after a brushing pass, clean it out and go on with the carding.

FLICK CARDING WORKSHOP

Flick carding uses about 2 in. (5 cm)-wide groups of lock fibers at a time. Put a strong cloth in your lap since the carder is literally flicked against the fiber (and your thigh) during this process. While holding the cut end of the fiber lock on your thigh, lightly hit the tips of the lock with the flick carder. Don't pull the fiber. Just bounce the carder on the tips. Turn the fiber over, and in the same lock formation, "flick" that side. Then flick the cut end the same way. This creates a lofty fiber in a parallel formation for worsted spinning, spinning from the fold, or a preparation that's been flick "teased" for drum carding.

DRUM CARDING WORKSHOP

Begin by (1) spreading a thin layer of fiber on the "bed" of the drum carder (the platform just before the small roller). Open any matted locks before starting to place them. Turn the carder handle in a clockwise direction and the fiber will pull into the carder, ending up on the large roller.

   Note: There will be fibers adhering to the small front roller. These fibers are rejects from the large roller and are probably shorter than the other fibers. Some spinners discard them, but I like to add them to novelty batts, where they create interesting noils (lumps and bumps).

   Continue to add fiber to the feed area until the carded fiber has nearly filled the pins of the large roller. When the carder is nearly full, stop adding fiber and turn the carder for several more rounds. (2) Then use the doffer/awl tool (the tool that looks like an ice pick) to take off the fiber batt. There is an open channel on the roller where the doffer can be slid under the batt and gently pulled up to separate the fibers and "break" the batt. (The fibers don't actually tear, but pull apart according to their staple length.) (3) Pick up the back end of the broken fiber batt and pull it off toward the back of the carder, using the doffer rod to pull stragglers. The fiber should come off the carder in one piece. (The rollers will turn as the fiber is pulled off.) Clean the carder with the small cleaning brush that should be attached to the carder. (This brush can also be used as a flick carder in a pinch.) It often takes two or three runs through the drum carder before the fiber is fully

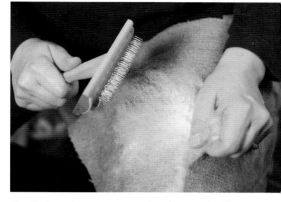

The flick carder process involves hitting the fiber tips with the carder using a snapping motion.

The drum carder process, step by step:

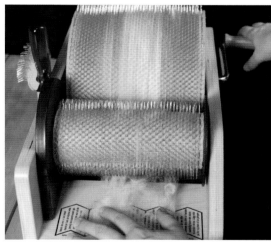

(1) Feeding fiber into the carder

(2) "Breaking" the fiber batt for removal

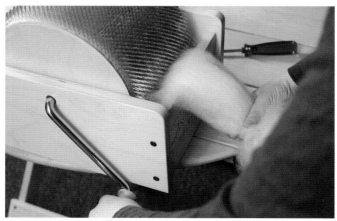

(3) Pulling the batt off the carder

carded. When running the batt through the carder for additional carding, split it into two sections and spread the fiber across the width of the carder before running it through. Hold the batt up to the light, and if you don't see any clumps or vegetation, it's ready to separate into thin sections and predraft for woolen spinning.

Note: Even though it's tempting, don't try to run the entire batt through on subsequent rounds, or pins may bend.

COMBING WORKSHOP

Combing (also called "jigging") is a method of straightening fibers into an extremely parallel configuration for worsted spinning. It leaves behind short ends of fiber ("noils" and "neps") not wanted in worsted spinning and readies the fiber for turning into sliver for spinning.

Note: Fiber blends should be similar in diameter and staple length, or the fibers will not blend well in combing.

Set up the combs by clamping one on a table with the tines pointing to the ceiling. (1) "Charge" the one clamped to the table by dressing it with fibers that have been aligned in as parallel a manner as possible, with the cut end of the fiber on the combs about three rows in and the fiber tips hanging. (The process of charging combs with wool is also called "lashing on.") This setup lets you work with the grain of the fiber scales, which is preferred in worsted spinning. Fill the tines to no more than one third of their depth.

(2) Take the other comb ("working" comb), turn it so its tines are horizontal, and, with a swinging motion from right to left (or left to right), comb the fibers off

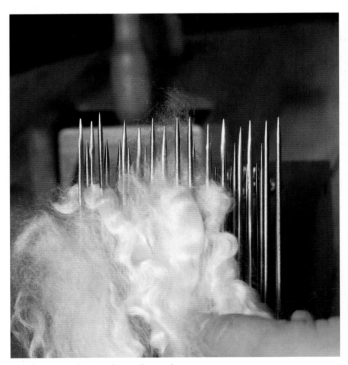

(1) Charging the combs with wool

(2) First half pass combing direction is sideways (right to left or left to right)

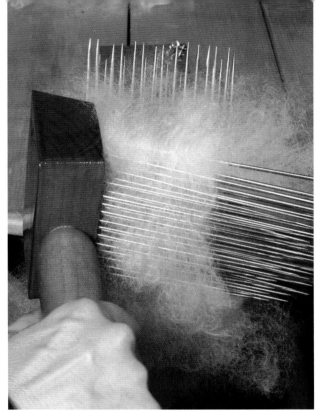

(3) Second half pass combing direction is vertical (top to bottom)   (4) Final combed fibers ready for the diz and worsted spinning.

the clamped comb. Start with the tips and work your way back so you don't get stuck in a mass of tangled locks. (Be careful when swinging at the fiber with this "Edward Scissorhands" tool. This work is best done with no one else in the room, including pets.) When most of the placed locks have been combed, what remains on the clamped comb is unusable in the worsted process. Put those short fibers aside for woolen spinning or to add to a creative spinning project.

   Note: The first staples to transfer to the working comb are the longest. If you're just separating out long guard hair from the short downy undercoat (for example, the "tog" from the "thel" in Icelandic wool), that may take only a few combing strokes.

   You're not done yet. (3) While standing to either side of the clamped comb, again turn the working comb tines horizontally, this time with tines facing away from you. With a vertical (top to bottom) swinging motion, comb the fiber from the working comb back to the clamped comb, and (4) the lock tips will once again be hanging off the clamped comb. Remove any short fiber ends from the working comb. This cycle of combing is called a complete "pass," and it usually takes two to three passes before the fiber is well prepared. When the fiber is well combed, end after a half pass so the fiber cut end is hanging off the working comb. The next step is to turn the combed fiber into a sliver with the help of a diz. (Are you starting to see the advantage of getting pre-prepared top for worsted spinning? Fiber combing requires a good deal of physical effort!)

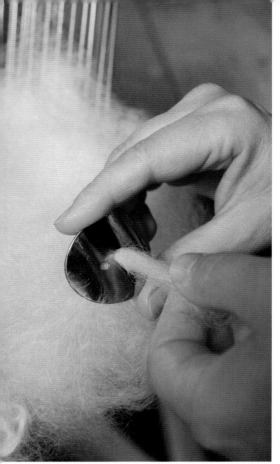

Using the diz to create roving from the combed fiber

SLIVER WORKSHOP: USING A DIZ

Pick a hole in the diz that is close to the size of the singles yarn you wish to spin (be sure it's not smaller than the yarn size). With the charged comb (or hackle) attached to the stand or table, take a fine crochet hook, or the orifice hook from a spinning wheel, and pull an end of the combed fiber through the hole. The concave side (back side) of the diz should be facing toward the comb so you're looking at the arched side (front side) of the diz while working. Continue to pull the fiber through the hole—moving it back and forth and side to side to facilitate an even sliver—and eventually there'll be no more fiber on the comb. (There may be some short ends left, but don't pull those through.) Assuming instructions were followed to end the combing with the cut end of the fiber, keep track of the beginning of the sliver by taping or knotting it. If you begin spinning with the taped or knotted end, you'll be spinning with the grain of the fiber for a true worsted spin.

CREATIVE FIBER BLENDING WORKSHOP

Why do spinners blend fibers? Sometimes it's an economical decision—to create a yarn out of an expensive fiber without the expense of using 100 percent of that fiber. The decision may also be fueled by a desire to have specific qualities in a yarn that can't be achieved by a single fiber. For example, silk added to soft wool makes a fiber with more strength and luster; mohair added to a medium-grade wool makes a fiber with more loft and softness.

Note: Uniform fibers spin better. For the best spinning, pick fibers with a micron diameter difference of no more than 10. If there is a greater variation in diameter, the coarser fibers will tend to float to the surface when spun, and the yarn will feel rougher than it should. Uniform staple lengths are also important since shorter fibers will tend to pull out of the yarn and pill if incompatibility between the fiber lengths and the twist allows that freedom. This sounds "fiber segregationist," but in general, protein fibers blend better with other protein fibers and cellulose fibers blend better with other cellulose. If you want to blend across fiber categories, choose fibers with a similar staple length and fiber diameter.

When blending, pay attention to the density of the fibers. The density of a fiber is based on its weight and volume quantity relative to other fibers. For example, 2 oz (57 g) of silk weighs the same as 2 oz (57 g) of angora, but by volume quantity, 2 oz (57 g) of silk is smaller than 2 oz (57 g) of angora, making silk denser than angora.

A volume of angora weighs considerably less compared with the same volume of wool fiber. Since angora has dominant characteristics, very little is needed to make a well-balanced blend.

Examples of more dense (heavier but less volume) fibers include silk, mohair, and alpaca. Examples of less dense (lighter weight but more volume) fibers include angora, cashmere, and qiviut.

Note: When you buy 2 oz (57 g) of a 50 percent silk and 50 percent cashmere blend, the blend is actually determined by the weight of each fiber type. Because cashmere weighs less than silk, you are actually getting more cashmere in this blend than silk.

Comparing two ounces of angora (left) with two ounces of silk (right)—it's obvious that the angora has physical dominance.

The physical volume of fibers also impacts the final quality of the yarn. For example, a blend of 50 percent angora (a less dense but large-volume fiber) will produce a yarn that dominates with the physical characteristics of angora. The tipping point for large-volume fiber dominance generally starts at 25 percent of the total fiber weight.

Part of the fun of blending comes from experimenting with the effects of blending different fibers in different percentages and seeing/feeling the results. But as in a cooking recipe, when too many ingredients have created a dish with fighting flavors, the same can be true in fiber blending. Keep blends to no more than three different fibers, or the yarn will be a hodgepodge of too many fiber "flavors." Such a yarn will have no real character. If you want to use several fibers in your yarn, mix up the fibers in the plying of the yarn rather than within a single. Different plies with different characteristics will be more distinctive than a muddy single consisting of many different fibers.

How to Blend

Many spinners prefer to do a "touchy-feely" kind of blending process, grabbing fibers and mixing them until the blend looks or feels right. This works fine if the blend doesn't need to be reproduced later. But consider the scenario of needing only 60 yd (54 m) more of handspun yarn to finish a fantastic wool/silk-blend sweater, but you used the touchy-feely method of measuring your blend and now cannot replicate it. That's a learning experience we all try to avoid. Instead, go to FA-6: Be Your Own Fiber Chemist: How to Blend Fibers (page 168) to try a solid method of creating a fiber blend without the guesswork: blending fibers by weight percentage. Then follow the process of dying and blending angora and wool in the Knit Workshop Dominique (page 143).

Note: For guidance in blending, note the percentage numbers that commercial fiber suppliers have used in their yarns.

Fibers can also be sent to a commercial mill for blending into roving, but check with the mill first to see if they can handle the fibers you want to blend. Some mills aren't able to blend fibers at all or don't have the special equipment needed to blend fine fibers.

Similar Fibers Fight for Yarn Domination!

Avoid making a 50/50 blend of spinning fibers that are similar in density. To make a successful yarn, the characteristics of one fiber should always dominate, or you'll be fighting with the other fiber's qualities in the spinning. The spinning method will be determined by the dominant fiber, since the dominant fiber holds the other fiber(s) in the twist and will respond first to the spinning method.

Looking Ahead at Dyeing

Blended fibers from different fiber categories won't accept dye equally. Nevertheless, a yarn made from such a blend can have a lovely heathery appearance. If dyeing across fiber categories, be aware that different fibers react differently to different pH levels in dyeing and may be damaged if dyed at the wrong pH for the fiber. (See the Dye Workshop section, page 71, for more on dyeing options.)

part 2　Spin Workshop

This workshop takes you through the process of the spin—from the history and equipment to the actual spinning methods—to help you create beautiful yarn in a variety of weights and fibers. Along the way, valuable tips and techniques are given for spinning from a knitter's perspective.

With every stitch, knitters can feel a historical connection to the generations that knit before them. Spinners have an even longer history, filled with great troubles and great joy.

ABOVE This more efficient production-oriented spindle wheel was a first step toward industrialization and allowed the common person to make more thread and yarn for their own use and to sell. In fact, from its design in the 1600s or 1700s until the height of industrialization in the mid-1800s, the Great Wheel, or walking wheel, was an essential piece of household equipment. *Library of Congress*

ABOVE RIGHT Today's principal wheel is the flyer wheel—sometimes called the Saxony wheel. On a flyer wheel, the yarn is wound onto the bobbin at the same time it is twisted, speeding up the process of spinning. These wheels had their origin in the 1500s when they were called flax wheels since they were mostly used for spinning flax. *Author's Collection*

A BRIEF HISTORY OF SPINNING

Although it's not known when the first spun fibers were created, archaeological evidence suggests that spinning began at the start of civilization, as we know it. The few existing archaeological garments tell us that flax and wool were among these early spun fibers. Most certainly, early spinners were the first "locavores," since only fibers from the spinner's region were available until trade routes opened up a wider selection. The first spinning tool was probably a stick, which later developed into a stick with a rock at the end of it, and finally became the hand spindles spinners use today.

We have to take a stratospheric leap ahead to the 1100s and late medieval Europe to see the first real evidence of modern advancement in the textile industry. During this time, the skills of fiber workers improved because the organization of the guild system advanced the industry's techniques. Guilds were built around a single craft, and men who practiced that craft as a profession were the only people allowed (forced, actually) to become members. During the Middle Ages, women held a subservient position in society, and although they were deeply involved in textile creation up to that time, they were not allowed to join the guilds. But they were allowed to participate in guild activity at the "lowly" level of washing fleece—and spinning. Despite the fact that women were excluded from the "higher" levels of the new textile industry, the guild system educated workers, and advancements were made.

The textile industry continued to expand, and by 1628, in England, the first spinning school was created to teach girls in poverty how to spin and knit. But these "spin schools" were actually factories, and the main education the girls received was in learning how to spin and knit standardized yarns. At this same time, workhouses employed and taught women in poverty to spin and weave, and correction houses called "spin houses" kept "incorrigible" and "lewd" women "in discipline" by teaching them a trade. From this time until about 1750, children, women living in poverty, and female convicts were the principal spinners, weavers, and knitters for the growing textile trades.

The mechanization of spinning, knitting, and weaving in the 1700s brought dramatic change to the textile industry. Prior to the industrialized era of the 1700s, all thread and yarn was laboriously spun by hand, so cloth and clothing were precious. When spinning became industrialized, spinning wheels became the machinery of home industry and leisure activity—and the fashion industry was given wings. More women started to spin in their homes to sell their own yarn in local markets to hand knitters, who might likewise turn around and sell their handknits. Leisure spinners had spinning parties that were regular social gatherings, much like the spinning groups and guilds of today. The industrial era freed women from lives of servitude to the wheel so that they could have lives that allowed the wheel to finally serve them.

Even though interest in leisure spinning has waxed and waned through the years (nearly dying out at the beginning of the 1900s), we've always returned to it. I think that spinning is a part of our DNA. The recent revival in the popularity of spinning is evidence of its continued importance as a touchstone in our lives.

Spinning in the Future

We don't need to hand spin for survival anymore—or do we? Our need to spin may now be for our spiritual, psychological, emotional, and intellectual survival. Along with being a means to make the yarn we really want, spinning soothes a deep primal desire to sit calmly and create. It's our escape from the mad rush of modern times—a place of solace in a world where there is less value attached to simple repetitive motion. Spinning puts us into a larger history that's connected to our ancestors. It gives productive purpose to our love of fibers, drawing us full circle. Men have even joined in on the "lowly" task, finding the spin centering and therapeutic. No matter what reason brings us to the wheel, we join a long heritage of others in a perpetual, hypnotic, healing rhythm attached to the end of a string.

An Ashford wheel in motion

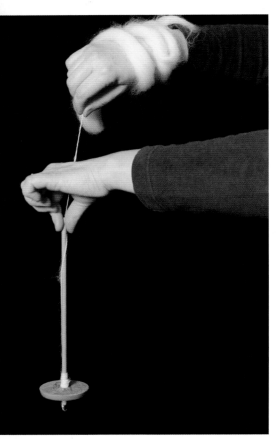

Spinning with a hand spindle, using the drop method

SPINNING TOOLS

The tools that actually do the spinning of fibers range from basic hand spindles to electric spinners that are the next step before the high-speed commercial spinning machines found in a spinning mill. But most hand spinners still use hand spindles or a manually operated wheel.

Hand Spindles

The hand spindle is the core of ancient and modern spinning. Even today, hand spindles are the most basic, portable, and economical spinning tools available. I first learned to spin on a drop spindle and, even though I prefer a wheel, the spindle was a great teacher. In my classes, I start students on drop spindles because I believe it gives the best feel for the spin and is a wonderful preparation for the wheel experience. And there's not much that can go wrong with a spindle, aside from breaking a shaft or snagging the yarn on a wood splinter.

There are two types of hand spindles: drop and supported. The drop spindle uses gravity as a force to help pull and draft the fiber. The supported spindle relies more on the spinner to control the drafting of the fibers, since the spindle rests on a surface (usually a bowl) and the spinner must create the force for the drafting.

Note: Supported spindles are useful when spinning short fibers that would break apart if subjected to the gravity forces of a drop spindle.

There's a plethora of different designs for hand spindles, from exotic hand-carved wood to ones you can make yourself from old CDs. They all take the basic form of a bottom, top, or middle whorl (the whorl is the big disk on the spindle), but within those three types of whorl placements, there's a wide variety of styles, weights, and sizes.

Note: For beginners, the more controllable spindles weigh between 1 and 3 oz (28 g and 85 g). Go to Beginning to Spin, page 51, to learn how to spin with a hand spindle.

Supported spindles are useful when spinning short fibers that would break apart if subjected to the gravity forces of a drop spindle.

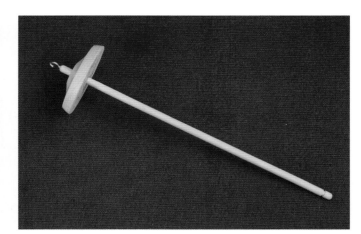

This top whorl spindle is convertible and may also be used as a bottom whorl spindle (as shown in the photo at the upper left).

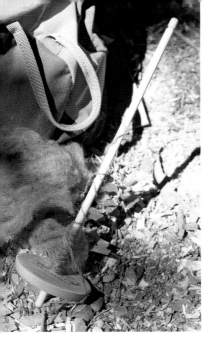

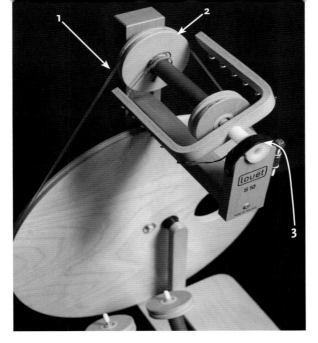

Spinning Wheels

Essentially, wheels are tools that expedite the spinning process. Considering the simplicity of the hand spindle, heads can also start to spin when considering all the different types of spinning wheels available: single-drive, double-drive, upright, Saxony, castle, Norwegian, flax, spindle, flyer-driven, bobbin-driven, Scotch and Irish tension…But in reality, all these wheels fall into three main types.

THREE PRINCIPAL WHEEL STYLES: BOBBIN LEAD, SINGLE DRIVE, AND DOUBLE DRIVE

Wheels have developed improvements during their relatively brief history, and these improvements can be seen in the style of their "drive" system (the parts that make the wheel and flyer move) and in their overall functioning. They are identified by names that reflect their key unique features.

Bobbin Lead/Bobbin-Driven (or Irish Tension)

This wheel has a single drive (one drive band), and that drive band pulls a whorl pulley on the bobbin, which pulls the flyer around. It also has an "Irish tension" brake band by the flyer orifice. Bobbin lead wheels are considered good wheels for spinning medium to bulky yarns. They are great beginner's wheels since there are fewer parts that need to be adjusted to achieve a consistent spin.

   Note: Mechanically, whorls function as pulleys so the words *whorl* and *pulley* are used interchangeably in the Spin section.

Single Drive/Flyer-Driven (or Scotch Tension)

These wheels have a drive band that turns the flyer whorl pulley and a brake tensioner (Scotch brake) to keep the bobbin under control, allowing the yarn to be pulled onto the bobbin. Single-drive/flyer-driven wheels are also very easy for beginning spinners to control.

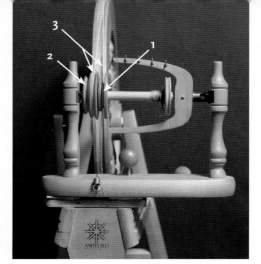

Ashford wheel, with double drive; 1. Bobbin whorl pin, 2. Flyer whorl and pulley, 3. Double drive

Standard spinning wheel parts: 1. Wheel, 2. The footman (located behind the wheel) connects the treadle to the wheel, 3. Treadle, 4. Maidens hold the flyer, the flyer holds the bobbin. The entire maiden and flyer area is called The Mother of All, 5. Brake and wheel tensioners, 6. Orifice, 7. Drive band

Double Drive

This wheel has a single drive band that doubles over to pull both the bobbin and the flyer whorl pulley. One part of the band turns the whorl to determine the wheel speed (see whorls and ratios below), and the other one turns the bobbin whorl pulley, and that action pulls the yarn onto the bobbin. The bobbin whorl pulley is always smaller than the flyer whorl pulley. The difference in size makes the bobbin turn faster than the flyer, pulling the yarn onto the bobbin. These wheels are versatile and have many drive speeds based on available whorl sizes. Because these wheels are also a bit more difficult to master, they are typically not the first choice for a beginner.

OTHER WHEEL FEATURES

After considering the basic wheel form, there are a few other features that are important to identifying a wheel and understanding how it may uniquely function.

Flyer Options

Every wheel manufacturer has a different style of flyer mechanism and ways to adjust the flyer. Some have hooks on the flyers, some have twisty wire yarn guides, and some flyers have guides that move along the length of the bobbin to automatically distribute the yarn to the bobbin. There are flyers with large orifices for spinning bulky yarns, some with small orifices, and others with unique orifices such as a delta guide that controls the yarn like the tip of a spindle on a spindle wheel. (See photo on page 47). And there are flyer adjustments that require twisting the maidens to set the bobbin or simply adjusting the flyer with a knob. In the end, the main task of all flyers is to hold the bobbin and twist fiber into yarn.

Whorls and Drive Ratios

The concept of whorls and drive ratios is not my favorite part of spinning. I don't care much about numbers. I just want to spin. And the fact is, you don't *have* to know anything about drive ratios to spin. But in this case, ignorance isn't bliss. If you understand the concepts behind the whorls and drive ratios of your wheel, you'll have an easier time getting the spin you want for the project you have in mind.

It's actually pretty simple if you don't get stuck on the math. Drive ratio refers

A MajaCraft Little Gem with a delta orifice guide; 1. Delta Orifice

to the number of times the flyer turns during one complete round of the wheel. Every wheel has a range of different drive ratios based on the selection of whorl pulleys that come with the wheel. The ratio number is actually based on the whorl size. A whorl with a 5:1 ratio means the whorl pulley makes the flyer spin around five times for every round of the wheel. A whorl with a 12:1 ratio means the whorl pulley makes the flyer spin around twelve times for every round of the wheel. Since the flyer is the mechanism that spins the fiber and the whorl pulley drives the flyer (this is also true for a bobbin-led wheel because the whorl pulley is part of the bobbin), the 5:1-ratio whorl will put less twist into the yarn per inch than the 12:1 ratio whorl. So a less-twisted, chunkier yarn can be spun with the 5:1 whorl. The 12:1 whorl can spin a finer yarn like a fingering weight, since that needs more twists per inch. The largest size whorl creates the slowest speed for the flyer, and the smallest whorl creates the fastest speed. The treadling speed does not affect the speed ratio of the flyer. No matter how fast you treadle, the wheel will still only cycle around once and the flyer will only spin around the corresponding number of times based on the whorl size. Check out Spin Numbers Workshop (page 62) for more on the effect of drive ratios.

Counting Ratios

It's easy to measure your wheel's drive ratios. Tie a string someplace on the wheel (the actual wheel that turns). Then tie another string on the flyer. Treadle very slowly and count the number of revolutions the flyer makes for one round of the wheel using the string as a starting point. The resulting number is the ratio for the whorl pulley that the drive band is wrapped around. If the last revolution wasn't complete, just round the last turn up or down to get the total flyer revolution count.

Single Treadle Versus Double Treadle

I spun for twenty-five years before I got a double-treadle wheel. Honestly, I don't have a preference. They each have their advantages and disadvantages. The double treadle lets you sit in balance, working both feet, but the single treadle lets you move around a bit more, providing more flexibility in your spinning position. In the end, only you can decide which one works best for you. Practice with the wheel before buying.

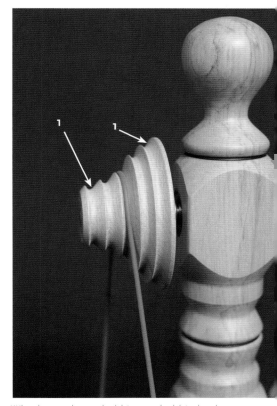

Whorls may be on bobbins on bobbin-lead wheels or separate whorl elements on flyer led wheels, as on this MajaCraft Little Gem. 1. This whorl pulley has drive ratios ranging between 13.1:1 to 4.9:1

For further guidance on selecting wheels, see Resources and Supplies (page 159).

Lazy Kate with a brake

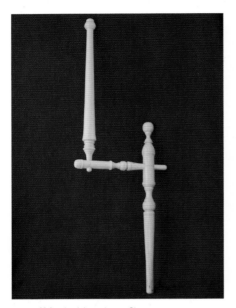

Distaff for holding bast fibers

Lazy Kate

An onboard Lazy Kate

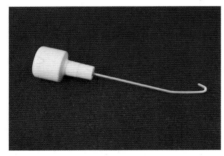

Orifice hook

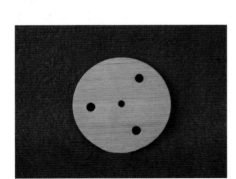

Plying disk

Additional Tools

These tools are helpful to complete the spinning experience. Some are essential to the wheel, such as an orifice hook and wheel oil, and others assist in spinning plies and unusual fibers, such as a Lazy Kate, plying disk, and distaff.

Distaff. Holds a strick of bast fiber for spinning. The distaff can be attached to a wheel or stand. Traditional distaffs can be hard to find, but any device will work (such as a broom handle or dowel) as long as it holds the bast fibers in place and allows an easy draw down for spinning.

Lazy Kate. Holds bobbins during the plying process. Every spinning wheel manufacturer has its own style of Kate. Some are onboard (built into the spinning wheel). There are Kates with brakes to hold the bobbins in tension and others that are quite simple in design. For more information about using a Lazy Kate, see Plying Workshop (page 63).

Orifice hook. Pulls yarn through the orifice. But there are other useful duties for an orifice hook, such as helping test the twist of a new fiber, pulling fiber through a diz, pulling singles through a plying disk (see below), finding the end of a broken single on the bobbin—and scratching your back!

Plying disk. If you don't want to use your fingers in a mad spider configuration when making multiple plies, this tool holds multiple strands of singles to help keep the singles from tangling during the plying process.

Wheel oil. Good maintenance is vital to the smooth operation of a spinning wheel, and a huge part of maintenance is making sure your wheel is well oiled. A good wheel oil to use is mineral oil, 30-weight oil, or lightweight machine oil (like the type used for sewing machines). The oil needs to drip into the wheel parts, so use a container that has a needle end rather than a spray nozzle. See SA-1: Wheel Maintenance— Become Your Wheel's Grease Monkey page 172, for more on oiling wheels.

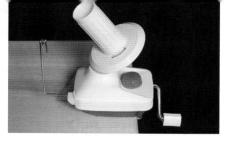

Ball winder

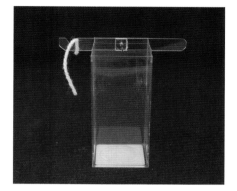

McMorran Balance

Tools for Yarn Finishing

No spinner's tool chest is complete without tools to finish the yarn. The following list includes equipment that both spinners and knitters often use, so you may already have a few of these handy items in your knitting arsenal.

Ball winder. Ball winders are ideal for making center-pull balls of yarn.

McMorran Balance. This is an easy-to-use tool that saves loads of time in measuring yarn. The balance is available in most spinning shops, and some craft and yarn shops. You just need a snippet of yarn to balance on the device and after a simple calculation you will know the number of yards in a pound of that yarn.

Niddy noddy. Used for wrapping spun yarn into skeins. They are available in wood or plastic. The plastic version is especially useful when finishing cotton and other cellulose fibers that need to be wet when setting the tension.

Nøstepinde. This traditional Norwegian tool is a ball-winding device and makes a fine center-pull ball simply by holding one end of the yarn against the shaft of the tool and winding the rest of the yarn around the shaft and into a ball shape. Slide the yarn off and you have a center-pull ball!

Swift. Also a knitter's tool, a swift is used as a skein holder for winding off skeins into balls. It can also substitute for a niddy noddy, but it isn't as accurate in wrapping specific yarn lengths.

Note: On a budget? Check out SA-2: Fiber Prep and Spinning Tools on a Budget (page 172) for inexpensive options to the standard fiber prep and spinning equipment.

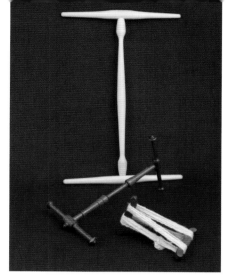

Niddy noddies

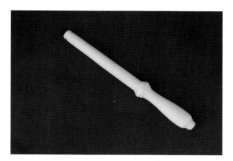

Nøstepinde

Umbrella swift

SPIN CONCEPT

Spinning is magic. Well, that's what people say when I demonstrate spinning in public settings. Yes, the visual effect of the turning of the wheel and the fiber morphing into yarn looks like alchemy. But in reality, spinning is one of the simplest of human activities. All it requires is a stick attached to a filament of fiber. Then twist the stick and pull. You're spinning!

In my beginning spinning classes, I'm always asked, "How long will it take to become a proficient spinner?" In his book *Hand Woolcombing and Spinning*, Peter Teal has a great answer to that question: "How long will it take? You should, if you practice for six hours a day, produce a fairly reasonable yarn in three days." With some exceptions, he's pretty accurate in his statement. So don't despair. Practice!

Twist: The Five Primary Spin Characteristics

The act of spinning is simply drawing out a group of fibers, twisting them, and repeating the motion. These few steps make a continuous strand—a.k.a. yarn! The more a fiber is twisted, the stronger and more rigid the strand becomes—that is, until it breaks from the tension. The less a fiber is twisted, the softer and less strong the strand becomes—until it breaks from the lack of spin. A good twist is the balance point between too much and too little tension. Spinning is all about achieving balance.

But of course, there's more to it than that. Let's begin with the five primary spin characteristics of a yarn:

1. Fiber type—protein, cellulose, cellulosic, synthetic, etc.
2. Spin method—how the fiber is actually spun, such as worsted, woolen, etc.
3. Wraps per inch—a spinner's equivalent to stitches per inch; this helps spinners determine what diameter of yarn they are spinning.
4. Spin twist—this involves the direction of the twist (to the right—Z-twist—or to the left—S-twist), the number of twists, and the angle of the twist.
5. Ply—the number of single strands of yarn making up the final yarn.

These five characteristics are the keys to selecting the most appropriate yarn construction for specific spinning and knitting projects. The first part of the book discussed fibers, so now it's time to dive into the other four characteristics. You can read the following pages on spin from start to finish or drop in as desired.

BEGINNING TO SPIN

Like getting into a car and checking the mirrors and adjusting the seat before driving, there are a few steps to take before beginning to "safely" spin.

Spinning with a Hand Spindle

Hand spindles are the most basic of spinning tools. Devote some time to practice coordinating your hand motions while spinning the spindle, and learning this technique will be pretty straightforward. Follow these instructions for either a top or bottom whorl spindle.

BODY POSITION FOR DROP SPINDLE SPINNING

You can either stand or sit while spinning. If standing, you'll have greater distance for practicing the technique before the yarn needs to be wrapped on the spindle, but sitting may give you more control of the spindle dance. Wrap your fiber supply around the wrist of the hand that will feed fiber to the spindle—this is usually the dominant hand (the right hand if you're right-handed and vice versa).

PREPARING THE DROP SPINDLE

Tie a leader of wool yarn (approximately 20 in. [0.5 m] in length) around the spindle shaft, close to the whorl on the side facing the hook. Bring the leader to the other side of the whorl and wrap it with a half hitch next to the whorl (see example, page 52). Bring the rest of the leader back to the top, wrap it a few times around the spindle shaft (if using a bottom whorl spindle), and with a backward *e* loop, wrap it on the hook (or the notch if using a convertible spindle). Now you're ready to attach your fiber and start spinning.

> ### Spinning on the Go
>
> If you find hand spindles too fussy or slow, don't despair and give up on spinning altogether. You don't have to get proficient on a hand spindle. Move on to a wheel before deciding that spinning just isn't your cup of tea. Even though I'm not terribly fond of hand spindles, I'm grateful to know how to spin with them, since they are extremely portable. They easily slip into a suitcase, backpack, or purse—just waiting for the opportunity to sample wonderful fibers while on the road.

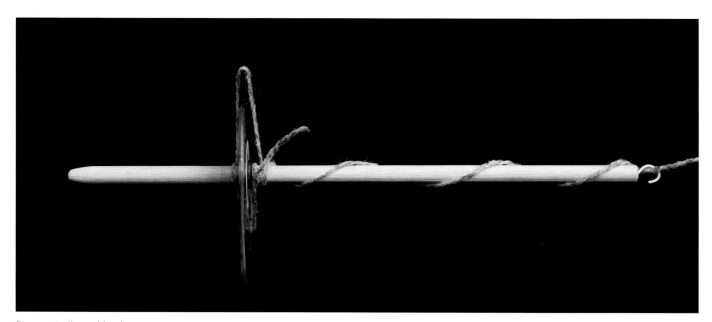

Drop spindle and leader setup

If the bobbin doesn't have a leader thread, tie that on by making a half-hitch loop (lark's head knot) as shown. Then make another half-hitch loop to secure the first one, or the first loop will just slip around the bobbin shaft when you start to spin. This method of tying the leader is called *a lark and a bight.*

HOW TO SPIN WITH A DROP SPINDLE

1. With the spindle suspended, lay the fiber supply end over the end of the leader, pinch the fingers of your dominant hand over the overlapped fibers on the leader end, and, with your other hand, twirl the spindle shaft to the right so the spindle starts to turn. In a few moments, you should see and feel the twist touch your pinched fingers.

2. When you feel the tension build in the twist, gingerly release your pinched fingers so the twist enters the overlapping fibers and the fibers wrap around the leader, becoming one.

3. Pinch your fingers again at the end of the well-formed twist, give the spindle another good twist to the right and start drawing the fibers back to create a drafting zone. (The drafting zone is a triangle of fiber just before where the twist begins.)

4. Release the pinch when the twist enters your fingers, let the twist enter the drafting zone, and pinch again at the top of the twisted area.

5. Give the spindle a twirl to the right when it slows down or starts to reverse to the left.

Keep repeating this motion of drafting, pinching, and twirling. When your spindle can no longer be spun without hitting the floor, unwrap the leader yarn around the shaft and wrap the new yarn next to the whorl (from the bottom up to make a more stable and balanced spindle spin), rewrap the shaft with yarn, and go back up to the hook to spin some more.

Congratulations! You've just made a connection to generations of spinners by spinning in the most ancient of spinning methods.

Note: The spin method on a supported spindle is not that different from the drop spindle method. The main difference is that a bowl or some type of support is needed to spin against.

Spinning with a Wheel

Before spinning with a wheel, follow these few simple steps to prepare the bobbins and wheel. **Special Note:** The rest of Spin Workshop focuses on wheel spinning but many of the basic concepts can be translated to hand spindles.

PREPARING THE WHEEL

First, prepare the bobbin.

Note: For most spinning, a wool leader works best since it grabs onto fibers better. The closer the leader is in diameter to the spun yarn, the better the join.

GET IT IN DRIVE

Put the drive band in place.

Single drive wheel: The drive band goes on the whorl pulley. If you have a Scotch tension brake, be sure it's in the right place on the bobbin whorl pulley.

Double drive wheel: Place one loop of the drive band on the flyer whorl pulley and the other loop on the bobbin whorl pulley. Be sure the flyer whorl is larger than the bobbin whorl or the drive band won't drive the flyer, leaving you spinning with no draw on the yarn.

Before going any further, clean and oil your wheel so all parts are working smoothly. You should clean and oil it at least every time you change a bobbin. (Refer to SA-1: Wheel Maintenance, page 172.)

Note to Beginning Spinners

I've met many spinners who intimidate the new spinner by throwing out concepts such as "ratios" and "WPI." or "TPI." Don't worry about those details for now. I don't mean to say you should ignore the technicalities, because that would mean no advancement in your practice. Just don't get stuck on the rules and numbers while starting out. So much of spinning is about how the twist feels and looks.

Single drive placement on Lendrum wheel

Double drive placement on Ashford wheel

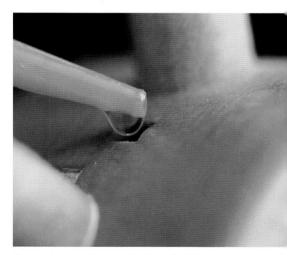

Remember to oil your wheel regularly!

Know your Zs and Ss

Turning the wheel clockwise creates a Z-twist spin in the yarn and is typically how most single yarns are spun. The wheel turns counterclockwise when plying, creating an S twist. (See more about twist direction on page 61.)

TEST THE DRIVE

If the wheel has a drive band tensioner, first adjust the tension by completely loosening the knob so the flyer doesn't move when the wheel is treadled. Also loosen the Scotch brake if the wheel has one.

USING THE TREADLE

Remove your shoes. Not only does treadling in stocking feet protect the wood of the wheel, it also allows you to better feel the treadle. Now, treadle the wheel, turning the wheel in a clockwise direction, for several minutes. Put yourself to sleep if you wish. Treadle and treadle. Get comfortable with the rhythm of the wheel. You are literally training your brain to accept the new information it's receiving about spinning. You may find yourself rocking back and forth. Breathe deeply with each treadle. Now dog-ear this page because, as you get going with your spinning, you'll want to come back to this beginning step just to renew your mind and take a break from patting your head and rubbing your stomach—you'll know what I mean later.

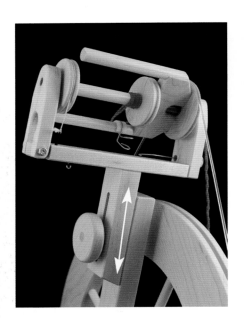

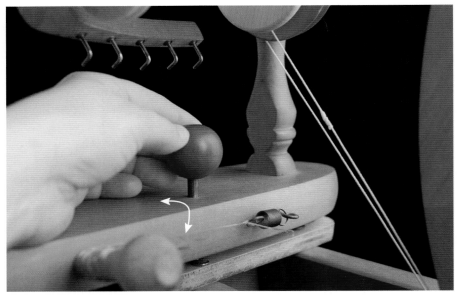

A couple of different styles of tensioners and brakes (Lendrum and Ashford). The tensioner subtly moves the drive band away or toward the flyer. This Lendrum wheel has a tensioner that moves the entire flyer up or down, thereby adjusting the drive band tension. This Ashford wheel tensioner is on the flat surface between the maidens and, when turned, moves the entire flyer area (mother-of-all) away from or toward the main wheel. When the flyer is moved away from the main wheel, the drive band is tightened, and when it is moved toward the main wheel, the band is loosened.

Predrafting the fiber

Give the fiber a test spin with your orifice hook.

PREDRAFTING FIBER

Before even touching fiber to the wheel or spindle, play with it. See how far it can be stretched until it pulls apart. This test will help give you a sense of the staple length, which is valuable information for knowing how to spin it. Use the orifice hook or a crochet hook to test how the fiber spins. Twist and pull to see how too much or too little tension affects the fiber. Note the texture of the fiber—whether it's slippery or has a gripping quality. See how the diameter and length of the fiber affects the amount of twist needed to hold the yarn together without breaking or corkscrewing.

SPIN!

With your dominant hand in front (since it's usually the most dexterous hand and feels the twist with more sensitivity) and the other in back, pull (draft) out a thin triangle from the fiber supply and overlay it on about 3 in. (8 cm) of yarn at the end of the bobbin leader. Tightly pinch the overlapped fibers with the index finger and thumb of your front hand so the twist doesn't move past the fingers and into the fiber supply when you start to spin the wheel.

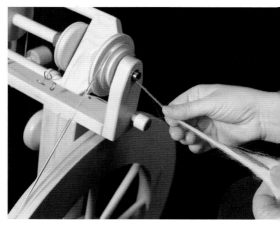

Beginning the spin—joining fiber to the leader

The spacing of hands while spinning often relates to the staple length of the spun fiber. Hold the fiber supply in your back hand at a distance behind your pinched fingers that's just short of the fiber's staple length. Relax this hand so the fiber can move smoothly into the triangle of fiber behind your front hand (the "drafting zone") when you start spinning.

Short Backward Draw

I think the easiest method for beginning spinners to learn is the short backward draw. This is a method of spinning that gives the spinner firm control of the draft and twist. I've found that this one aspect of control makes it easier for the body and mind to adjust to learning to treadle and spin at the same time. It's also a worsted spin method that quickly leads to learning the woolen draw methods.

1. Begin by putting your focus on the pinched forward fingers. With your back hand, pull (draw) the fiber supply back a little from your pinched fingers until the fiber between your hands (the drafting zone) starts to release and slide apart.

2. Start to treadle the wheel so it moves in a clockwise direction (to the right). Use your back hand to push the wheel to get it going if you must. Don't release your forward pinched fingers. Tension should start to build in the leader and into the overlying fiber supply until you feel it in the fingers of your front hand.

3. Slightly release your pinched fingers to allow the twist to enter the drafting zone, slide your fingers back to the end of the drafting zone, and pinch again at the end of the twist. Stop treadling and take a look at how the twist energy twisted the fibers that were in the drafting zone.

4. Repeat this sequence in a fluid movement without stopping (pinch the forward hand, draw back the fiber with the back hand, and slide the forward pinch back to pinch again at the end of the twist), and you're spinning!

   Note: To join new fibers to the yarn, just spread the end of the spun yarn into a fan that's nearly the staple length of the fibers. Overlap that end with a similar fan from the end of the fiber supply. Spin twist into the connection while drafting back and continue with spinning.

   When there's a flow to your movement, move on to Spin Methods to fine-tune your spin to incorporate the best spin draw for the fiber and the yarn you're making.

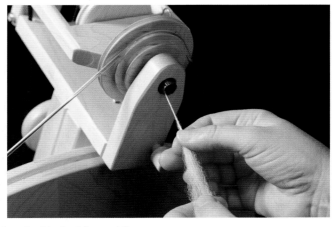

Step 1—Pinched forward fingers

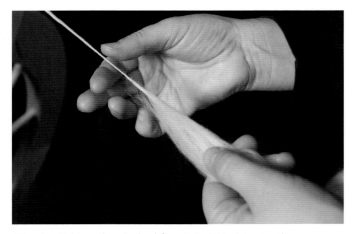

Step 3—Release the pinched fingers to let twist enter the drafting zone

Initial Troubleshooting

If you're not getting any draw in or much twist in the fiber, tighten the brake very slightly. If the fiber is flying out of your hands and onto the wheel with no twist, loosen the brake very slightly. It doesn't take a dramatic amount of adjustment for dramatic results in the takeup. If adjusting the brake doesn't help, also try tightening or loosening the drive band tension.

Note: If you are having trouble drafting and treadling at the same time, enlist someone to slowly turn the drive wheel by hand while you practice drafting.

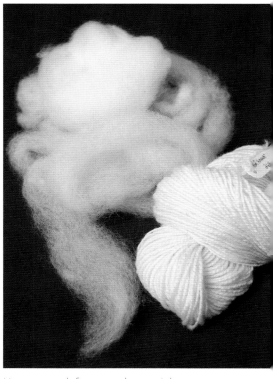

SPIN METHODS

You would think that after eons of spinning experience there would be certain set spinning methods that everyone follows. On the contrary, it seems that for all the spinning teachers in the world, there are just as many variations in spinning methods. But there's one thing all these spinning approaches have in common: They are all based on worsted and woolen spinning techniques.

Worsted or Woolen Spin

Worsted and woolen are not just spinning techniques, they are the essence of spinning. When you know how to produce both types of spin, you will be able to spin any fiber. A worsted-spun yarn is strong and smooth with great durability. A woolen-spun yarn is soft and warm with limited durability.

Fiber choice plays a role in selecting a spin method. The best spin method enhances the fiber qualities. A fiber with a relaxed crimp (fewer than 7 crimps per inch [2.5 cm] or no crimp), luster, strength, and length will spin the best with a worsted spin that keeps the fibers parallel so the luster can be emphasized, and the strength and straight fibers complemented. A short fiber (typically under 3 in., or 7.5 cm) with great crimp will spin best with a woolen spin, as the woolen method makes the most of the great qualities of the shorter length, crimp, softness, loft, and warmth.

WORSTED SPIN METHOD

Key point: Twist stays in front of the hands.

A worsted spin is best for yarns that are destined for garments receiving hard use or needing good resilience. Good projects for worsted-spun yarns are socks, lace, and other items that require good stitch definition and endurance.

Worsted-spun yarn is spun from combed fibers that have been properly separated and aligned, creating uniformity in the fiber direction and length. The parallel alignment is kept right into the spin. A worsted-spun yarn produces a fabric that is crisp and strong.

To spin worsted yarn, use a drawing method that gives you the most control for keeping the fibers as uniform as possible. (See Draw Methods, page 58.)

Unspun top, left; worsted yarn, right

Rolag, left; woolen yarn, right

WOOLEN SPIN METHOD

Key point: Twist is allowed between the hands.

A woolen spin is best for yarns that are destined for warm, soft garments. Think of the warm, cozy qualities of a big wooly sweater, and you'll have a sense of the innate quality of a woolen spin. Good projects for woolen-spun yarn are sweaters, hats, mittens, and any items that are enhanced by a yarn that contains softness, warmth, and elasticity and doesn't require strong stitch definition, high strength, or resistance to wear.

Woolen-spun yarn is spun from carded fiber that is aligned in many directions. The yarn may be spun from a carded rolag, roving, or top that is spun from "the fold" (top spun from the fold may also be considered a semi-woolen). The goal is to have a light, fluffy yarn with a lot of air pockets. A woolen-spun yarn produces a fabric that is warm and soft.

When spinning woolen yarn, allow more room in the drafting zone to enable the multidirectional fibers to catch the twist. Choose a drawing method that puts twist in the drafting zone. (See Draw Methods, below.)

In-Between Yarns: The Semis Explained

These are "in-between" yarns—neither fully worsted nor fully woolen but having qualities of both types of spin. Spinners have different ideas about whether the "semi" description refers to the preparation or the spin. I define it from the spin perspective:

Semi-worsted yarn is drawn/spun worsted from a woolen preparation. It has less stitch definition and is a bit loftier than a full worsted-spun yarn.

Semi-woolen yarn is drawn/spun woolen from a worsted preparation. It has more stitch definition and is a bit smoother than a full woolen-spun yarn.

Many spinners use one of the "semi" techniques nearly exclusively. There's nothing wrong with that if the result is good. Choose the spin method you think is best for your project. This is why we spin rather than buy our yarn at the local yarn shop. It's the apex of creative freedom for knitters.

DRAW METHODS

Worsted and woolen spinning methods each use particular techniques for drawing out the fiber prior to the spin. (Drawing the fiber means attenuating it for the twist that turns it into a strand of yarn.) But this is where the spin methods require a bit of fudging on your part. Most spinners spin with a combination of draws, even within the same yarn and spinning method. I'll play the teacher here: Learn the different draw methods and what kind of yarns they are meant to produce before starting to mix them up. It doesn't take long to get a feeling for the draw methods—although it is a brain exercise to quickly move from a forward to a backward draw!

Spinning for the Left and Right Brain

When just beginning to spin, set a timer for a break every fifteen minutes. Since spinning uses thought and visual processes that simultaneously stimulate the left and right side of the brain, this break will give your brain a chance to process the new patterns it's making and give your body a chance to release some of the tension you're probably experiencing.

Short Backward Draw—for Worsted Spinning

This was the method recommended on page 56 for beginning spinners and the method used when you want to have the most control of the twist in your yarn.

Note: At first, there may be clumps of yarn at the transition points in the pinch, but in time you will become more proficient, and these clumps will even out.

Medium and Long Draw—for Woolen Spinning

In these methods, occasionally you will still pinch with the front hand, but not so tightly since that hand needs to allow twist to move behind it into the drafting zone. The front hand becomes a facilitator of the twist and not a tight controller. The back hand moves backward at the rate of the twist entering the fibers, and the front hand moves along the yarn as needed to adjust the twist. (It's like an elongated version of the short backward draw, but without the tight front hand tension.) Focus more on the back hand and watch where the twist is going. The back hand needs to keep the twist ahead of it and pinch the fibers when it's time to feed the yarn onto the wheel. This is a fast spinning method. As you get adept, you can open your movements into a long draw by releasing the front hand completely and making a more elongated stroke while pulling back with the back hand, allowing more twist to back up into the fiber. This long draw movement is like the backward draw of an archer's bow. The long draw looks like magic and will impress your family and friends.

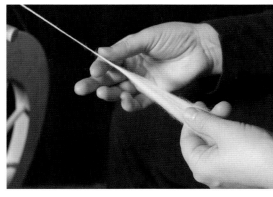

Medium draw, woolen spin method

Long draw, woolen spin method

Spinning from the Fold—for Semi-Worsted Spinning in a Short Draw and Semi-Woolen Spinning in a Long Draw

This is the spin of spiders. This method is mainly used to control slippery fibers from a combed top and for spinning long staple fibers. It decreases luster and strength, but makes a loftier knitting yarn with a little more elasticity.

1. Pull off a staple length of fiber from your fiber supply and fold it over the index finger of your back hand. Pull a few fibers forward to the tip of your finger (or along the first joint of your index finger) and hold the fiber against the yarn coming from the wheel and begin to spin. The fibers should quickly catch the yarn.

2. Spin from the tip or joint of the finger only, adjusting the fiber draw-off as you're spinning so it continues to pull from both sides of the fingertip/joint and the fiber remains folded over the finger. The draw-off of the fiber forms a V.

3. Pull your hand back until the twist suits your needs and release the yarn to wrap on the bobbin. Keep pulling back, allowing twist to pick up the fibers, and then feed the yarn to the wheel. This move is similar to the long draw bow move, but not as elongated. You will feel like a spider spinning a web. You can use your front hand to adjust the spin, but with the exception of the short draw semi-worsted spin, this is essentially a one-handed technique. When spinning from the fold as worsted, the yarn will have a bit more loft than a true worsted yarn.

   Note: Having trouble with your spinning? Go to SA-7: Troubleshooting Your Wheel and Spin Technique on page 178, and you will most likely find your problem and the solution. If not, sometimes a human touch is needed. Look for a spinning guild or shop in your area that has a help class or someone who can personally walk you through your problem. You may also be able to find a private teacher. There are also loads of websites with "how-to" videos and social networking sites covering spinner's issues.

When to Move to a New Bobbin

When the bobbin has filled evenly or when you've used up a certain portion of the fiber you intended to spin (provided you're making a multiple-ply yarn), it's time to replace the full bobbin with an empty one and spin that one to roughly the same level as the first.

   Note: Bobbin capacity is not standard between wheel brands. As you become familiar with your wheel, you'll get a sense of how many yards/meters will fit onto the bobbins based on the characteristics of the spin. A McMorran balance may also help determine a closer estimate of the number of yards/meters of yarn on the bobbin.

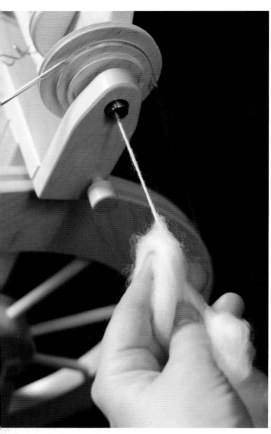
Spin from the fold method

TWIST

Twist is what holds yarn together. If the yarn kinks back into multiple coils or even breaks, there's too much twist in the spin. A yarn that's too loosely spun —a rare occurrence for a beginner—will be so loosely twisted that it doesn't hold together.

Note: The length of a fiber staple can affect the amount of twist your yarn needs. The longer the staple, the less twist is needed to hold the yarn together; the shorter the staple, the more twist is needed.

Z- and S-Twist Direction

There are two different directions of twist: clockwise and counterclockwise. The clockwise direction is called a "Z twist" since the yarn twist direction resembles the slant in the letter *Z*. This is the direction in which most singles yarns are spun. The counterclockwise direction is called an "S twist" since the yarn twist resembles the slant in the letter *S*. This is the direction in which most plies are spun. Another way to remember these spin directions is to write the letters in the air with your finger. The direction used at the very beginning of writing each letter is the direction in which the wheel should spin.

Note: Thin, overspun yarn is called "twit"—maybe because you're a twit if you keep overspinning!

Important Test: Checking Your Spun Yarn

Spin until your yarn is even and fairly kink free. The amount of time it takes to get an even yarn varies. Even experienced spinners can sit down at a wheel and take some time to get the wheel and their hand motions to agree before they have an even yarn. Try to relax. As you've probably experienced in knitting, your state of mind is a big factor in the final outcome of the work.

When you're ready, pull out about 2 ft (61 cm) of spun yarn from the bobbin and let it coil back on itself. Congratulations! You have just presented the first test of a spun yarn. What you see in this coiled single yarn is what the final plied yarn will look like if you hold your twist consistently throughout the spinning. (The assumption is that yarn will be plied, as most yarns are.) If you're happy with the look of the twist, cut off the coiled yarn and knot it at the cut ends. Then dunk it into warm water to allow the twist to set. Hold both ends of the yarn so it loops toward the floor. If it hangs in an open loop with no corkscrewing twist, the yarn is considered "balanced." That means if you continue to spin and ply the yarn to match the sample (the "control" yarn), it will knit up as a balanced (unbiased) material (no leaning left or right). Use this control yarn as your guide for the rest of your spinning project to maintain a balanced and consistent yarn.

Note: A yarn meant to remain a single does not benefit from this twist test. Singles yarns will always twist back on themselves. The only way to settle a singles yarn is by hanging it wet under tension. Some spinners will also slightly felt singles yarn to set the twist for knitting.

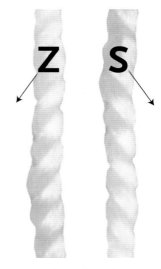

Examples of Z- (left) and S-twist (right) yarns

Coil back workshop test

This is a good time to figure the wraps per inch (WPI) and twists per inch (TPI) of the control yarn, recording the numbers in your record keeping book. (See Spin Numbers Workshop, below, and SA-8: Record Keeping for Spinning, page 179, for a sample control card and record-keeping sheet.) These numbers will help keep the yarn consistent and be a guide for replicating the yarn. (Be sure when comparing the control yarn to the just-spun yarn, you hold both under the same tension.) This is also a good time to spin up more yarn and do a sample swatch to be sure you are spinning the yarn you want for your knitting project.

SPIN NUMBERS WORKSHOP: A PATH TO SPIN CONSISTENCY

Spinning is a freeing, creative activity. But there are times you may want to match a commercial yarn, have a yarn that fits a knitting pattern, or just feel like a master of spinning. Taking control of the spin will help with these goals. But to take control, a little math is necessary.

WPI: Wraps Per Inch

WPI is a measurement of the number of yarn wraps that fit within a 1-in. (2.5 cm) measure. It's one way to monitor consistency in the spin. Every time we sit down to the wheel, we're in a different mind-set and have a different body tension, and this affects our spin. So keeping an eye on the WPI can help keep us true to the yarn we started making. Although not a completely reliable measuring method, it is a guide for creating a yarn that will be the right knitting weight for a project. See SA-3: Yarn Measurement Systems, page 174, to find out how to measure WPI.

TPI: Twists Per Inch

As with WPI, TPI can be measured in singles, but it's most useful in the plying process. TPI is the number of twists the spun yarn has made in 1 in. (2.5 cm). Measuring TPI is another way to make the yarn more consistent. See SA-3: Yarn Measurement Systems, page 174, to find out how to measure TPI.

Whorl Drive Ratio Numbers and Yarn Twist

Whorl drive ratios directly relate to yarn twist numbers. Here are some examples to explain the relationship:

- In a 5:1 whorl drive ratio, the flyer turns five times for every wheel revolution, creating five twists in the yarn for that one revolution. This is a twist rate that pulls the yarn onto the bobbin quickly, so you will need to feed the yarn into the wheel faster since it will corkscrew backward much more quickly at only five revolutions per wheel round. This rate of drive makes a thicker yarn.

- A 12:1 ratio makes twelve twists in the yarn for one wheel revolution. To make a good twist without corkscrewing backward, you need a thinner amount of yarn to take up the twelve revolutions, and you will need to feed the yarn into the wheel more slowly to achieve the twelve revolutions per wheel round. This rate of drive makes a thinner yarn.

Note: For heavyweight yarns, use a large whorl and quickly feed in the yarn. For fine yarns, use a small whorl and slowly feed in the yarn. Of course, the fiber you are using needs to be compatible with a heavy or thin yarn. Practice by spinning with different whorls and types of fibers to see how your wheel's drive ratios change the spin.

PLYING WORKSHOP

Psst. Over here … I've got something for you. Handspun and plied yarn. Knitters' nirvana!

Plying is twisting single-plied strands together to make a yarn that is balanced in the twist, stronger than a single ply, and stable for knitting. Plying turns the twist in a completely opposite direction from the singles, thereby equalizing the twist through the strands for a "balanced" yarn, perfect for knitting.

It's best to wait to ply the singles until after they've had a chance to rest on the bobbins overnight so the fiber can "learn" to hold the twist. The rest time will set a stable twist in the singles and also make the plying more stable.

Note: Your body has a memory of how you spun the singles, so spin all the singles for your project first to help the final yarn be more consistent in appearance. If you have a lot of yarn to spin, keep extra bobbins on hand for storage. Some spinners rewrap their filled bobbins prior to plying since the rewrapping process balances some of the unevenness in the singles. But winding the yarn into balls may negatively affect the twist of the singles and make the plying inconsistent. If you need to wind your singles into balls, be consistent and do all of them.

TOP A plied yarn measuring 10 wraps per inch (2.5 cm)

ABOVE A plied yarn showing 3.5 twists per inch (TPI). (Measured by a total of 7 bumps to an inch [2.5 cm] divided by the 2 plies.)

A beautiful skein of two-plied yarn

Whorl Size Matters

Consider the quality of the singles' twist and the quality you'd like in the final yarn and select the whorl size based on the desired ply twist. For a tight twist in the ply, select a smaller whorl than the whorl used in the singles. To loosen the twist, select a larger whorl for plying. Typically, a larger whorl is used in plying since it's more common for the ply to need to relax the singles. A whorl that's one size larger than the whorl used for the singles is a good place to start.

Prepare the Bobbins

Note: If you are using balls for plying, skip this step.

You will need a Lazy Kate or a modification of a Lazy Kate to hold your bobbins. Be sure the yarn is coming off the bobbins in the same direction, or the yarn will fly all over the place when you start the ply.

Start the Ply

Tie the two singles to the leader on the empty bobbin. There are many methods for holding the singles for plying. Any method that gives consistency in the plying is fine. I've found that a one-handed hold gives a more even ply, so I hold the plies in my dominant hand, palm face up, with a finger between the fibers to help hold an even plying angle. My other hand adjusts the singles to come off the Lazy Kate at a steady, equal pace. For a two-ply, I often separate the strands by putting one above my leg and one under it. To be consistent in the ply, it's best to keep the same ply hold for all the yarn in a project and the bobbins at a moderate, even tension throughout the plying process.

Turn the wheel in a reverse direction from the singles spin, or the singles will untwist. So if you are spinning singles as a Z-twist yarn (with the wheel spinning in a clockwise, right-handed wheel direction), spin the ply as an S-twist yarn (with a counter-clockwise, left-handed wheel direction). When plying, you are facilitating the single strands to become a yarn, so don't hang on to the yarn tightly, but let the wheel pull the yarn onto the bobbin. This is your time to relax and let the wheel work for you.

Role of Twist Angle

Different yarn qualities are determined by adjusting the twist angle. Use the twist chart in SA-3: Yarn Measurement Systems, page 174, as a guide for picking the twist angle for the yarn.

Multiple Plying

All plies are plied together from singles. So no matter the number of plies, tie them all to the bobbin leader. If there are more than four plies, a plying disk will help hold them. (See Spinning Tools, page 44.) Adding plies makes a smoother yarn, but also takes away from stitch definition. If the knitting project needs good individual stitch definition, such as in lacework, spin a two-ply yarn. Consider spinning three or four plies for less-defined stitchwork.

Three-ply set up for a Lazy Kate

g techniques: Tying singles to bobbin leader | Plying two singles together | Plying three singles together.

Another type of multiple ply is a cable. Cables are first plied as two or more singles and then plied in the opposite direction with two or more plied groups. Cable singles need to have a lot of twist to survive this multiple plying technique. The resulting yarn is very strong. Fittingly, cabled yarn gives great definition to the other kind of cabling: cable knitting!

THE FINISHING ACT: WRAPPING UP THE SPIN

When the spinning and plying are done, there are still a few more steps before the yarn is truly finished. You've got that lovely yarn on the bobbins, all plied up with nowhere to go. *Au contraire!* Next stop: the niddy noddy, a valuable tool that seemingly magically turns spun yarn into a skein. Wrapping yarn into skeins is an essential step for setting the twist and for prepping the yarn for dyeing.

Winding Skeins on a Niddy Noddy

To begin, adjust the niddy noddy so that the top and bottom arms are turned, making a twisted "I" with the top and bottom arms parallel to each other. The niddy noddy can be wrapped when the yarn is still on the wheel. Release the wheel's brake tension and pull the yarn out of the orifice and hooks. (Tie down the flyer so it doesn't catch on the yarn as it's being unwound.) Or put the bobbin on a Lazy Kate and make the skein from there.

Note: A niddy noddy should never be glued in place. The ability of the tool to twist its arms is essential to its operation. If the tool has loose arms, just put some beeswax on the wood, stick some fiber into the arm holes, or wet the wood a bit so it swells slightly and makes the seal tighter.

Sample Now to Avoid Surprises Later

Avoid jumping into a project without first spinning a test length of yarn. If making a plied yarn, spin several yards and ply them together. Then test the yarn by actually knitting it in the stitch your pattern requires.

Hold or tie the end of the yarn to the center shaft. Hold the niddy noddy in one hand with the top arm pointing toward you and start wrapping the yarn up to the farthest end of the top arm. Wrap the yarn around the outside of the top arm and then down to the bottom right arm, wrapping from the farthest to the closest side, then up to the closest top arm, over and down to the bottom left arm and back to the first arm the yarn went across at the start. Continue this way to the end of the yarn. You are actually making a continuous circle with the yarn. When you get to the end of the yarn, wrap to a point where you can easily tie the beginning of the yarn to the end.

Use pieces of scrap yarn to tie the skein in at least four places with figure-eight ties. (Use undyed yarn for the ties if you plan to dye the skein.) Fine and novelty yarns need up to eight ties since they have a greater tendency to get tangled in the final wash and the dye process. Do not tie tightly! If the skeins are tied tightly and the yarn is dyed, the tied areas will remain undyed, resulting in a tie-dyed look.

Twist the arms back into a flat "I" formation to release the tension from the skein and slip the skein off the niddy noddy. If the yarn is really twisty or easily felted, wrap it into a twisted skein to keep it from tangling more or felting while being set in water, but open the skein back to its loop form when it's time to dry the yarn.

Note: Use a CPVC skein blocker, plastic niddy noddy, or plastic bobbins as a skein blocker for holding cotton yarn while setting the twist. (See SA-2: Fiber Prep and Spinning Tools on a Budget, page 172, for more information on CPVC skein blockers and how to make your own.)

Time for a Wash and Set: Setting the Twist

If a twist isn't set, the yarn will do all kinds of amazing—and unexpected—twists and turns in your knitting. So setting the twist is an essential last step before you can use your lovely new handspun yarn.

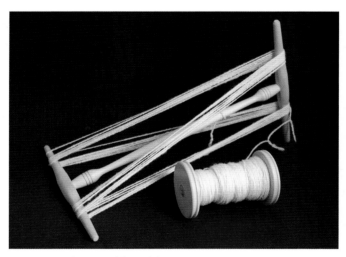

Yarn wrapped on a niddy noddy

Yarn wrapped on niddy noddy with figure-eight ties

WOOL YARN

Put the yarn into a warm, slightly soapy bath using a soap with a neutral pH (such as Synthrapol, Eucalan, or even a neutral pH dishwashing soap such as Dawn) until it's soaked through. To rinse, fill a tub or utility sink with cool water and completely submerge the skein. Don't be tempted to swish the yarn around in the water, or it could felt. Empty the rinse water and fill the tub again, this time adding a cup of vinegar to the cool water to be sure all soap residue rinses out. (To be completely safe, I do this even when using the rinse-free soaps such as Eucalan.) Gently squeeze out the water from the skein between baths. Once again, fill the tub or sink with cool rinse water and submerge the yarn again to make sure the yarn is free of vinegar. If you skip this final rinse, the acid state of the vinegar will damage the wool in time. Some spinners add a drop of essential oil to the final rinse to help deter pests. But beware of adding any oils if you plan to dye the fiber, as oils will affect the dyeability of the fiber.

Help the skein to dry by either running it through the spin cycle of your washer (top-loading washers only!), gently rolling it up in a towel and squeezing without force, or using an old salad spinner as a centrifuge to remove the excess water. Lay it flat on a drying rack or hang with light tension to dry. (Spray water bottles are great devices for hanging on the skein as a weight, and you can easily adjust their weight by adding or removing water from the bottle.)

Note: Singles yarn needs its twist set under heavier tension. If you try to dry it without sufficient tension, it will twist into a coil shape and be a wild, energized yarn that knits up unpredictably.

CELLULOSE/SEED HAIR YARN

Cellulose/seed fibers require a constant tension during the finishing. Cotton needs to be boiled for at least forty-five minutes to set the twist and remove the natural oil from the fiber. Boil the fiber in a pot with 1 tbsp (15 g) of a neutral pH soap and, optionally, 2 tbsp (15 g) of soda ash (also called "washing soda"—see Dye Workshop, page 71). Rinse in lukewarm water (no vinegar). Express the extra water by machine or towel, and dry it with heavy tension.

CELLULOSE/BAST YARN

To get the softest yarn, boil the skein in a soapy, neutral pH water for thirty minutes to an hour. This softens the gummy material in the bast fiber. Then place the yarn in a lukewarm water bath (no vinegar) to rinse. Express the extra water by machine or towel, and hang it with moderate tension to dry.

SYNTHETIC YARN

Wash in a warm, soapy bath and rinse (vinegar is unnecessary). Express the extra water with a machine or towel and hang it with moderate tension to dry.

When the skein is dry, twist it up into a hank or roll it into a ball and start knitting. If you're planning to dye it, leave it in the skein with all ties in place. Go to FA-8: Fiber Storage and Pests, page 170, for advice on how to store yarn.

Skein in a hank wrap

Fulling

For a woolen yarn, the softness and loft of the woolen spin can be enhanced by "fulling" it. Fine fibers, such as angora, yak, cashmere, and blends of these fibers will soften and bloom after fulling. This process also strengthens yarns spun with delicate fibers, making the fiber less likely to loosen from the yarn when it's knit or worn.

There are two fulling methods:

Method 1: While in the hot wash water, push a plunger into the wool several times, rinse the fiber in cold water, and plunger it again in hot water. (Take care to not overdo the plunging, or the yarn will felt.) Lay it flat for drying.

Method 2: After washing, whack the yarn a few times on a countertop edge. This will slightly open the woolen spin and make the yarn softer. Lay it flat for drying.

Spinning to Knit

Knitters are best served by hand-spun yarns that are designed from the start to suit the unique twists and wraps inherent to knitting. Here are a few tips to assist in spinning yarns best suited for knitting.

- When comfortable with the spin rhythm for a project, stop to knit gauge swatches using several needles before evaluating the yarn's appropriateness. Also periodically check in with your control yarn to help keep the yarn consistent.

- If the yarn is overtwisted after the twist is set (a problem mostly for singles yarns) there are a few options to save it:
  - Choose a knitting stitch other than stockinette (which emphasizes the twist problem by leaning the fabric in the opposite direction of the overtwist).
  - Use a garter stitch or a mix of purls and knits to even out the twist.
  - If stockinette is essential, try knitting into the back of the stitches to balance the twist.

- Single-ply yarns won't wear well, and their unbalanced twist will probably create a twisted fabric when knit in the round. Therefore, it's best to knit single-ply yarns in flat constructions.

- Yarns with two plies are good for detailed stitchwork (like lace) that the crisp plies can accentuate.

- Hand-spun yarns for knitting are often spun with twist angles of between 5 degrees and 35 degrees. Yarns with angles above 35 degrees are considered hard twist and most often used by weavers.

- Yarns that have three or more plies tend to fill in the stitches and are best used for garments that don't need well-defined individual stitches or for lofty garments needing warmth.

- Blends and knitting: The more even the blend, the more even the knitted fabric will be.

- Yarn plied in a Z direction is best for crocheting and twined knitting since that twist direction is amenable to the inherent twist direction of the crochet and twisted knit stitch.

- Knit directly from roving. This is a great method of knitting a garment that will be fulled later. But roving is difficult to knit. A very light hand is needed so the fiber doesn't fall apart.

Note: If you're not certain what type of yarn is best to spin for a project, knit a swatch with a commercially spun yarn that you would consider for a similar project, and in your spinning, try to "copy" some of the characteristics of the commercial yarn by using the guidelines found in SA-4: Tips for Matching Commercial Yarn, page 176. This test can also give you an idea of the amount of yarn you will need to spin for the project.

SPINNING JUST FOR THE ZEN OF IT

Spinning has been with us since before we had knowledge of the turning earth. It's part of our eternal pulse. When spinning, we're moving energy with each turn of the wheel, connecting forward and backward in time, drawing all of existence to the center of our actions. As all of creation is in flux and movement, spinning evokes the spirit of creation and energizes the soul. Yogis believe that a person's level of awareness is reflected in their reason for spinning. The lowest level of awareness is spinning to sell the yarn, next is spinning to weave, then spinning to gift the yarn. The highest awareness is spinning for pure meditation.

When you're comfortable with how your body relates to the wheel or spindle, you will find that spinning can open your mind and become a practice similar to meditation. It's meditation with the knitter's ultimate benefit: the creation of yarn, so your next meditative practice—knitting!—may begin.

Tips for Getting into a Spinning Zone

- Stretches, like shoulder rolls and hand extensions, can relieve tension in spinning—and knitting. Breathe deeply while stretching.

- Count your treadle strokes and pace your breathing to match the strokes. You will become more relaxed as you spin, and your yarn will become more evenly spun.

- To improve technique and really feel the spin, wear a blindfold, close your eyes, or bring your wheel into a dark room. This exercise will give you more confidence and help develop hand and finger sensitivity and control.

- Use the opposite hands from the ones you normally use as your forward and backward spinning hands. This switch is not only helpful to develop greater skill in spinning, but also charges different areas of the brain, keeping your mind alert.

- Every so often, release all expectations of your spinning and just spin to spin with no product in mind. You will find yourself breathing the spin, in and out. You may find it helpful to use essential oils like lavender and listen to relaxing music, paced to your spinning speed. Get into the rhythm of the spin, and you may even find yourself starting to fall asleep while spinning! When my mind can't settle down, I often take out my wheel and spin simply for meditation.

> *"When times are tough I sit down to spin during the news broadcasts, with therapeutic results. Knitting, as you well know, is therapy too."*
>
> —Elizabeth Zimmermann, *Knitter's Almanac*

Although not a technical spinning method, cupping the fiber mass within your hands will help you feel the give and take of the wheel and fiber. But your fiber must be *very* well prepared for it to not be taken en mass onto the wheel!

part 3　Dye Workshop

Y ou may choose to enjoy your handspun yarn in its original form—naked and unadorned. But this book is about all aspects of creating that piece of creative genius called yarn. This workshop walks you through the history of dyes, discusses the different dyes on the market today, and provides guidance on tools and step-by-step dyeing methods that you can replicate at home.

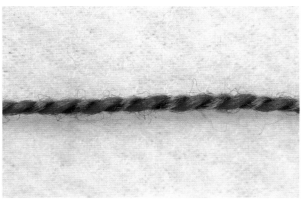

This painting by an unknown artist depicts early dyers tending a dye vat during Medieval times.
Universal History Archive/Photolibrary

A BRIEF HISTORY OF DYEING

The first known pigments can still be seen as prehistoric paintings on cave walls. They were mineral based—not dyes, but more like a paint or stain.

So what is dye? Dye is made of soluble compounds suspended in a medium that only dye fiber while in liquid form. When the compounds contact a fiber, they are diffused into the fiber, resulting in their color being transferred to the fiber's cells. Dyes may have been contemporary to cave painters, but since textiles haven't survived through the years like pigment on solid walls, the date of their origin can't be proven.

Just as the first spun fibers came from areas in which the spinner lived, the same was true of dyes. Dyers in certain regions of the world became specialized in the dye plants of their area. As trade routes opened up, dye plants began to cross borders and influence other regions, leading to advancement in dye techniques as competition and desire grew for the same dyestuff.

Some historians believe that Egypt was the first civilization to record its dye work. Egyptian dye pots consisted of madder (red), safflower (red and pink), indigo (blue), cochineal (red), archil (red), alkanet (red), buckthorn (yellow), saffron (yellow), and mulberry (red or purple). It's thought that the Egyptians also created the process of mordanting (fixing) colors that's still used today in natural dyeing, although the Chinese and Indians also claim this piece of history.

Of all the dye colors in ancient times, purple was the most esteemed. It was a rare color, requiring 10,000 mollusks for 1 g (0.04 oz) of dye. Some historical accounts say that if Nero (the Roman emperor) saw anyone outside of the royal family wearing purple, they were punished with death. (That had to affect the color trends of ancient Rome!)

Even though many dyes held an esteemed position in society, throughout early history, dyers held a lowly position. They were the experimenters—the "magicians" of the time (more accurately, the early "scientists") who were not trusted to be part of general society. Men are believed to have been the principal dyers in this outcast profession, since they are the only people shown on drawings depicting the profession at work, and all dye records found to date from this time were written by men. Of course, women may have been omitted from the historical record, but due to the high-risk nature of the work, it's unlikely that women served an active role.

As with spinning, the guilds of the Medieval and Renaissance periods encouraged advancement in dye technique. Dyers became better skilled at developing mordants and dyeing procedures, and brighter colors were created. Colors were made more stable, and the dyers themselves became more important. An example of their esteemed status was evident when guilds developed a system to organize the use of water in cities and towns just so dyers would have clean water for their dye process. Dyeing finally came out of the dark ages and into a bright new world—albeit, a secretive world. Akin to great security around today's corporate trade secrets, guilds kept dyer's notes under strict lock and key. Nevertheless, in time, dye "trade secrets" leaked out, and the resulting competition became one of the driving forces behind advancements in the dye industry as it moved toward the future.

Dyeing to Heal—and Put on Eyeliner

Early alchemists (our modern-day pharmacists and chemists) advanced the dye industry. Fueled by a desire to develop new substances, these visionaries experimented with new methods of extracting and processing solids and liquids for medicines and beauty products. Some of the experiments eventually became dye colors. Alchemists made the color vermillion from sulfur and mercury, and the color gold from sulfur, tin, and mercury. But these innovators died young—no doubt because of their work with these very toxic elements.

The post-Renaissance humanistic era of the 1700s marked significant advancement in dyeing science. New elements such as cobalt, manganese, and chlorine were discovered, and a uniform system of measurement in chemistry was established. The modern-day pharmaceutical industry got its start in this early age of chemistry, and some of the experiments led to new dye formulas.

When the textile industry became mechanized in the 1800s, so did the dye industry. Soon dye plants were grown in large-scale production. A dyer, Michel-Eugene Chevreul, created the first chromatic color wheel, making the mixing of

Dyes, Intrigue, and Empires—and You Thought You Were Just Dyeing a Pretty Red!

- Mining of the mordant alum became the "petroleum industry" of the Middle Ages, and even the papacy had alum holdings.

- The "discovery" of the West Indies and the Americas led to a new source for dyes that produced reds. These new red dyes were costly, and the high cost in turn elevated the status of the color red, changing the garments of religious and royal elite from purple to red.

- The story of cochineal is closely associated with the Spanish conquests in the Americas during the 1500s. The Spanish established plantations of cactus in the Americas to meet the mounting desire in Europe for the cactus-loving bug and its rich, red dye. Cochineal ultimately decimated worldwide demand for madder—the previously favored red dye. (Thank cochineal for your bottle of Bordeaux. When cochineal became the favored red dye of Europe, French madder farmers turned their fields over to the growing of grapes for wine. This started the French wine industry that we enjoy today.)

- Brazilwood, a plant that produces a red, orange, or brown colored dye, was not named after the country, but rather the country was named after the dye plant.

Yellow dye powder with mortar and pestle. One of the earliest examples of dyed fabric dates to 6000 BC—it was dyed yellow.

colors more reliable. He was also one of the first chemists to explore the potential of synthesizing color elements from plants. This set the stage for the first synthetic dyes, which were born out of necessity due to the strain put on natural dye resources from the ever-expanding textile industry of the mid-1800s.

A Brave New Synthetic World

We have the mosquito to thank for synthetic dyes. In 1856, William Henry Perkin, a teenage English chemistry student, developed the first synthetic dye while attempting to synthesize quinine for malaria patients. His experiment became the color mauve. It came from a base of coal tar and led to other synthetic (aniline) dyes that were developed in a similar method. These dyes were made from natural substances that were manipulated into a dye structure through a chemical process (that is, organic chemistry—the science of carbon and hydrogen structures). Following Perkin's discovery, a tidal wave of chemists made attempts to create the next great dye. The first water-soluble acid dye was developed in 1862. By 1868, the structure of madder was recreated in a lab. It was chemically identical to natural madder, but it contained no impurities, was fast in color (didn't fade), and was less expensive. In 1880, indigo was synthesized for the first time, and the synthetic dye industry of today was born.

ABOUT DYES TODAY

There are two categories of contemporary dyes: natural (made from an animal, vegetable, or mineral source) and synthetic (made from chemically synthesized natural and petrochemical material). In the eco-conscious world of today, synthetic dyes often provoke scorn and heated opinions. This is a somewhat unfair position. Let me try to put reality into focus on the good and bad of both natural and synthetic dyes.

The Naturals

What is it about the lure of natural dyes? Is it the romance of picking the delicate flower and watching as it swirls in a hot bath, releasing its color essence? Experiencing the penetration of color as it enters the fiber, essentially merging the sun, earth, and sky to create the color we envision? Or is it the fact that natural dyes seem more real than a powder from a can? Perhaps it's just that natural dyeing balances us. When we use natural dyes, we think about the earth and how ancient methods of dyeing are still viable—and best of all, we don't have to buy all the ingredients. There's no denying that natural dyes put us in touch with the earth. They can be locally gathered—usually at no or minor cost—and are pleasing to process into dye. Whatever drives the passion for dyeing naturally, we must admit: It's a strong force.

Getting down to reality, natural dyeing often requires a lot of dyestuff to create enough dye for just one dye session (often 50 to 100 percent of the weight of the fiber), perhaps depleting the natural regrowth of flowers and plants in the

A couple varieties of mushrooms—
a commonly found natural dye stuff

process, and in the case of mordants, stripping the ground of minerals. If we had to rely only on natural dyes today, the dye industry would negatively impact our natural resources in a dramatic way because of the huge amount of natural material needed to successfully dye on a large scale. In addition, natural dye colors are not easily reproducible; are often not fast (in both literal time and color-stability terms); are sometimes unpredictable; have varying methods of processing requiring some advance knowledge specific to the dyestuff and process; can be seasonal in supply; have color options limited by dyestuff and additives; may require ecologically toxic mordants (it takes only 0.1 oz [3 g] of alum to kill a child—1 oz [30 g] for an adult); and the dyestuff itself can even consist of toxic or deadly elements (as in the case of some mushrooms).

The Synthetics

Synthetic dyes require less product to create, so they don't deplete as great a quantity of the earth's natural resources as natural dyes do. Synthetic dyes are reproducible; are fast; are usually predictable; follow universal dye methods; dye relatively quickly; are commonly available to buy; have a nearly unlimited number of color options; do not require mordants or dangerous fixatives; and have low or no toxicity, depending on the manufacturer and dye color (exception: synthetic black contains chromium, which is toxic).

But synthetics are synthesized from petrochemicals and this is their Achille's heel. The same substances could be produced from other carbon sources, but it takes a substantially larger quantity—at a greater financial cost with potentially greater environmental damage—to match what petrochemicals offer. So, for now, they are petrochemically synthesized, and that's also not ecologically optimal.

The Best Dyeing Method

Quite honestly, the best dyeing method for the earth and our health would be not to dye at all. Looking at the realities of both dyeing realms, there is no truly environmentally friendly dyeing process—just degrees of eco-friendly based on the chemicals and procedures being employed.

There's a *lot* of misinformation in the world about the facts of dyeing. Misinformed dyers without chemistry backgrounds spread more misinformation, and, when the cyber world is involved, myths become truths. There are two classes of synthetic dyes: industrial and home. The home dye market contains less toxic dyes than the industrial dye market, yet many of the studies about the toxicity of synthetic dyes refer to statistics coming from industrial dyeing. This is like comparing apples to oranges. Because of intense consumer focus on the synthetic dye industry, the United States, Canada, Europe, and a few other countries heavily regulate and regularly test synthetic dyes for their environmental impact. As a result of this vocal interest, more synthetic dyes are being created as "low-impact" dyes—meaning they've been designed with no or few heavy metal particles, resulting in a dye that contains no or few environmentally hazardous by-products.

Since natural dyers are mostly home dyers and their own regulators of safe dyeing procedures, one can only hope that self-regulation of natural dyeing is effective. But I'll bet many home natural dyers are pouring mordants such as tin, chrome, and alum down the drain, thinking they aren't doing enough dyeing to affect the environment. Those mordants should not be put into the sewer system in any quantities and should either be eliminated in the dye bath through exhaustion or evaporated and disposed of in an appropriate manner—*sometimes* as hazardous waste.

No matter which dye method you choose, the most important consideration is to be responsible. Responsibility starts by being knowledgeable about the dye process and following safe dyeing practices *every time* you dye, whether you are using natural or synthetic dyes. Wear a dust mask when working with the dry dyestuff of both natural and synthetic dyes. The fine dye powder of synthetic acid and fiber-reactive dyes can be a lung irritant, but, with a few exceptions, is not toxic. Dry natural dyestuff and mordants may also irritate the lungs, and more of these may be toxic. Vapors from acid dye cooking are generally not toxic, but may irritate the lungs of sensitive people. Natural-dye cooking vapors have a greater chance of being toxic (especially if you are dyeing with poisonous plants or fungi). A vapor mask is recommended for those who have lung sensitivities because of over-exposure and to prevent the possibility of developing sensitivities because of over-exposure to the vapors of either the natural or synthetic dyes. I wear a vapor mask as a precaution since I spend a good deal of time in the dye lab and don't want to develop sensitivities that would end my dyeing days.

Dyeing is an industry that has always changed with the times, from the early alchemists to the modern-day innovators. I'm hopeful that a modern-day alchemist will develop a dye that is totally eco-friendly, safe to use for all fibers, and fast. In the meantime, enjoy whatever type of dyeing suits your needs or interest while following the best dye methods for you and the planet.

Until we have safer, truly earth-friendly dyes, I've picked dyes for Dye Workshop that have the fewest issues with safety and eco-concerns, yet are effective in dyeing our *Yarn Works* fibers.

DETERMINING A FIBER'S DYEABILITY

The dyeability of a fiber is relative to the cellular characteristics of the particular fiber. Wool dyes very well due to its unique scale structure and great ability to absorb moisture (including dye), especially when the fiber is well scoured and in an acid environment, such as found in the acid dyeing process.

Cellulose fibers have a cellular structure that is less favorable to accepting dye, so the fiber reactive dye process, which creates an alkaline environment to open up the cellulose fiber cells to accept dye, is the most effective.

The unique physical characteristics of different fibers also influence dyeability and the dye appearance. The long guard fibers (awl) of angora are hollow and do not deeply absorb dye. Some fibers have a cuticle that inhibits dye absorption. And some fibers with a natural sheen (such as silk) will reflect more light back to the eye and, when dyed, appear lighter in tone than a fiber with little or no natural sheen (such as cotton).

Note: Silk is less slippery when dyed, so you may want to wait to spin it until after dyeing. Cultivated silk has a brighter surface than other silks and will give the brightest dyed colors. Tussah (wild) silk has a natural, buff tone and will give a rich, overdyed color.

Dyed silk: on the left is cultivated silk and on the right is honey tussah silk

When you know the unique dye characteristics of the fiber you are using, you can prepare for possible surprises or achieve intentional unique dye effects—such as creating a heathered color by dyeing unlike fiber types, such as protein and cellulose, in the same dye pot with only one dye method. Fiber-Reactive Dye Workshop (page 103) has more detail on specific fiber characteristics along with notes on the dyes suited for specific fibers.

Dyeing to Knit

The appearance of dye color is affected by the way the yarn is knit. Since knit stitches lie back farther than purl stitches, purling certain stitches will bring those colors forward and enhance them. When knitting a color pattern such as Fair Isle, the color stitch being worked for the main pattern can be held to the front of the other colors to help it dominate in the knitting.

If you have a yarn that's been dyed with too many bold color areas, try knitting with an open stitch, such as lace, to break up the dominating color effect. Or, if possible, adjust your needle size to change the knitting gauge and the overall look.

A yarn that's dyed in a solid color will stand out better in a color pattern than one that has a heathered appearance. Similarly, a knit pattern that has lots of detailed stitches will also look best when knit with a solid-color yarn.

If skeins of dyed yarn are unevenly dyed, knit by alternating skeins every other row to make the knit material appear more uniform.

Acid dyed fibers from Hanna Knit Workshop project (page 125). Left to right: in fleece form, carded, and after spinning

The Best Dye Time in the Life of a Fiber

Because there are so many dye methods and options, it can be hard to know when is the right time to dye a fiber. Here are some considerations to help you pick a dye time that's best for your particular fiber and final purpose.

You can dye your fiber

- Just after washing the raw fleece—if dyed with a strong color saturation, the final result will make an even tone in the final yarn, since the dye color will be evenly distributed throughout the fiber by the time it's prepared for spinning. This is also the best time to dye if you are at all nervous about the dye process ruining your fiber or are uncertain about your color choices, since you have little time investment in the process up to this point.

- After carding or combing—providing more opportunity to control color in the yarn since you can keep the colors in their dye groups for spinning.

- After singles have been spun—to achieve individual color strands (also called "marled" yarn) or hand-painted effects.

- After the yarn has been spun, plied, and the twist set. If kettle dyed, the yarn color will be the most even of any of the dyeing methods. When hand painted, the color will be the most controlled to suit a unique, although less reproducible, colorway. The downside is that it's more difficult to fix dye problems at this end stage.

Note: If you want to reproduce a color, record keeping is vital. There's nothing more frustrating than having a great color that memory can't recreate. Look to DA-7: Record Keeping for Dyeing, page 185, for a record-keeping dye journal form and photocopy it for your dyeing workshops.

Note: The fibers highlighted in the *Yarn Works* Dye Workshops are all naturally light in color and were selected for their suitability for dyeing. To encourage creativity, I've kept the instructions generic, letting you fill in the blanks for your fiber and color preferences. The hope is that this chapter will be a guide to help you proceed on your own to other dyeing experiments with added confidence.

Being able to dye our own fiber and yarn is the apex of creativity for knitters. Color can make our yarn truly distinctive. Unfortunately, I've found that many people back away from the dyeing process, thinking it involves messy, complicated, and/or dangerous procedures. But the fact is, a degree in chemistry is not needed to dye yarn. Yes, there are certainly dye processes that border on the complex (such as natural and fiber-reactive dyeing), but there are also one-step synthetic dyes with a process nearly as easy as heating water. If you feel at all threatened by dyeing, think of it in terms of cooking or baking. Similar principles apply. You need to measure accurately and "cook" the ingredients thoroughly and safely. But in the end, if the recipe is followed, you'll have a "dish" that's absolutely delicious to look at and knit with!

Note: Dye Workshop focuses on metric measures (grams, liters, and milliliters) since it's a more accurate and easier-to-follow measuring system for the dye process.

MEET THE DYES

Even though household dyers have a wide palette of dye types to choose between, there are only a handful of dyes that are in common use today, mainly because they are generally less toxic and easier for the household dyer to use. The main headings for these dye types are natural and synthetic. Under the heading of synthetic, the main types of dyes are acid (for protein fibers) and fiber reactive (for cellulose fibers).

NATURAL DYES

Since natural dye choices are nearly as varied as all living matter on earth, to help guide the discussion, I'll focus on three of the most historically significant natural dyes: cochineal, madder, and indigo. Both protein and cellulose fibers may be dyed with these natural dyes, although different processing methods are required for the two fiber groups. (See Natural Dye Workshop, page 92.)

COCHINEAL

Cochineal, an Aztec name meaning "the blood of the prickly pear," is derived from a small, grain-sized beetle primarily found on the prickly pear (*Opuntia*) cactus. The dye pigment comes from a carminic acid in the bug's body that deters predators from eating them. Ironically, it's the same carminic acid that drives human predators (harvesters) to collect them two to four times a year as a fiber and food colorant. The bugs are dried and crushed to make the rich, red dyestuff. Approximately 9,000 insects are needed for 57 g (2 oz) of dye.

Note: Cochineal bugs are also commonly used as a food coloring, although in food ingredient listings, the dyestuff is referred to as "carmine" or "carminic acid."

MADDER

The other significant red dye is *rubia tinctorum*—dyer's madder. It's made from the dried, ground-up root of a two- to three-year-old madder plant. This plant is native to the eastern Mediterranean and central Asia, but is found in cultivated form in temperate regions all over the world. It takes only 113 g (4 oz) of madder root to dye 227 g (½ lb) of wool.

INDIGO

The dyestuff of indigo comes from a plant in the legume family. There are many species of indigo; the most common for dyeing come from *indigofera*. It takes 45 kg (100 lb) of leaves to produce 113 g (4 oz) of the dyestuff. The dried leaves are ground into a powder prior to dyeing. This powder is insoluble in water, but when a reducing agent such as thiourea dioxide is added to the dye bath, indigo powder is converted into a water-soluble form. When fiber is put into the dye bath, the now-soluble dye is absorbed by to the fiber and turns green. When the fiber is removed from the vat and exposed to oxygen, the indigo turns back into its insoluble form and the fiber turns blue.

Note: For more information on natural dyes, see the Bibliography on page 160 for a list of recommended sources.

Cochineal bugs

Madder roots

Pre-reduced indigo powder on left and pure indigo crystals on right

Powdered dyes are easy to measure and dissolve quickly in hot water.

Synthetic Dyes

Although there are several different synthetic dyes to choose between, I'll focus on two synthetic dye types that are the most used today: acid dyes for protein and polyamide (nylon) fibers, and fiber reactive dyes for cellulose fibers. They are the easiest synthetic dyes to work with and the safest for the home dyer. (See Acid Dye Workshop: Protein Fibers, page 100, and Fiber-Reactive Dye Workshop: Cellulose/Bast Fibers, page 103.)

ACID DYE

Protein and polyamide (nylon) fibers are the only fibers that are chemically compatible with acid dyes. To be dyed, protein fibers must first become positively charged with acid to attract the negatively charged dye molecules to the fiber and allow it to diffuse into the fiber cells. Although the name is scary, the acid in acid dye is merely household vinegar (or food-grade citric acid).

For the projects in this book, I've used the Jacquard brand of acid dye, which only requires the addition of 5 percent acetic acid (household white vinegar) or citric acid crystals to fix the color.

Eco Note: Neither vinegar nor citric acid is an environmental danger since they break down biologically. As long as the acid dye doesn't contain heavy metals (such as chromium or lead), the dye will also safely break down biologically. (See the manufacturer's specifications for the dye chemical breakdowns.)

Note: Dye baths exhaust more efficiently with citric acid crystals since they contain 56 percent acetic acid, allowing for more dye bonding with the fiber than with household vinegar (typically 5 percent acetic acid). The crystals have an added benefit of no vinegar smell.

Another option is all-in-one acid dye, such as Gaywool by Louet, which has the acid ingredient already added to the dye powder. All-in-one dyes cost more because of this convenience. Most professional dyers recommend Lanaset/Sabraset dyes for superior wash- and lightfastness, although this dye needs leveling salt (Glauber's salt) for even color distribution, costs more than other acid dyes, and is a somewhat "fussier" method of dyeing more suited for experienced dyers.

Acid dyes (left) and fiber-reactive dyes (right) are packaged in powder form.

Fiber-Reactive Dye

Fiber-reactive dyes, created in 1956, are best suited for cellulose fibers. Fiber-reactive dyes form a bond with fiber dye sites through a chemical reaction, resulting in the dye molecule actually becoming a part of the fiber molecule. This "covalent" bond is stronger than the chemical bond made with acid dyes and very wash- and lightfast. The cellulose dye projects in this book were dyed with Jacquard Procion MX dyes (a common brand of fiber-reactive dye).

Glauber's salt is added to fiber-reactive dye baths as a dye leveler to even out absorption. The salt slows the processing, allowing the fiber to absorb more dye before it's permanently fixed on the fiber. The dye bath needs a high pH environment for dye bonding (10.5 pH is best), so soda ash is also added to raise the alkalinity. No heating of the dye bath is needed with Procion MX dyes.

Eco Note: Both salt and soda ash do not break down biologically, remaining as salts, so they may adversely salinate the ecosystem.

Note: Protein fibers can be dyed with fiber-reactive dyes, but the high pH soda ash needs to be replaced with vinegar or citric acid to avoid damaging the protein fiber. Dye colors may not be consistent on protein fibers, so the final result is unpredictable; plus not all of the dye may be absorbed by the protein fibers, the fiber-reactive dye won't exhaust completely. Since this method essentially turns fiber-reactive dye into acid dye, it's better to dye protein fibers with acid dyes to get more predictable, efficient, and environmentally friendly results.

Even though silk is a protein fiber, it can be dyed with either the acid or fiber reactive methods, since it isn't damaged as readily by alkaline conditions.

Other Common "Household" Dyes (not included in the Dye Workshops)

Kool-Aid, Easter egg dye tablets, and food-coloring dyes—these are acid dyes for protein fibers. (Kool-Aid already contains the acid needed in the form of citric acid crystals.) Instruction on dyeing with these nontoxic dyes is easily found online. These dyes aren't as wash- or lightfast as other acid dyes, but they are great alternative dyes if children are involved in the process. Even though they are nontoxic, take caution to not inhale the powder form of these dyes.

All-purpose dyes, such as Rit (also called union dyes)—these are "one-size-fits-all" dyes for nearly all fiber types. They compensate for the different fiber types with different processing methods. They are less eco-friendly than other dyes because they contain a concoction of chemicals designed to dye a wider variety of fibers. Since not all the dye particles/chemicals are able to chemically bond to the particular fiber being dyed, excess dye particles/chemicals float loose in the dye bath as waste. Some of these particles may be hazardous.

Note: You may have heard of "disperse" dye. This is a dye used exclusively for dyeing synthetic fibers such as polyester. The chemical carrier in this dye acts as a softener to break down the tough synthetic fibers allowing the dye to be absorbed. Because of this strong chemical, disperse dye is more toxic than most dyes available today and, even though it can be readily purchased, home dyers seldom use it due to its toxicity.

Revealing the True Dye Soda: The Difference between Baking Soda, Household Washing Soda, and Soda Ash

Soda ash is a sodium carbonate that increases the alkaline nature of a dye bath (that is, it increases its pH). Baking soda is sodium *bicarbonate*. It's slower reacting and doesn't have the same effectiveness in a dye bath as household washing soda or soda ash. But even though household washing soda and soda ash are both made of the more ideal sodium carbonate, many washing sodas for household cleaning contain bleach or other additives to help brighten and may be formulated at a weaker strength for the household market. In addition, the bleach and additives often found in household washing soda can damage fiber. More washing soda is also needed to raise the pH sufficiently for the dye reaction, making washing soda a more expensive dye assist. So that leaves us with soda ash as the best, true, full-strength sodium carbonate to increase the pH of our alkaline dye processes. It's available through art and dye supply shops. (See Resources and Supplies on page 159.)

SUPPLIES AND TOOLS FOR DYEING

What follows is a general list of supplies and tools that may be needed for your dye process, so not all of these may be necessary for the dye process you choose. Before beginning to collect any items, check your particular dye method for the ones that apply to your situation.

Note: Supply and tool sources are listed in Resources and Supplies, page 159.

Supplies (see Dye Workshops for specific dye method tools)

- dye—see specific dye method for type
- mordants and assists (for natural dyeing; see dye method for ingredients needed)
- white vinegar or citric acid crystals (for acid dyeing)
- soda ash and Glauber's salt (for fiber-reactive dyeing)
- urea (for hand painting with fiber-reactive dye)
- neutral pH soap—Synthrapol or a liquid dishwashing soap such as Dawn

Suggested Tools

Note: Aside from a microwave and stove/hot plate, none of these tools should be used for food after being used for dyeing.

COOKING EQUIPMENT OPTIONS

- nonreactive pot (stainless steel, glass, or enamel). Do not use aluminum or iron. If using an enamel pot, there should be no chips in the enamel. Use a pot that's as large as you can find and will fit on your cooking device. You will never regret getting a large pot that has at least a 15 L (16-qt) capacity. (My favorite is a 15 L [16-qt] white enamel pot so I can really see the color of the dye and the fiber being soaked.)
- slow cooker (Crock-Pot)
- microwave—preferably not in a kitchen
- vegetable steamer
- plastic tubs (for dye methods that don't require heating)
- stove or hot plate—preferably not in a kitchen. A hot plate is especially useful when cooking natural dyestuff outdoors. (My favorite cooking surface is an induction hot plate, since it doesn't have a dangerous flame and has a digital temperature setting with a timer shutoff. It can be used inside or outside, as long as there's an electric outlet nearby.)

MEASURING AND MIXING

- measuring spoons
- digital scale to measure both fiber and dyestuff from 1 g (0.01 oz). (A jeweler's scale with a 1 g (0.01 oz) measure is a fairly inexpensive scale specifically for weighing dyes.)

- heat-resistant measuring cups
- stainless steel spoons, glass rods, or chopsticks (wood or stainless steel)
- instant-read cooking thermometer or candy thermometer
- clean-up cloths and wet sponges (if using reusable rags, wash them separately from other laundry)
- dye remover to clean surfaces (often standard kitchen cleaners will remove dye from surfaces)
- wet mop
- microwave-safe glass pans and bowls
- microwavable plastic wrap (the kind that seals to the container)
- buckets for soaking and washing fiber

ABOVE LEFT Some of the general tools used for dyeing: slow cooker, pot, steamer, plastic tub, and hot plate.

ABOVE RIGHT General tools to have on hand: measuring cups and spoons, scale, cups, glass rods/sticks, thermometer, cleanup rags, liquid cleanser, glass bowl, plastic wrap

A jeweler's digital scale is great for measuring dyestuff.

ABOVE LEFT For safety, be sure to use the following: apron, dust mask, gloves, and potholders.

ABOVE RIGHT Optional supplies

CLOTHING AND SAFETY EQUIPMENT

- dust mask—always wear one when mixing dyes
- gloves. A pair of heat-resistant rubber gloves is best for hot cooking methods, but for greater flexibility of grip, lightweight first aid or painter's disposable gloves are adequate for non-hot situations. Some dyers use a product called Liquid Gloves before putting on other safety gloves to help keep rogue dye from dyeing their hands.
- apron (for keeping clothes clean and also to protect from spills of hot liquids or chemicals)
- potholders (for hot dye-cooking methods)

OPTIONAL

- graduated pipette and pipette bulb for measuring small quantities of dye solution
- pH strips for measuring the pH of the exhausted dye bath prior to disposing it
- face mask rated for fumes
- safety glasses (for dye bath splashes)
- calculator
- note paper/dye record keeping form (DA-7: Record Keeping for Dyeing: A Dye Journal, page 185)
- color wheel
- mortar and pestle
- stainless steel whisk for mixing dye solution
- lingerie laundry bags with zipper (to contain fibers—not for microwave cooking method)
- zipper-style freezer plastic bags (to contain fibers for microwave cooking method)

- plastic or stainless steel funnel
- cheesecloth (to contain fibers)
- paint strainer or fine coffee filter (to strain dye solution)
- timer
- full-spectrum lights
- clothes washing machine (top loading)

PRACTICE SAFE DYEING IN YOUR KITCHEN

It's ideal to have a space separate from your kitchen to use for dyeing, but if the kitchen is your only option, follow these basic rules.

- Mix the dry dyestuff away from the kitchen, keeping the dye material away from any foodstuff.
- Don't use old food containers to store dyes or other dyeing ingredients, and do not store dye materials around foodstuff.
- Ventilate well while dyeing, and spotlessly clean the area before using it again for cooking.

OTHER SAFE DYEING RECOMMENDATIONS

- The best dye solution storage containers are glass. If you wish to use a plastic container, be sure it is stamped with the code: HDPE 1. This identifies the plastic as a high-density polyethylene that withstands most solutions from the household dye process. Other plastics aren't as resistant to dye solutions and can leak over time.
- Keep all supplies marked with their real ingredients and away from children.
- Store dyestuff in a dark, cool, and dry location.
- Cover tables with thick plastic or vinyl tablecloths, preferably in white so you can see dye colors without distraction. (I use old shower curtains.)
- Clean up dye spills with a wet sponge, cloth, or mop.
- Arrange for good ventilation, even if using a mask. If using a fan to aid in ventilation, turn it off when working with dry dyestuff.
- Do not automatically put a natural dye bath down the drain. (See Dye Bath Disposal, page 105).
- Use common sense. Avoid eating or drinking while dyeing and avoid dyeing if pregnant, breast feeding, or unwell.

HOW TO PREPARE FIBERS AND DYES

As you ready a kitchen to prepare a special recipe, you must prepare fibers and dye prior to dyeing.

The Five Steps of Fiber Prep

Note: Raw fiber with grease must be scoured before beginning these steps. See FA-3: How to Clean Raw Fleece, page 164.

1. **Weigh the dry fiber/yarn.**

   Record the weight (preferably in metrics). *All dye calculations will be based on the dry fiber weight so this step is vital.*

2. **Contain fiber and yarn.**

   All loose fibers should be put in some sort of containment. Use a wrap of cheesecloth tied with string (undyed so dye won't bleed from the tie) or a small laundry bag for washing lingerie. (Remember, if using cotton wraps or bags, they will also dye in a fiber-reactive dye process.) If using a microwave cooking process, freezer bags (slightly open for venting) may be used for containing loose fibers.

   Roving can be loosely tied into bundles or placed in cheesecloth or lingerie bags for dyeing.

   Spun yarn needs to be in skein form and tied with a loose figure-eight knot in at least four to eight places (see Spin Workshop, page 41).

3. **"Wet out" the fiber.**

   Before the fiber can be dyed, soak it in a warm, soapy bath to clean it in preparation for evenly accepting the dye. If dyeing with an acid method, combine "wetting out" with the presoak step on next page.

All fiber and yarn should be weighed before beginning the dye process.

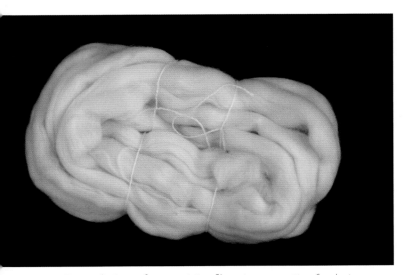
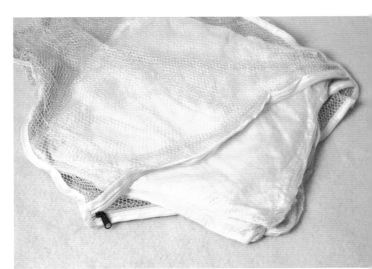

Two techniques for containing fibers in preparation for dyeing:
LEFT: Roving tied in a bundle. **RIGHT:** Silk hankies placed in a lingerie bag.

NATURAL DYEING ONLY: USING MORDANTS—THE "AMBASSADORS" OF NATURAL DYEING

Mordants chemically prepare fiber to accept most natural dyestuff (some natural dyestuff, such as indigo and weld, don't require mordanting of the fiber). You could say mordants create an environment of friendship between the dyestuff and the fiber. They also set up what dye color will result on the fiber, depending on the particular chemistry of the dyestuff, mordant, and fiber, as well as the processing method. Some natural dyestuff is mordanted after dyeing, but in Dye Workshop, we will work only with premordanted techniques.

Premordanting Prep

Premordanting is done after wetting out the fiber. In premordanting, the clean fiber is usually heated in a mordant solution for a period of time specified by tested recipes. See the Natural Dye Workshop on page 92 for how to prepare fiber with an alum mordant.

ACID DYEING ONLY: ACID PRESOAK—COMBINES THE WETTING-OUT STEP WITH AN ACID PRESOAK

For 100 g (3.5 oz) of fiber—increase proportionately for other weights.

Soak fibers for 30 minutes in an acid presoak of 37 ml (2.5 tbsp) white vinegar or 4 g (¾ tsp) of citric acid crystals and 2.5 ml (½ tsp) of a neutral pH soap (such as Synthrapol) for every 3.8 L (1 gal) of hot water. Do not rinse. Squeeze out excess water from the fiber before dyeing.

Note: Silk requires a longer presoak, from 30 minutes to 1 hour, to allow the bath water to penetrate the fiber. But beware of soaking silk for too long, since it can be damaged by acid in the presoak bath. You'll know it's soaked through when the silk sinks to the bottom of your soaking container.

FIBER-REACTIVE DYEING ONLY (CELLULOSE AND CELLULOSIC FIBERS): PRESOAK METHODS

For 100 g (3.5 oz) of fiber—increase proportionately for other weights.

Immersion dyeing. Soak fibers for 1 hour in a boiling water bath of 2.5 ml (½ tsp) Synthrapol for every 3.8 L (1 gal) of water. Rinse fibers in clear, hot water after soaking.

Hand painting or LWI (low water immersion).—First, wash fibers by soaking them for 1 hour in a boiling water bath of 2.5 ml (½ tsp) Synthrapol for every 3.8 L (1 gal) of water. Rinse fibers in clear, hot water after soaking. Soak fibers for an additional hour in an alkaline presoak of 75 ml (5 tbsp) of soda ash for every 3.8 L (1 gal) of warm water (add more soda ash if necessary to reach a pH of 10.5). Do not rinse. Squeeze out excess water from the fiber. (The soaking solution can be reused a few times in future dye sessions before being disposed.)

Dye in Lots If You're Going to Dye Lots

Like commercial yarn dye lots, dyes vary from lot to lot, so you'll find that trying to match a color based on a predyed swatch isn't always reliable. Even if you're using a synthetic dye from the same dye lot, you may see a slight color variation from one dye session to the next just based on differences in the hardness of the water or slight changes in the water temperature. So if you're dyeing yarn or fiber for a large project, dye it all together to avoid any color surprises.

Tied roving entering a presoak bath

4. **Calculate the amount of dye powder, solution, or dyestuff.**

    The final dye saturation is not determined by the amount of dye put into the pot, but rather by the ratios of dye, dye water, and fiber.

THE MATH OF DYEING

The formulas for calculating dye stock have always flummoxed me. I'm "math phobic," and just looking at numbers in formulas can send me into a cold sweat. But being able to measure dye that's reproducible is the true test of a good dye barista—so in Dye Workshop, I've tried to make the formulas and calculations as friendly as possible by giving specific examples and making the language clear. I recommend that you play with the formulas in advance of beginning your dye session so you really understand them. Measure twice—dye once! A calculator will be very helpful.

Calculating Depth of Shade (DOS)

The first consideration in calculating dye quantity is what depth of color shade you wish to dye. DOS is a guide to the amount of dye that's needed for dyeing particular shades and is measured by the percentage of dye to the weight of the fiber or yarn to be dyed. See DA-4: Measuring Dye Powder Using the Standard DOS (Depth of Shade) Formula, page 182, for how to calculate DOS.

Measuring Dye Powder

Dye may be measured using volume measures, such as spoon measures, or by scale weight. The scale weight option is more accurate and is the system I use in Dye Workshop. It's a more reliable measurement, since spoon measures can vary greatly based on the user and the dye powder properties. Plus, the weight system is absolutely reproducible, and that's important if you ever want to replicate your results. You will need a digital scale that records grams. If you want to mix smaller amounts of dye than your scale permits, you can make concentrated dye stock solutions (see below) and use those in your measurements.

Concentrated dye stock in solution

Concentrated dye stock solution should be stored in a labeled bottle.

Measuring Dye Stock Solution

Working with powdered dyes is made easier and safer by creating concentrated dye stock solutions. The dye is then available to use as you wish, for either immersion dyeing (by mixing it with a proportionate amount of water) or for hand painting, which uses many different hand application techniques, often directly from the dye solution or as a dilution (Creative Dyeing Workshop, page 106). Dye stock solution is made from dry dye powder premixed with water into a concentrated form (something like frozen orange juice concentrate). Go to DA-5: Recipe for Concentrated Dye Stock Solutions, page 183, for instruction on mixing stock solutions.

Measuring Natural Dyestuff

Many natural dye recipes require dyestuff in quantities as much as 50 to 100 percent of fiber weight. See your specific natural dyeing recipe for the amount of dyestuff needed.

5. **Prepare for the cooking method to be used: kettle, vat, steamer, slow cooker, microwave.** See The Dye Workshops for the traditional kettle and vat methods.

ALTERNATIVE DYE WORKSHOP COOKING METHODS

A slow cooker or microwave may be used instead of a kettle for immersion dyeing. They are also great tools for cooking hand painted fibers and for steam setting dyes.

Slow Cooker

This method follows the same setup steps used for kettle dyeing, but the pot is more evenly heated than in kettle dyeing and heats up much more slowly. It's a good cooking method for delicate fibers. A slow cooker pot can be used for steaming, low water immersion dyeing, and hand painting (Creative Dyeing Workshop, page 106). Test the slow cooker in advance to see how long it takes to reach the required temperature and note at which setting the slow cooker should be set to maintain the correct heat for the dye and fiber. When the temperature is stable, follow the standard cooking method for the dyestuff. Do not reuse the slow cooker for food after using it for dyeing!

Slow cooker pot with dye and fiber

Microwave with dyestuff

Note: It's not recommended to use a microwave for food after using it for dye cooking, although, depending on the dye method, many people do this with no ill effect. At the very least, clean and air it out well after dyeing.

Microwave

Often used for steaming, hand painting, or LWI (low water immersion) dyeing, microwaves can also be used to rapidly cook using the standard immersion method. They are perfect for dyeing delicate fibers that may be prone to felting.

Note: In LWI dyeing, if the fiber is dry between dye application areas, it could burn (even flame) in the cooking process. Be sure the fiber is entirely wet and put a "heat sink" (a small open container holding water) in a corner of the microwave to help keep the fiber from drying out and catching fire.

1. Place the hand-painted or dye-immersed fiber into a microwave-safe bowl, using plastic wrap to seal the bowl and leaving an unsealed gap of about an inch (2.5 cm) to vent the steam. (If the cooking container is not vented, there will be an explosion of dye in the microwave. If using plastic freezer bags as a cooking container, they must be open about an inch [2.5 cm] for venting.)

2. Place the contained fiber into the microwave, close the door, and start the cooking at 100 percent power for 3 minutes. (See below for instructions for other wattages.) Watch the process carefully to be sure there are no signs of burning or boiling fiber.

3. After the first 3 minutes, open the door, check the fiber and container seal, and reset the microwave for 100 percent power and another 3 minutes. If cooked longer and/or at hotter temperatures, the fiber may felt or even burn. The dye process is done when the dye bath is clear or nearly clear.

4. When cool enough to handle, remove the container from the microwave.

5. Let the fiber cool to room temperature while still in the cooking container. Then gently remove it from the container and finish according to the dye and fiber requirements.

Tip: Check the Wattage

Cooking times and powers given here are based on a 1,000-watt microwave. A microwave with less wattage will require more cooking time and power. A microwave with more wattage will require less cooking time and power for the same time intervals. Experiment with a 30-second difference in time and 10 percent difference in power for every 200 watts. Silk should be cooked at a lower power level (70 percent) than wool (100 percent).

Steam Setting

This method uses a steam chamber made just for dyeing (or a vegetable steamer, slow cooker, or microwave) with just an inch (2.5 cm) or so of water in the bottom of the container. Then the chamber or pot is heated for the time required by the dyeing method. This is a great way to dye silk without damaging the heat-sensitive fiber.

THE DYE WORKSHOPS

The following workshops move step by step through the dyeing process using immersion methods of dyeing with the natural dyes of cochineal, madder, and indigo (page 92); Jacquard Acid Dye for protein/nylon/silk fibers (page 100); and Procion MX fiber-reactive dye for cellulose/bast fibers (page 103). The workshops are presented like open recipes, so you may fill in your own calculations and reuse the recipes in the future.

Note: The use of the word *fiber* may be interchangeable with *spun yarn* in the following recipes.

Our Goal Is...to Be Exhausted!

An exhausted bath is one in which dyestuff wasn't wasted and the best color has been attained with the dye used. It also leaves the least amount of potentially hazardous dye materials in the wastewater. Accurate measurements of fiber, dyestuff, assists, and dye liquor (water) are all important to the ultimate goal of an exhausted bath. The following Dye Workshops use dye measurements that try to achieve an "exhausted" dye bath, but even so, not all dye baths may become exhausted, depending on the dye chemistry and dyeing particulars. In fact, due to their chemistry, fiber-reactive baths are less able to become exhausted.

Note: If dyeing a fiber that's been blended from different fiber categories, pick a dye method that's best for the majority of the fiber blend. For example, if the fiber is 80 percent silk and 20 percent flax, dye it with acid dyes; if the blend is 80 percent flax and 20 percent silk, use a fiber-reactive dyeing method. Either method creates a variegated effect in the final fiber or yarn, since the dyes won't take evenly in a mixed fiber blend. The bath may not completely exhaust when dyeing different fiber types. If a more even dye tone is desired when dyeing differ-ent types of loose fibers, try dyeing the fibers separately and blending them prior to spinning.

Exhausted dye bath

Fiber blend with variegation in dyed color

General Dyeing Tips and Troubleshooting

- When dye touches fiber, it immediately "strikes" (dyes) the fiber where it touches, so mix the dye into the dye pot before putting in the fiber, or it will be unevenly dyed.
- Gently turn the fiber in the pot so it has a chance to dye evenly. Do not stir, or—in the case of wool and fine protein fibers—felting may result.
- If the water is high in iron content, colors may be less bright. Get a water softener that removes iron or use distilled water for dyeing.
- If dye washes out of the fiber in the final wash, it may be due to three conditions:
  1. Oversaturation of dyestuff in the bath. (Weigh the dyestuff and fiber more carefully next time.)
  2. The fiber wasn't receptive to the dye or dye process. (Review the dye or process.)
  3. The dye cooking or processing was incomplete. (More time is needed in the cooking or processing stages.)

NATURAL DYE WORKSHOP

Consistency in color is always an issue when using natural dyestuff. Because of this, it's best to naturally dye for a project that won't require more than one dye bath. Remember that the first step for all workshops is to *weigh the dry fiber*. This weight is vital to all the ingredient measurements that are necessary in your dye process.

Note: There are a multitude of different dyeing methods for nearly every natural dye material. For Natural Dye Workshop, I chose the methods that are the least fussy yet produce satisfying results. Both cochineal and madder may be dyed without premordanting the fiber (for *substantive* dyeing), but the dye results are better if the fiber is premordanted (for *adjective* dyeing). Indigo doesn't need mordanting (it's a *vat dye* requiring fermentation). See DA-1: Dye Workshop Definitions on page 180 for definitions of these terms.

Because of all the steps involved in the natural dyeing of protein and cellulose fibers, I've narrowed our focus to protein fibers for the cochineal and madder workshops, and to cellulose fibers for the indigo workshop.

Premordanting (for the Cochineal and Madder Workshops)

I've used alum (aluminum potassium sulfate/potash alum) as a mordant for both protein fiber workshops since it's less eco-hazardous than other mordants and produces great colors in cochineal and madder dyeing. This is not the alum used in cooking (aluminum ammonium sulfate) or the alum used in gardening (aluminum sulfate)—both of which are weaker than potash alum. When alum is used with tartaric acid/cream of tartar (also a stronger version than the one used in cooking), the absorption of dye into the fiber is greater and the bath exhausts better. Cream of tartar reduces the pH of the mordant bath, making mordanting more efficient

Mordant pot with yarn

for protein fibers. Potash alum and cream of tartar are available through art and dye supply shops (see Resources and Supplies, page 159).

Note: Mordanting can be done far in advance of dyeing—even months before dyeing. Be sure to completely dry the mordanted fiber before storing and tag it with the name of the mordant.

Alum Recipe

Ingredients for mordanting 100 g (3.5 oz) of protein fiber/yarn
(adjust all ingredients proportionally for other weights)

- 10 g potash alum (10 percent of fiber weight)
- 7 g cream of tartar (7 percent of fiber weight)
- 3.8 L (1 gal) water

Wet out the fiber before mordanting (see page 86). Dissolve the alum and cream of tartar in 235 ml (1 cup) of boiling water. Put this mixture into a nonreactive pot and add 3.8L (1 gal) water. Add the wet fiber and slowly bring the temperature up to a simmer (180°F–200°F, or 82°C–93°C) and let it simmer for an hour. (Exception: Bring silk fiber to a simmer and turn off the heat, allowing the fiber to cool.) Cool the pot to lukewarm and remove the fiber. Wash and rinse it in cool water. The fiber can be dyed before it dries, or dried and stored for future dyeing.

Note: The alum solution can be reused a few more times without refreshing, and then can be refreshed by adding half the alum and tartaric acid. When the mordant solution has served its purpose, or after about two or three additional mordanting soaks, pour it out for disposal with lots of water in an acid-loving garden. (Do not put the alum mordant in one garden location more than twice during a year.)

Cochineal—for Pink-Red Tones

This recipe is for protein fibers only. (Note that silk requires a lower cooking temperature.)

Ingredients for 100 g (3.5 oz) of fiber
(adjust all ingredients proportionally for other weights and/or for lighter or darker tones)

- 5 g (0.2 oz) cochineal bugs—A powder concentrate may also be used, but the dye quantity will need to be adjusted per the concentrate instructions. This recipe only addresses dyeing with the actual bugs.
- 3.8 L (1 gal) water
- Small, nonreactive pot for soaking bugs
- Large, 14 L (15-qt) nonreactive cooking pot
- Stainless steel strainer and/or paper coffee filter

Premordant the protein fiber with alum (see Alum Recipe, above).

Straining cochineal bugs from dye liquor

The alpaca fiber for Róisín Knit Workshop project (page 139) was dyed with cochineal.

DYE EXTRACTION

1. Put the cochineal bugs in a small, nonreactive pot with enough water to cover, and soak them for at least 3 hours to overnight. After soaking, boil the cochineal bugs and soaking water for 15 minutes, adding more water if necessary to cover the dyestuff.
2. Strain the resulting dye liquor into the main dye pot, being careful to not allow any bugs to pass into the pot. (A paper coffee filter works well as a strainer. I like to place a stainless steel strainer under the coffee filter to catch any rogue bugs that might float off the sides of the coffee filter as the solution is being strained. After extracting the dye, the bugs can be put in a compost pile or disposed of as waste.)

DYE PROCESS FOR PROTEIN FIBER

1. Add 3.8 L (1 gal) cold water to the main dye pot and put the premordanted fibers into the dye bath. Add more water if the fiber isn't swimming in the pot.
2. Slowly bring the heat up to 180°F–200°F (82°C–93°C) and let it simmer for 1½ hours or until the fiber is the desired color. (For silk, see note below.) Let the fiber sit in the dye pot until it's completely cool.

    Note: Don't put silk into the dye bath until the bath has simmered for at least 1 hour. Then add the silk fiber, bring to a simmer, and turn the heat off, allowing the fiber to cool.
3. Gently remove the fiber from the cooking container (see Dye Bath Disposal, page 105) and wash it first in a bath of cool water to catch any loose dye particles, then in a warm bath of water with neutral pH detergent (such as Synthrapol) before rinsing in subsequent baths of progressively cooler water until the rinse water is clear.

    Note: Before the last rinse, add 30 ml (2 tbsp) of white vinegar or 5 ml (1 tsp) of dissolved citric acid crystals to a soaking bath and follow that bath with one more rinse bath of clear water.
4. Spin-dry the fiber in the spin cycle of a clothes washer or gently squeeze the fiber between layers of a bath towel.

5. Lay fiber flat or hang to dry. If you dyed roving or top and the fibers seem to be compacted, give the fiber a slight tug between your hands until the compaction opens up. See notes on finishing yarns in Spin Workshop, page 41.

Madder—for Red-Orange Tones

This recipe is for protein fibers only. Cellulose fibers require a different method. See Resources for more information sources for natural dyeing.

Ingredients for 100 g (3.5 oz) of fiber
(adjust all ingredients proportionally for other weights and/or for lighter or darker tones)

- 150 g (5.3 oz) dried madder roots (1½ times the weight of the fiber)—A concentrated powder may also be used, but the dye quantity will need to be adjusted per the concentrate instructions
- 3.8 L (1 gal) water for dye bath (additional water is required for root soaking and dye extraction)
- Nonreactive pot for soaking madder (of a size to fit madder and soaking water)
- Large, 14 L (15-qt) nonreactive cooking pot
- Stainless steel strainer and/or paper coffee filter

Premordant the protein fiber with alum (see Alum Recipe, page 93).

DYE EXTRACTION

1. Chop up the madder roots into small pieces (about 1–2 in. [2.5–5 cm] long).
2. Soak the madder root pieces in enough water to cover for at least 18 hours.
3. Drain off the soaking water and cover the root pieces again with fresh water.
4. Put the madder and the new soaking water in a small nonreactive pot and heat it slowly to a simmer (no more than 180°F [82°C]). *Do not allow the madder solution to boil or your dye will turn brown.* Let the solution cook for about 1–2 hours, depending on the depth of dye you desire.

DYE PROCESS FOR PROTEIN FIBER

1. Strain the resulting dye liquor from the extraction process and add the liquor to a nonreactive pot containing 3.8 L (1 gal) cold water for each 100 g (3.5 oz) of fiber. (The remaining madder root pieces may be dried for a future dye session, although they should not be allowed to become moldy, so spread them out with good air circulation while drying. Also know that the resulting dye will be lighter in color.)
2. Put the premordanted fibers into the dye bath. Add more water if the fiber isn't swimming in the pot.

The natural dye, madder, was used for the yarn created for the Vallkulla Knit Workshop project (page 120).

Straining soaked madder roots

3. Slowly bring the heat to 180°F (82°C) and let it cook for 1 hour or until the fiber is the desired color.

4. After cooking, let the fiber sit in the dye pot until it's completely cool or for up to 2 days. (The dye sets best if the fiber is allowed to sit in the dye bath for 24–48 hours.)

5. Gently remove the fiber from the cooking container (see Dye Bath Disposal, page 105) and wash it first in a bath of cool water to catch any loose dye particles, then in a warm bath of water with neutral pH detergent (such as Synthrapol), before rinsing in subsequent baths of progressively cooler water until the rinse water is clear.

   Note: Before the last rinse, add 30 ml (2 tbsp) of white vinegar or 5 ml (1 tsp) of dissolved citric acid crystals to a soaking bath and follow that bath with one more rinse bath of clear water.

6. Spin-dry the fiber in the spin cycle of a clothes washer or gently squeeze the fiber between layers of a bath towel.

7. Lay flat or hang to dry. If you dyed roving or top and the fibers seem to be compacted, give the fiber sliver a slight tug between your hands until the compaction opens up. See notes on finishing yarns in Spin Workshop, page 41.

   Note: If you have unexhausted dye bath water from either the cochineal or madder dye sessions, you can reuse it for future dyeing by storing the solution in a glass container in a cool, dark location. It should remain viable for a couple of months, but the dye strength will probably yield a lighter color.

Yarn being dyed with madder for the Knit Workshop project Vallkulla (page 120).

Indigo—Blue Tones

The alkaline nature of an indigo dye bath is especially conducive to dyeing cellulose fiber. Protein fibers also dye well with indigo, but the dye bath must be heated, and a few other dye bath ingredients must be as substituted to accommodate the unique needs of protein fibers in an indigo vat. This Dye Workshop only focuses on the indigo dye process for cellulose fibers. For more details on indigo dyeing for protein fibers, see the natural dying books in Resources, page 159.

There are many different types of indigo vat preparations to choose from, from the oldest form of natural fermentation indigo vats (some of which may use yeast and sugar, wheat bran and madder, fruit or urine to ferment the vat) to vats that use strong chemical assists. The natural fermentation methods can be very fussy and time-consuming, and they use natural indigo, which contain many impurities and may produce inconsistent color (much natural indigo has only 80 percent blue in its content). I've found that the entire natural indigo dyeing process is not easy for the casual dyer. In fact, there are dyers who have specialized careers in mixing and maintaining indigo dye vats!

In the interest of keeping this Dye Workshop easy to follow and the rate of success high for the novice dyer, I have chosen to use an indigo vat that is a happy medium between the natural process and the chemical process. This vat isn't truly a natural dye, but it uses fewer chemicals than the easiest of the indigo vats, is quicker to work up, has no impurities, holds a truer color, and requires less "babysitting" than vats with natural fermentation methods.

Indigo dyed cotton roving for Knit Workshop project Bene (see page 149)

AN EASIER BLUE: PREREDUCED INDIGO

This type of indigo, although chemically identical to natural indigo, is synthetically produced, so it is technically not a natural dye. Yet it's hard to call it truly synthetic since it is identical to natural indigo in all chemical aspects, except it lacks the impurities found in most natural indigo. It also has less environmental impact than some forms of natural indigo dyeing that require caustic lye to prepare the dye for the vat. The prereduced aspect means it requires less fermentation time and works up quicker into a vat than natural indigo. It's made in a crystallized form that dissolves better in water than natural indigo, costs less, and produces a more stabilized blue than natural indigo. Prereduced indigo is the primary type of indigo used in most indigo dyeing today. In fact, many dyers who say they dye with a natural indigo are actually using this prereduced synthetic form of indigo without realizing its synthetic base! The dye process (after dye and vat preparation) is essentially the same as the natural indigo process, but only half the quantity of dye is needed, since prereduced indigo is more efficient.

Ingredients

- 40 g (1.4 oz, or 5 tbsp) prereduced indigo—This amount makes a 12 L (approximately 3 gal) vat and can dye 454 g (1 lb) of fiber medium to dark blue. The vat can be refreshed with the addition of more dye and Thiox—see sidebar on Babysitting the Blue, page 100
- 24 g (2 tbsp) thiourea dioxide—also called Thiox (This is an oxygen reducer—oxygen oxidizes the dye and destroys the dye solution.)
- 190 g (7 oz) soda ash
- 12 L (approximately 3 gal) water
- 19 L (5 gal) plastic painter's pail (or a similar tall, cylindrical container with a lid)

All fibers must be wetted out before going through the indigo dye process (see page 86). No mordanting is required.

Note: Prereduced indigo uses comparatively safe and nontoxic ingredients, but caution should still be used. The dye stains easily and the vat fumes are quite nasty, so indigo is best dyed outdoors. Even outdoors, you should wear gloves and a respirator mask.

INDIGO DYE PROCESS: CELLULOSE FIBERS

1. Fill a large, cylindrical pail (the "vat") with 12 L (about 3 gal) water at no more than 70°F (21°C). (The container shape is important to allow less oxygen to enter the dye bath and to force the fiber to sink deeper into the vat, away from oxygen on the surface.)
2. Add 24 g (2 tbsp) Thiox and the prereduced indigo to the pail (vat) and gently stir. (There will be fumes, so be sure to wear a mask!)
3. Dissolve the soda ash in 475 ml (2 cups) of boiling water until it dissolves. Add this to the vat and stir *gently* in one circular direction. If you stir too vigorously, you will add extra oxygen into the vat. The vat liquid should turn a yellow-green, and a bronze or copper film (the "flower") will develop on the surface. End the stirring by scraping the stir stick along the inside of the vat and slowly pull the stick out. Let the vat rest for about 3 hours.
4. When ready to dye, check to see that the vat is yellow-green and the correct temperature for the cellulose fiber (no more than 70°F [21°C]). If the vat appears blue, there's too much oxygen, so add more Thiox—add 20 g (0.5 tsp) Thiox dissolved in 118 ml (4 fl oz) hot water and wait 15 minutes for the color to change. Add more if needed.
5. Gently remove the flower skim from the vat with a paper or foam plate. (Keep the skim to put back on the vat when done dyeing.) To avoid introducing more oxygen into the vat, be sure the presoak water is well squeezed out of the fiber. Then, very slowly, put the wetted-out fiber into the vat.
6. When the fiber is fully submerged, wait 1–3 minutes and very slowly take it back out. It will emerge a yellow-green and turn to blue as air oxidizes the dye. If you want a darker blue, wait 15 minutes and dip the fiber again.

A bundle of cotton roving is dipped into the indigo vat.

The dipped cotton roving immediately turns blue when pulled out of the vat.

7. To finish, wait until the fiber has dried to be sure the dye has fully oxidized before following the dye finishing steps.

   Note: To get a darker blue, dip the fiber several times rather than soak it in the vat. Soaking the fiber produces a dye result that rubs off with wear (this is also called "crocking"), but dipping (with 15-minute pauses between dips as noted above) allows the indigo to bond better with the fiber. Two to three values of blue are lost after washing and drying, so dye a deeper tone than you want in your final fiber.

8. Wash the fiber first in a bath of cool water to catch any loose dye particles, then in a warm bath of water and neutral pH detergent (such as Synthrapol) before rinsing in subsequent baths of progressively cooler water until the rinse water is clear.

9. Spin-dry the fiber in the spin cycle of a clothes washer or gently squeeze the fiber between layers of a bath towel.

10. Lay flat or hang to dry. If you dyed roving or top and the fibers seem to be compacted, give the fiber sliver a slight tug between your hands until the compaction opens up. See notes on finishing yarns in Spin Workshop, page 41.

When you are done with the indigo vat, slip the "flower" back on the top of the vat solution, stir in a circular direction as before, and put a tight lid on the vat. This vat solution can last for several weeks or even months if you tend it or use it occasionally. See Dye Bath Disposal on page 105 for how to dispose of the spent vat.

Babysitting the Blue— How to Tend an Indigo Vat

If the vat solution looks blue-green or you see blue particles suspended in the solution, reduce the vat by adding 2 g (0.5 tsp) thiourea dioxide dissolved in 118 ml (4 fl oz) hot water and wait about 15 minutes for the solution to appear yellowish-green again. If the vat appears milky, add 4 g (1 tsp) of soda ash dissolved in 118 ml (4 fl oz) hot water. If the color is weak or the vat solution is gray and watery, it's best to start over with a new vat.

Overdyeing Naturally

Natural dyes can be overdyed to achieve different colors as long as the processing chemistry and fiber content allow overdyeing. Dull, naturally dyed fibers can be overdyed with synthetic dye, but a synthetically dyed fiber overdyed with a natural dye will not be very successful, since there are fewer cellular areas on the fiber for dye to penetrate or bond with after synthetic dyeing.

After spinning, the Bene project cotton yarn was put on a CPVC stretcher and boiled to set the twist.

ACID DYE WORKSHOP: PROTEIN FIBERS

This workshop leads you through the process of immersion dyeing protein fibers, which include animal fibers, silk, and nylon. I suggest you use DA-8, the Worksheet for Jacquard Acid Dye Immersion Dyeing on page 185 to enter the specific weights and measures you follow while dyeing the fiber. Keeping good records will enable you to recreate dye results later.

Ingredients for 100 g (3.5 oz) of fiber
(adjust all ingredients proportionally for other weights and/or for lighter or darker tones) (see Supplies and Tools for Dying, page 82, for general workshop supplies)

- Acid dye (these instructions were written for Jacquard Acid Dyes)
- 5 percent acetic acid (household white vinegar) or citric acid crystals
- Large, 14 L (15-qt) nonreactive cooking pot

Note: 17.5 g (1 tbsp) of citric acid crystals equals 207 ml (14 tbsp or 7 fl oz) of 5 percent acetic acid (white household vinegar) and is enough to dye 454 g (1 lb) of fiber.

ABOVE LEFT Preparing the acid dye liquor for the fiber cooking process

ABOVE RIGHT A rich red acid dye liquor ready for the dye pot

ACID DYE IMMERSION DYEING PROCESS

1. Weigh the dry fiber. Wet out the fiber by presoaking in soap and vinegar. (See wetting out instructions, page 86.)

    Soak fibers for 30 minutes in an acid presoak of 44 ml (3 tbsp) white vinegar or 4.5 g (1 tsp) of citric acid crystals and 2.5 ml (½ tsp) of a neutral pH soap (such as Synthrapol) for every 3.8 L (1 gal) of hot water. Do not rinse. Squeeze out excess water from the fiber before dyeing.

2. Measure the dye powder according to the DOS desired (DA-4: Measuring Dye Powder Using the Standard DOS (Depth of Shade) Formula, page 182) and put it in 120 ml (½ cup) boiling water to dissolve the powder, or mix a dye stock solution (DA-5: Recipe for Concentrated Dye Stock Solutions, page 183).

3. In a nonreactive pot, put the amount of water (dye liquor) required for the fiber weight, subtracting the dye solution volume from the proportions above.

4. Add the dye solution to the pot and stir.

5. Gently place the wetted fiber into the pot and slowly heat the pot to the cooking temperature indicated in the formula above. Occasionally lift and turn the fiber so it dyes evenly while the temperature is rising.

6. When at the indicated temperature, move the fiber to the side (or momentarily lift it out) and pour in the vinegar or dissolved citric acid crystals. Do not pour the vinegar or citric acid solution directly onto the fiber, or spots will result.

7. Tend the dye bath for 30 minutes, while occasionally and gently moving the fiber around in the bath to keep even dye coverage. Do not stir aggressively! If the dye has not exhausted in the bath, add more vinegar or citric acid (about half the original amount) and continue cooking until all or most of the dye has exhausted.

8. After cooking, leave the fiber in the dye bath and let the cooking container cool.

9. Gently remove the fiber from the cooking container (see Dye Bath Disposal, page 105), and wash it first in a bath of cool water to catch any loose dye particles,

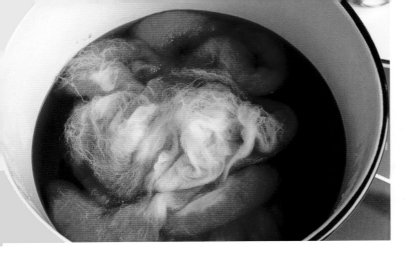

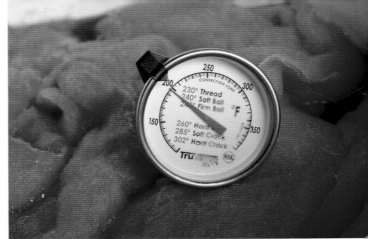

ABOVE LEFT Roving soaking up dye during the acid dyeing immersion process

ABOVE RIGHT The dye pot temperature must be watched closely to avoid boiling the fiber and felting it.

An exhausted dye bath. All the dye has entered the fiber, leaving the dye bath clear.

then in a warm bath of water and a neutral pH detergent (such as Synthrapol), before rinsing in subsequent baths of progressively cooler water until the rinse water is clear.

   Note: Before the last rinse, add 30 ml (2 tbsp) of white vinegar or 5 ml (1 tsp) of dissolved citric acid crystals) to a soaking bath and follow that bath with one more rinse bath of clear water.

10. Spin-dry the fiber in the spin cycle of a clothes washer or gently squeeze the fiber between layers of a bath towel.

11. Lay fiber flat or hang to dry. If you dyed roving or top and the fibers seem to be compacted, give the fiber a slight tug between your hands until the compaction opens up. See notes on finishing yarns in Spin Workshop, page 41.

FIBER-REACTIVE DYE WORKSHOP: CELLULOSE/BAST FIBER

This workshop leads you through the process of immersion dyeing cellulose/bast fibers, which include cotton and flax/linen. Use DA-9: Worksheet for Fiber-Reactive Procion MX Dye on page 186 to enter specific weights and measures as you dye. Keeping good records will allow you to recreate the results later.

Ingredients for 100 g (3.5 oz) of fiber

(adjust all ingredients proportionally for other weights and/or for lighter or darker tones) (see Supplies and Tools for Dying, page 82, for general workshop supplies)

- Dye (these instructions were written for Procion MX fiber-reactive dyes)
- Glauber's salt
- Soda ash
- A nonreactive pail or tub for soaking the fiber while dyeing (plastic works well)

FIBER-REACTIVE IMMERSION DYEING PROCESS

1. Weigh the dry fiber.
2. Wet out the fiber by presoaking in soap and soda ash. (See instructions on page 86.)
3. Measure the dye powder according to the DOS desired (DA-4, page 182) and put it in 118 ml (½ cups) boiling hot water to dissolve the powder, or mix a stock solution of dye (DA-5, page 183).
4. In a plastic pail or nonreactive pot, add the amount of water (dye liquor at 86°F [30°C]) required for the fiber weight, subtracting the dye, salt, and soda ash solution volumes from the total (see the volume formulas in DA-9, page 186).
5. Dissolve the Glauber's salt in lukewarm water, measuring the water as part of the dye bath/liquor.
6. Gently place the wetted fiber into the pail/pot and let it soak for 15 minutes, occasionally lifting and turning the fiber.
7. Lift the fiber out of the soak and add the dye solution to the pail/pot. Replace the fiber and stir occasionally for 30 minutes.
8. Dissolve the soda ash in warm water (measuring the water as part of the total dye bath liquor).
9. Move the fiber to the side (or momentarily lift it out) and gradually add the soda ash solution to the dye pail/pot. Do not pour the solution directly onto the fiber or dark spots will appear.
10. Tend the dye bath for 45 minutes, while occasionally and gently moving the fiber around in the bath to ensure even dye coverage. The dye bath will probably not be totally exhausted, and that's common for fiber-reactive dyes.
11. After dyeing, gently remove the fiber from the dye bath (see Dye Bath Disposal, page 105) and wash it first in a bath of cool water to catch any loose dye particles, then in a hot bath of water and neutral pH detergent (such as Synthrapol),

Dye weighing

Mixing dye into solution

Fibers as it first enters the bath

The fiber-reactive dyeing process.

Fiber at the end of the dye cooking

before rinsing in subsequent baths of progressively cooler water until the rinse water is clear.

12. Spin-dry the fiber in the spin cycle of a clothes washer or gently squeeze the fiber between layers of a bath towel.

13. Lay fiber flat or hang to dry. If you dyed roving or top and the fibers seem to be compacted, give the fiber a slight tug between your hands until the compaction opens up. See notes on finishing yarns in Spin Workshop, page 41.

Dye Bath Disposal

Being a responsible dyer means being a safe and ecologically responsible dyer. Here are some guidelines to follow for cleaning up your dye bath and dye space.

NATURAL DYES

The dyestuff and mordants determine the proper disposal method for natural dyestuff. You will need to evaporate and dispose of the bath as hazardous waste if it contains tin, chromium, and other toxic materials. Research your natural dyestuff in advance to know what ingredients may be toxic. The natural dyeing books listed in the Resources section (page 159) will help guide you on matters of toxicity. When a natural dye bath is exhausted and/or doesn't have dangerous mordants or dyestuff, it can be put down a drain. Dye baths that use alum in the mordanting and are exhausted may be poured, with copious amounts of water, on a gravel driveway or garden. Beware that animals may be attracted to dump sites if any salts remain in the bath. If you have any questions about disposal, contact a local environmental agency for proper disposal methods. If the dye bath doesn't have harmful elements, follow the steps below for pH testing before pouring the bath down the drain or outside.

Eco Note: The natural dyestuff in *Yarn Works* projects (including those used in indigo dyeing) do not contain hazardous materials.

ACID AND FIBER-REACTIVE DYES

Eco Note: This step is optional since pH of the waste water from home dyeing has a negligible effect on the environment but it's recommended for dyers who wish to be fully eco-responsible.

Check the pH level of your dye bath after dyeing. If it's highly acidic (has a pH several levels under 7), add soda ash (or its less desirable cousin, baking soda, if you don't have soda ash)—dissolving 14 g (1 tbsp) at a time in boiling water first—until the level reaches 7 (neutral pH). If the dye bath is highly alkaline (has a pH several levels over 7), add white vinegar or citric acid—5 ml (1 tsp) at a time—until a neutral pH state is reached. When a neutral pH has been achieved, pour the dye bath down the drain. The exception is if you've used a black with chromium in the formula or another color with potentially harmful ingredients. For those baths, allow the liquid to evaporate and dispose of the resulting sludge as a hazardous waste. Refer to the dye manufacturer's safety sheets (easily available online) for the safety specifications of each color.

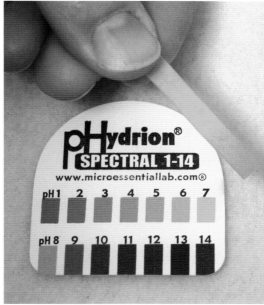

Using a pH tester in dye bath—7 is neutral pH.

Clean Up

Wipe counters and the floor with a wet cloth when done. In home dyeing, safety is your responsibility. No one is looking over your shoulder to monitor the methods you choose to use. So be safe and be a good steward of the environment.

Whether immersion dyed or hand painted, a world of magical color opens up when you dye your own fiber and yarn.

REFLECTIONS ON THE DYE WORKSHOPS

While doing research for Dye Workshop, I found nearly as many dye methods as there are dyers. Dyeing is a science that still welcomes *safe* experimentation. There's also an appealing "surprise" element to the dye process. Even when following the rules to the letter, you may still discover your carefully dyed yarn isn't quite the color you thought it would be. But as long as you know the fiber characteristics, its dye-ability, and some of the science behind how the dye process works, your work in the Dye Workshop can be open for a bit of surprise and still achieve satisfying results.

CREATIVE DYEING WORKSHOP

I have something to confess: I'm often guilty of turning my dye workshop into a play zone during my dye sessions. This is the place to really become a creative dyer, complete with beakers and boiling brews. Creative dyeing involves hand painting fiber and yarn, mixing fiber colors and materials for spinning, and just about anything you can imagine to make the most unique dyed and handspun yarns.

I often prefer to dye in a creative way, mixing and diluting at will. It's sometimes not a reproducible practice, but gosh darn, it's fun! Nevertheless, there are three rules in my dye work from which I never stray. Keep these in mind as you begin this workshop:

1. Safety—which should be an obvious, solid fixture in the workshop (see Clothing and Safety Equipment on page 84 for more details).
2. A solid understanding of your fiber's structure and qualities—or it may not survive the creative dye workshop. For example, if you try to dye a cellulose fiber by cooking it in an acid dye bath, you will have a fiber that will be damaged by cooking or by the acidic nature of the dye bath (see Meet the Fibers, page 12 for details about a specific fiber).
3. Ecological impact—use good judgment!

Dyes

I've focused this workshop on acid dyes, since they are the simplest to use in creative dyeing, are stable for manipulating into creative techniques, have a wide range of controllable color variations, and work with the protein fibers that most spinners and knitters prefer. If you want to creatively dye cellulose fiber, keep in mind that fiber-reactive dyes require urea to keep the dye from drying out during the curing time. Otherwise, fiber-reactive dyes may be hand painted or applied like acid dyes. It's also possible to use natural dyes in creative techniques, and a few of the methods described here may translate to natural dyeing, but due to the huge number of different natural dyeing techniques, I've chosen to not dive into those deep waters in this book.

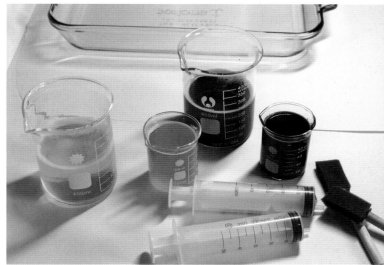

Tools

The tools of creative dyeing include anything you might use in creative painting. The sky's the limit on what you choose to use, as long as it gives you the results you are seeking.

- concentrated dye stock (see DA-5: Recipe for Concentrated Dye Stock Solutions, page 183).

In addition to the standard Dye Workshop tools, you may wish to acquire the following for Hand-Painting Dye Workshops:

- small foam paintbrushes
- squirt and spray bottles
- spice shaker jars
- plastic spoons
- sponges
- syringes (without needles)
- canning jars of various sizes
- white coffee filters or white paper towels to test dye stock colors

Useful tools from Spin Workshop include the following:

- hackles
- combs
- carders

Hand Painting

Hand painting yarns or fibers doesn't necessarily mean painting with a brush, although that is one method that can be used. Instead, the term *hand painting* is more the description of a dye process in which concentrated dye stock is applied onto the fiber by hand rather than by using an immersion method.

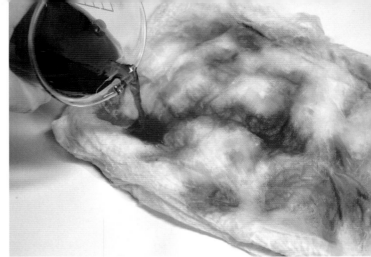

The hand-painting process, step by step, for the Knit Workshop project Sylph, using hand-painted silk hankies (see page 146).

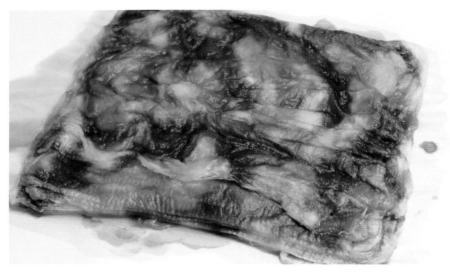

Recipe Modifications for Preparing Stock Solutions for Hand Painting

Acid Dye (Jacquard Brand) Stock Solution Modification

Add 14.8 ml (1 tbsp) vinegar or 4.9 ml (1 tsp) citric acid crystals to every 100 ml (about 7 tbsp) of concentrated dye solution.

Fiber-Reactive Dye (Procion MX Brand) Stock Solution Modification

Fiber-reactive concentrated dye solutions need to be made from urea water when used in hand painting. The urea water keeps the fiber moist during the curing time.

Add 100 g (9 tbsp) urea to 1 liter (approximately 1 qt) of lukewarm water. Use 250 ml (1 C) of this solution to make up each dye concentrate, adjusting the dye amounts proportionally according to the DOS for 250 ml (1 C) of stock solution. Just before using, add 4.9 ml (1 tsp) of dissolved soda ash to the stock solution. (Dissolve the soda ash in advance by stirring it into no more than 30 ml [2 tbsp] of hot water.)

When applied in regular sequences, hand-painted yarn produces a pattern in the knitting, like the commercial computer-created patterned yarns that knit up into jacquard or striped patterns when knit as socks. When applied in a less regular way, hand-painted yarn will knit into a variegated color effect, creating an impression of color rather than specific color patterns.

Start dyeing the lightest colors first, followed by progressively darker tones. Leave undyed space between colors if you don't want the colors to bleed together and create new colors. Trial and error will help determine how much space is needed between colors for your fiber and dye method. Let the dyed yarn sit for at least 15 minutes between color applications, since it may take that long for the dye to absorb and spread along the fibers.

Dyes for hand painting and most creative dyeing processes are first mixed as concentrated dye solutions and then diluted according to the method chosen for dyeing the fiber/yarn. Be sure your concentrated dye stock contains an acid ingredient (vinegar or citric acid) for acid dyeing, or urea and soda ash for fiber-reactive dyeing (refer to the instructions on page 103).

Dye osmosis is also called ombré dyeing.

Dyeing by Osmosis

This dye process uses the scientific property of osmosis to gradually dye different parts of a fiber (or yarn) just by dipping the different parts into dye solutions.

1. First, wet the fiber/yarn to facilitate the dye transfer and absorption.

2. Mix the colors desired for the dye, using a dilution of concentrated dye stock. Place the mixed colors into different glass canning jars.

3. Place an end of the wetted fiber/yarn into one of the dye jars. Drape the rest of the undyed fiber/yarn into subsequent dye jars of different colors. Let the fiber soak up the dye until the different dye sections are about 1 in. (2.5 cm) apart. Remove the fiber and lay it on a length of plastic wrap or kraft paper and allow the colors to move closer together until they touch or nearly touch. You can press the color areas toward each other if necessary to remove a gap between the colors, but be careful not to overlap the colors or there'll be an additional mixed color "blip" between the desired colors.

4. Finish the fiber according to the dye cooking method chosen for the fiber. (See methods below)

Sprinkle Dyeing

IMPORTANT SAFETY NOTE: Be sure to wear a mask when working with dye powder.

1. Put dry dye powder into a spice shaker jar and, after wetting out the fiber, sprinkle dye powder on the wet fiber.

2. Wait a few minutes for the color to soak into the fiber before processing it with the cooking method desired.

Cooking Methods for Hand-Painted Acid Dyes

Since hand painting means the dye is applied prior to the cooking process, the method of cooking the dyed fiber is more open ended.

KETTLE

A nonreactive kettle can be used to process hand-painted fiber using the immersion technique, or it can serve as a steaming pot for steam setting. The following methods are similar, but Option 1 starts with a fiber that has been overall dyed one color, and other colors are individually overdyed on that color, and Option 2 shows how to dye fiber with individual colors without an additional color base. The colors added to the fiber in Option 1 will be affected by the base dye color (for example, yellow will turn green when blue is added over it), and the colors of Option 2 will be more pure, only blending into other colors where the dye colors soak into each other. Option 3 may use either method of dye application, but the cooking method is steam setting the dyes (a good method for silk since it doesn't like hot cooking temperatures).

Option 1: Immersion Process

1. Prepare a dye pot with one main color that is lighter than the other colors to be dyed. Heat the pot to the appropriate temperature based on the immersion-dyeing recipe on page 87.
2. Wet the fiber according to the instructions on page 86. Place the wetted fiber into the pot and let it cook for about 15 minutes.
3. Add another color (the next shade darker than the first) directly to the fiber in the pot, in areas you wish to dye. Let this color cook for 15 minutes.
4. Continue with other colors, allowing them to cook for 15 minutes between color additions (this reduces the potential muddiness that might result when too many colors bleed and cook together). Cook the finished fiber at a simmer for 30 minutes and finish per instructions on page 103.

Option 2: Immersion Process

1. Prepare a dye pot with water only. Heat the pot to the appropriate temperature based on the immersion-dyeing recipe on page 87.
2. Wet the fiber according to the instructions on page 86. Place the wetted fiber into the pot.
3. Add a dye stock color directly to one area of the fiber in the pot. Do not stir.
4. Continue adding other colors to undyed areas of the fiber, leaving a small undyed space between colors if you don't want colors to bleed together. Colors can be added one after the other without a wait time if you keep a good space between color applications. Do not stir! Cook the finished fiber at a simmer for 30 minutes and finish per instructions on page 103.

Figure A

Figure B

Figure C

Figure D

The steam-set dye process, step by step

Option 3: Steam-Set Process

1. Cover 1 in. (2.5 cm) of the bottom of a dye pot with water and put a vegetable steamer in the pot. (Figure A)
2. Prepare your dye as a concentrated solution, diluting as desired for color tones.
3. Put the wetted-out fiber into the vegetable steamer, cover the pot with a lid, and heat until steam results. (Figure B)
4. Pour one dye color onto the fiber as desired, allowing the dye to soak in for at least 15 minutes. (Figure C)
5. Continue with the other colors, resting between dye applications for at least 15 minutes.
6. Let the dyed fiber steam while covered for an additional 15 minutes. (Figure D)
7. Finish per instructions on page 103.

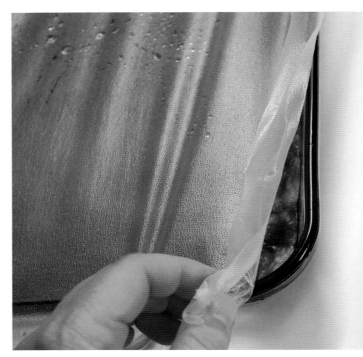

ABOVE LEFT To finish the hand-painting technique using the microwave, place the fiber in a microwave-safe dish and cover with plastic wrap.
ABOVE RIGHT the Sylph project silk hankies are ready for cooking.

MICROWAVE

Hand-paint the fiber according to whatever method you choose. Then follow the instructions for microwave cooking on page 90, but don't add additional water to the fiber's cooking container. Be sure to have a heat sink (see page 90) in the microwave when cooking so the fiber doesn't burn.

SLOW COOKER

Processing hand-painted fibers with a slow cooker is identical to both the immersion kettle and steam-set kettle methods above. Alternative Dye Workshop Cooking Methods (page 89) has specifics on how to cook with a slow cooker.

Breathing Life Back into Colors That "Go Bad"

As long as the "bad" color isn't really dark, you may be able to redye it with another color. The rules of color blending apply somewhat to overdyeing, although they aren't as reliable. The dye color will be going over existing dye on the fiber, and if that dye is a darker color, success will be limited. The best results occur when overdyeing a light color with medium to dark colors.

GOING BEYOND THE DYE WORKSHOP

Dyeing can be so much more than putting color to fiber. This section encourages you to open your world to seeing color in a different way.

Creative Inspiration

How do you focus on a color choice when the world of color is spinning around you? You can choose the natural world (flowers, leaves, rocks) and objects (food, photos, artwork, even paint chips), then record the color through photography, bring the object to the Dye Workshop, or just rely on memory. Color may even be felt through music or emotions. Inspiration can be in anything.

Causes to Dye For

Get a group of spinning and knitting friends together and throw a dyeing party! Turn it into a "Dye for a Cause" party and donate the final knitted items to your charity of choice. How about a pink party for breast cancer research? Or a blue party for arthritis, red for heart disease, or green for organ donation? Put out dye pots with the color of your cause and either provide fiber (or yarn) or have your spinning friends bring their own spun yarn or fiber to dye. At the end of the party, hand out a charity knitting pattern to use for knitting the garment that suits the particular charity chosen.

The color gradations in an old tree stump provided the inspiration for these two beautiful rust-colored skeins for the Catherine Knit Workshop project (page 156).

The lovely purple hue of a flower inspired the color of this yarn, used in the Hanna spinning sock Knitting Workshop project (page 125).

part 4 Knit Workshop

As knitters, we are at home in the world of yarn and needles. So this section brings our journey as spinners and dyers back home to our beloved passion: hand knitting. But this time, we'll be knitting with our own creations—hand-spun and hand-dyed yarn!

William Lee of Woodborough, England, invented the first hand-powered knitting machine in 1589. It's said he invented it because a woman he loved spent too much time with her knitting needles, ignoring his efforts to be her suitor. So he vowed to take her needles away forever by creating a knitting device. (If it's true, there's more to the story, but the conclusion is he died penniless in France, and she married another man who truly appreciated her needles.) *Universal History Archive/Photolibrary*

A BRIEF HISTORY OF KNITTING WITH HAND-SPUN YARNS

Prior to the 1800s, there is little historical acknowledgment of the work of knitting with hand-spun yarn. Archaeologists believe that the first hand-spun yarns were made for weaving. Prehistoric weavings from hand-spun yarns have been found in archaeological records, but the discoveries to date of the samples that look most like hand knitting (some earlier artifacts were proven to be *nålbinding* or another form of knot work) have come from a much later time period—perhaps as late as AD 1100. There was also no word for *knitting* in early history, so when it was described, it was possibly lumped in with weaving. Without samples to support knitting's existence, it may have flown under the radar of historical record or was simply not developed until later. The most we know about early hand knitting is that children, women, and men all knit as a profession until the Industrial Age, when women became the knitting-machine operators and primary hand knitters.

The most common articles made by early hand knitters were stockings knit from hand-spun yarn. Around 1589, the first hand-powered knitting machine was created in an attempt to relieve the toil of hand knitters. Even with the new hand-powered knitting machines, it appears that all knitting was still made from hand-spun yarn until the power mechanization of yarn and knitting became standardized in the 1700s and 1800s.

After the Industrial Age took over the work of hand spinners and knitters, groups of women continued to spin and knit for leisure. Knitting patterns were first widely published around 1830, promoting more interest in leisure knitting. Being able to spin and knit was a highly regarded part of civilized American society in the 1800s. This practicality and civility, I think, remains one of the captivating aspects of spinning and knitting today.

Spinning and knitting remained a means of economic and physical survival for quite some time among those in the working class and in remote areas of the world, including pioneer America. There are still a few regions of the world where hand spinning and knitting continue to play roles in economic survival. Among these are South America (Andean hand-spun and hand-knit sweaters), Russia (hand-spun and hand-knit Orenburg lace); Turkey, Kazakhstan, and Afghanistan (Tajik hand-spun and hand-knit mittens and slippers); Africa (Tanzanian hand-spun cotton for weaving and knitting); Nepal (hand-spun hemp and nettle); Canada (Cowichan hand-spun and hand-knit sweaters); Falkland Islands (hand-spun yarn); and the United States (Navajo Nation hand-spun yarn).

The Andean people of Peru and Bolivia continue to hand spin and knit to financially support their families and villages, keeping their traditions alive for future generations. Some Andean knitters also hand dye their yarn, often using natural dye methods that have been passed along for centuries in their culture. © *Michele Burgess/Alamy*

PATTERNS

I've designed these patterns to showcase the beauty of hand-spun, hand-dyed yarn, but with each pattern, you have the option of using commercial yarns to complete the projects. Because the yarn market is ever-changing, I haven't given specific yarn brands, but have suggested gauge, fiber weight, and other details that will help you pick a commercial yarn. You can follow the instructions word for word or modify them with your own spinning and dyeing creations as you experiment with other fibers and colors. The projects require smaller amounts of yarn and are therefore quicker to spin for. Each pattern presents a different knitting technique to interest knitters of all abilities. I've assumed that the knitter attempting these patterns has basic knitting ability (knowledge of casting on, knitting, purling, and binding off).

The patterns were knit using wool, alpaca fleece, wool/angora blend, silk, cellulose seed and bast, or synthetic fiber groups. At the end of the patterns, you will find a chart on how I prepared, spun, and dyed each yarn prior to knitting the project(s) and notes on my own discoveries, good and bad, during the spinning and dyeing of the yarn. My hope is that by following a fiber from source to final project, you will gain the knowledge to create your own workshops for spinning, dyeing, and knitting fibers.

A Knitter's Trick for Determining Needle Size— Applied to Spun Yarn

Place a knitting needle on top of two lengths of spun yarn or, using a needle gauge tool, pull two lengths of spun yarn through the needle gauge hole that fits it the best (the two strands of yarn should just touch the sides of the hole). The needle that matches the width of the doubled yarn strands (or the hole size on the needle gauge that best fits the yarn) provides a good starting point when estimating the best needle size to achieve an even fabric with the spun yarn.

A comparable needle size can also be found by looking at the crimp of the raw fiber. A knitting needle that fits into the width of one crimp of the fiber will probably be a good size for an appropriate project with that fiber.

ABOVE Hanna, the source of the fleece for Vallkulla, Hanna, and Sami patterns.

RIGHT Sue Ross, a noted sheep expert in the American Upper Midwest sheep industry, owns Woolen Meadow Farm. Every spring, Sue opens her farm to spinners for her annual sheep-shearing event. Minnesota spinners favor her farm for having high-quality fleece. Sue hand sews the coats that the sheep are wearing. She puts the coats on when the sheep come off pasture in the fall and start eating hay, and leaves them on until shearing time. The coats are made of a special material that allows the wool to breathe yet protects it from VG and dirt. Our lab subject, Hanna, was sheared along with twenty-two other sheep at the farm.

A Special Note about the Fiber of Vallkulla, Hanna, and Sami Knit Workshop Projects

The Vallkulla, Hanna, and Sami pattern yarns were all created from the fibers of a single raw wool fleece.

- **Fiber Source:** Hanna, a ¼ Corriedale (medium wool), ⅛ Romney (long wool), ⅛ Lincoln (long wool), and ½ Border Leicester (long wool) cross.
- **Fiber Supplier:** Sue Ross of Woolen Meadow Farm, Delano, Minnesota.
- **Fleece Stats:** The average staple length was 5 in (13 cm). The staple crimp was 5–8 cpi (per 2.5 cm). These characteristics put Hanna's fleece in the fineness category of medium wool with a medium to long staple. Total weight after shearing and skirting: 6.75 lb (3.1 kg). The fleece could have been sorted into wool grades, but I kept the fleece intact and processed it all together.
- **Cleaning/Scouring Process for Fleece:** Washing-machine soaking method (see FLA-X). Total weight after cleaning/scouring: 4.86 lb (2.2 kg).
- **Fiber Preparation:** I used three different methods of preparation for the three different Knit Workshop projects: Drum carding, combing, and hand carding.
- **Spin Method:** A medium/long wool like Hanna's can be spun either woolen or worsted. This type of wool is ideal for beginning spinners since the defined crimp and the long staple helps to develop and keep the twist, making a controlled spin much easier. I chose to spin her wool with the woolen, worsted, and semi-worsted techniques based on the preparation methods needed for the projects.

- **Final Yarn:** DK semi-woolen 2-ply for Vallkulla mitts, page 120; DK 2-ply worsted for Hanna socks, page 125; and bulky single-ply woolen for Sami mittens, page 130.
- **Dye Process:** Sami—acid immersion; Vallkulla—natural dye immersion (madder); Hanna—acid immersion (all dyed as spun yarn)

See the Natural Dye Workshop, page 92, and Acid Dye Workshop, page 100, to follow the different wool-dyeing methods.

During the scouring process for Hanna's fleece, 1.89 lb (680 g) of grease and VG were washed out of the fleece—that's 28 percent of the original weight of Hanna's coat! But compared with the average wool fleece, Hanna's fleece was quite clean, with average grease.

One bag full of Hanna's fleece, weighing 6.75 pounds (3 kg)

Hand-spun, hand-dyed yarns, all from Hanna's fleece. Clockwise from left: Woolen spun single ply (for Sami); worsted spun two ply (for Hanna); and semi-woolen spun two ply (for Vallkulla)

Vallkulla:
Twined Fingerless Mitts

This project was spun as a Z-twist yarn from a wool fleece. I envision these fingerless mitts as the ideal handwear for the Vallkulla—the women who spend their summers in the cool highland forests of Sweden, grazing and tending their milk cows and goats— so I named them after these hardy women. If you don't have any animals to milk, they are also great for any cold-weather activity in which you need to have your fingers free. Consider knitting a pair for winter spinning! They are especially well suited for drop-spindle spinning since the cuff material makes a great surface for wrapping your fiber supply while it waits to be drafted.

The Twined Knitting Technique

Hold both strands of the working yarn (one from the center of the ball and the other from the outside of the ball) in your working hand and separate the strands with your index finger. (Even though, historically, stitches are typically "thrown" when knit in twined knitting, I've found it doesn't matter if you "throw" the stitches with your right hand or "pick" with your left. Either method can be modified to create the same results.) Knit the first stitch with one of the strands. To knit the next stitch, pick up the other strand and wrap it clockwise *over* the first strand and knit. Then pick up the first strand again, wrap that clockwise around the strand just used for the second stitch, and knit the next stitch. Keep alternating strands in this manner for each stitch. If you are knitting correctly, the back (wrong side) of your work will have an even "twining" of stitches that run in the same direction.

Purled twined stitches are worked in the same manner, but with both yarns held to the front of the work as with a normal purl stitch. The yarns are wrapped clockwise around each other with the new yarn coming *under* the yarn from the previous stitch.

The mitts are begun with a long-tail cast-on. Although this cast-on method isn't a traditional twined-knitting cast-on, it works well in this pattern. I chose to use both a simplified cast-on and a basic pattern of knits and purls that I typically teach to my students because they give the beginning twined knitter a more expedient first experience

SKILL LEVEL

Intermediate ⬤⬤⬤▭

SIZES

Woman's small (medium, large) Instructions are given for smallest size, with larger sizes in parentheses. When only one number is given, it applies to all sizes.

FINISHED MEASUREMENTS

Circumference: 6 (7½, 9)" [15 (19, 23) cm] at wrist
Length: 6½ (7¼, 7¾)" [16.5 (18.5, 19.5) cm] or as desired

MATERIALS

 Z-plied wool yarn: 135 (167, 201) yd [123.5 (153, 184) m] /3.5 (3.9, 4.7) oz [89 (110, 133) g]

- Commercial yarn equivalent: DK weight, preferably plied Z
- Size 4 (3.5mm) double-pointed needles or size needed to obtain gauge
- Waste yarn
- Tapestry needle
- Stitch markers (optional)

GAUGE

24 sts and 24 rnds = 4" (10 cm) in twined knitting.
Adjust needle size as necessary to obtain correct gauge.

PATTERN STITCH

Note: All stitches are worked in the twined-knitting style. A chart is provided for those preferring to work from charts.

TWINED DIAMONDS CHART

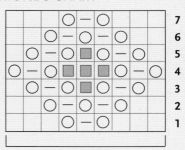

9-st repeat

STITCH KEY

▭	Standard twine knit stitch
○	Twined purl
−	Twined knit with previously purled strand carried in front
◼	Standard twine knit with purl strand moved to back

Note: On Rnd 4 where the 2 twined-purl sts come together between the pattern repeats; twine-purl the first stitch as usual, then return this strand to the back and bring the second strand to the front and twine-purl strand at the front and continue as shown on the chart.

in this fairly time-consuming knitting technique. I've found that after learning these basic twined techniques, the knitter gains confidence to advance to learning other twined cast-on methods and unique pattern stitches, such as chain paths and crook stitches.

Yarn Management

It's much easier to knit in the twined style if you put your ball into a "yarn bra," available at many yarn shops. You can also make your own from cut-up lengths of panty-hose or from netting that is used as packaging material at grocery or liquor stores.

Your working strands will become twisted around each other, making it necessary to stop at the end of each row to untwist your yarns; an easy way to do this is to put a needle through the ball of yarn (anchoring the yarn ends) and let the ball spin until the twist is undone.

About Twined Knitting

Twined knitting is a technique believed to have originated in Sweden, where it's called *tvåändsstickning* (two-ended knitting). The technique creates a fabric of double thickness. Historically, it was popular in the northern, forested regions of Sweden, where dense woolen wear was needed for the cold, snowy winters. In twined knitting, both ends of a ball of yarn are used at the same time. Stitches are worked by using one end for one stitch, then the other end for the next stitch, and continuing to alternate the ends throughout. A center-pull ball of yarn is necessary so you can work with both ends of the yarn. It is best to use a yarn that's been plied in the Z direction (clockwise) for twined knitting because the direction of the plying complements the twist inherent in this knitting technique. (S-plied yarns untwist when knit with the twined method.)

Twined Diamonds (multiple of 9 sts)

Rnd 1: *K3, p1, k1 keeping yarn from previous purl st on RS, p1, k3; rep from * around.

Rnd 2: *K2, [p1, k1 keeping yarn from previous purl st on RS] twice, p1, k2; rep from * around.

Rnd 3: *K1, p1, k1 keeping yarn from previous purl st on RS, p1, k1 moving yarn from previous purl st to WS, p1, k1 keeping yarn from previous purl st on RS, p1, k1; rep from * around.

Rnd 4: *P1, k1 keeping yarn from previous purl st on RS, p1, k3 with both yarns in back, p1, k1 keeping yarn from previous purl st on RS, p1 and take yarn to back; rep from * around.

Rnd 5: Rep Rnd 3.

Rnd 6: Rep Rnd 2.

Rnd 7: Rep Rnd 1.

Pattern Notes

- The size may be customized in increments of approximately 1½" (4 cm) by increasing or decreasing the cast-on count by 9 stitches.
- For ease in reading the pattern, instructions are written as standard knit or purl or variations (such as decreases or increases), but all stitches are worked in the twined-knitting style.

Instructions
RIGHT MITT

Make a slip knot with both ends of the yarn (one from the inside of the ball, one from the outside) and put it on a dpn. Using long-tail method and both ends of the yarn, CO 36 (45, 54) sts (not counting the first slip knot). Remove the first slip knot and distribute the sts evenly onto 3 dpns. Mark beg of rnd and join, taking care not to twist sts.

Knit 1 rnd.

Purl 1 rnd.

Knit 1 rnd.

Work 7 rnds, repeating the 9-st Twined Diamonds pat 4 (5, 6) times around.

Knit 1 rnd.

Purl 1 rnd.

Knit 6 rnds.

Cuff pattern

THUMB GUSSET

Inc rnd: *K18 (23, 27), kfb, knit to end of rnd—37 (46, 55) sts.

Rep Inc rnd 7 (9, 11) more times—44 (55, 66) sts.

Knit 4 (6, 8) rnds even.

HOLD THUMB STITCHES

Next rnd: K18 (23, 27); place the next 12 (15, 18) sts on waste yarn for the thumb; CO 4 (5, 6) sts (the "gap" sts) using both strands and long-tail CO; knit to end of rnd—36 (45, 54) sts.

Knit 6 rnds or until piece measures 3 rnds short of length desired.

Purl 1 rnd.

Knit 1 rnd.

BO in twined sequence by using every other strand in the BO.

THUMB

Transfer the 12 (15, 18) thumb gusset sts to 2 dpns; join yarn and knit across thumb gusset sts, then pick up and knit 2 sts before the gap sts, 4 (5, 6) across the gap, and 2 sts after the gap sts—20 (24, 28) sts. **Note:** *The additional sts on each side of the gap sts help close the space between the gap and the thumb gusset and provide more ease in the thumb.*

I usually pick up at least half of the gauge stitches-per-inch when shaping a thumb. These sts are decreased on next rnd.

Next rnd: K11 (14, 17), [k2tog] twice, k2 (3, 4), [k2tog] twice, working last dec with first st of next rnd; mark new beg of rnd—16 (20, 24) sts.

Knit 6 rnds or until thumb is 3 rnds short of length desired.

Purl 1 rnd.

Knit 1 rnd.

BO all thumb sts in twined sequence.

Weave in all ends.

LEFT MITT

Work as for Right Mitt to Thumb gusset

THUMB GUSSET

Inc rnd: K16 (21, 25) sts, kfb, knit to end of rnd—37 (46, 55) sts.

Rep Inc rnd 7 (9, 11) more times—44 (55, 66) sts.

Knit 4 (6, 8) rnds even.

Next rnd: K16 (21, 25); place next 12 (15, 18) sts on a holder for the thumb; CO 4 (5, 6) sts (the "gap" sts) using both strands and long-tail CO; knit to end of rnd—36 (45, 54) sts. Redistribute sts evenly on needles as necessary. Complete as for Right Mitt.

Details for Vallkulla Spinning and Dyeing

SPIN

Fiber type: Wool (from Hanna—Border Leicester mix, see page 118)

Fiber source: Woolen Meadow Farm

Fiber preparation: Scoured and drum-carded fleece; dyed after spinning

Weight after preparation: 4.6 oz (130 g)

Wheel and whorl used (singles and ply): Lendrum wheel; singles whorl: 8:1, ply whorl: 7:1

Spin method: Semi-woolen

Singles details
  spin direction: S
  wpi: 22

Ply details
  number of plies: 2
  spin direction: Z
  tpi: 5
  wpi: 13
  twist angle: 30°

Final yarn weight / length: 3.9 oz (110 g) / 167 yd (152.5 m)

Finishing techniques: Soaked in warm, soapy water; spun out excess water in washing machine and hung with light tension to dry. I mordanted the yarn at a later date in preparation for the natural dyeing process.

After the Spin Workshop reflections: A drum-carded fleece preparation wasn't ideal for this fleece. I didn't sort the fleece into zones before washing, so it had some short staples mixed in with the longer ones. The drum carder didn't process these shorter fibers in the fleece very evenly and they needed to be discarded during the semi-woolen spinning process, resulting in about a 15 percent reduction of the final spinning yield.

DYE

Dye type/brand: Natural dye—madder root

Color: Natural orange/red

Quantity of Dye: 165 g (5.8 oz) dry madder root (1.5x the weight of the yarn to achieve a darker hue)

Dye process followed: I mordanted the yarn with alum and cream of tartar (according to instructions in Dye Workshop, page 93), and then dyed with the immersion kettle method (see page 110 for process).

After the Dye Workshop reflections: I soaked the madder roots for 18 hours, then discarded the soak water and covered the roots with fresh water and cooked them for 2 hours over a slow heat. After straining the roots from the resulting dye liquor, the liquor was poured into the dye bath, the yarn was added, and the bath simmered for 1 hour. The yarn cooled in the dye bath for 48 hours before I washed and finished it.

See the Natural Dye Workshop, page 92, and Acid Dye Workshop, page 100, to follow the possible dye methods for wool (protein) fiber.

Hanna:
Socks for Peaceful Spinning

This sock honors Knit Workshop's wool fleece provider, Hanna. I found sheep charms to add to the back of the socks as a fun element to symbolize the fiber origin, attaching them to drop earring findings that I sewed into the sock fabric at the center back.

The wool was spun with a worsted prep and spin, which brings out the luster in Hanna's Border Leicester–cross fleece and makes this sock quite long wearing. The snug footlet shaping is perfect for keeping your feet warm without being too bulky while wheel spinning, and the decorative firm ribbing in the cuff gives this simple sock an elegant touch and keeps the sock from sliding off the foot while treadling. You can adjust the length of the cuff as you desire by knitting the ribbing to a longer length, although then you may want to make the cuff a bit wider for a more comfortable fit (see Pattern Notes below). If desired, a simpler k2, p1 rib will substitute for the more complicated cuff ribbing.

Pattern Notes

- This is a great beginning sock knitter's project and a quick project for experienced sock knitters. Prior experience with double-pointed needles is helpful.
- The instructions are written for double-pointed needles, but can be modified for knitting on two 24-inch circular needles. See note on page 128.

- A tighter join between needles on the first round is achieved by adding one additional stitch to your cast-on. Slip the last cast-on stitch (on the RH needle) to the LH needle next to the first cast-on stitch. Knit these 2 stitches together on the first round. This will eliminate a common problem of gapping between stitches in the join of the first round.
- If you want to use the Cuff Rib pattern to make a longer cuff than indicated in the pattern instructions, increase your cast-on stitch count by at least 6 stitches so the cuff will fit better up the leg. You will need to decrease any extra stitches by k2tog at evenly spaced intervals on the knit round following the Cuff Rib until you have the number of stitches indicated for your size at the end of the cuff.

Pattern Stitch

CUFF RIB (MULTIPLE OF 3 STS)

Rnd 1: Purl all sts LOOSELY.

Rnd 2: *K3tog but leave the 3 sts on LH needle and just pull the new st to the RH needle; knit the top (first) st

SKILL LEVEL

Easy ◖■■☐☐

SIZES

Woman's small (medium, large) for wearer's foot circumference of 7¼ (8¼, 9½)" (18.5 [21, 24] cm). Instructions are given for smallest size, with larger sizes in parentheses. When only one number is given, it applies to all sizes.

FINISHED MEASUREMENTS

Circumference: 7¼ (8, 9½)" [18.5 (20.5, 24) cm]
Length: 8 (9¼, 10)" [20.5 (23.5, 25.5) cm] or as desired

MATERIALS

 2-ply worsted-spun wool yarn: 113 (150, 187) yd [103 (137, 171) m]/ 2.2 (2.9, 3.6) oz [62 (83, 103g)]. As much as ⅓ more yarn may be needed if the cuff is lengthened.

- Commercial yarn equivalent: DK weight
- Size 3 (3.25 mm) double-pointed needles (set of 4) or size needed to obtain gauge
- Tapestry needle
- Stitch marker

GAUGE

22 sts and 36 rnds = 4" (10 cm) in St st.
Adjust needle size as necessary to obtain correct gauge.

Cuff pattern

in the k3tog group, pulling the st you knit into off the needle; knit the remaining 2 sts (of the k3tog) together tbl —this will be a tight st, made even tighter if your previous purl rnd was not purled loosely; rep from * around.

Rnd 3: Knit all sts.

Rep Rnds 1–3 for pat.

Instructions

CUFF

CO 39 (45, 51) sts. Distribute sts on dpns (each dpn should have a multiple of 3 sts), mark beg of rnd and join, taking care not to twist sts.

Work 3-rnd Cuff Rib pat twice or to desired cuff length, then work Rnd 1 once more.

Knit 1 rnd and inc 1 (dec 1, inc 1) st—40 (44, 52) sts.

HEEL FLAP

Set-up rows: K10 (11, 14); turn; p20 (22, 26) for heel flap. Leave remaining 20 (22, 26) unworked sts on single dpn to work later for instep.

Work heel flap back and forth using 2 dpns as follows:

Row 1 (RS): *Sl 1, k1; rep from * to end.

Row 2: Sl 1, purl to end.

Rep [Rows 1 and 2] 9 (10, 11) more times. There should be 10 (11, 12) chain-like selvedge sts on both sides of the flap, plus an additional stitch from the Set-up row.

TURN HEEL

Row 1 (RS): K11 (13, 15), ssk, k1, turn, leaving rem sts unworked.

Row 2: Sl 1, p3 (5, 5), p2tog, p1, turn.

Row 3: Sl 1, knit to 1 st before gap, ssk, k1, turn.

Row 4: Sl 1, purl to 1 st before gap, p2tog, p1, turn.

Repeat Rows 3 and 4 until all heel sts have been worked, ending after a WS row—12 (14, 16) sts rem.

GUSSET

Take pause to note needle numbers and how the needles will be set up to finish the heel shaping. (Needle 1 will be used to knit across the heel sts and pick up the first set of gusset sts; Needle 2 will be used to knit across the instep sts; Needle 3 will be used to pick up the second set of gusset sts and knit across half the heel sts.)

If you are working with 2 circular needles, Needle 1 will be used to work the heel/sole sts and both sets of gusset sts (equivalent to Needles 1 and 3 above) and Needle 2 will be used to work the instep sts.

Pick-up rnd: Needle 1: Knit across heel sts; pick up and knit 11 (12, 13) sts along side of heel flap; Needle 2: knit across 20 (22, 26) instep sts; Needle 3: pick up and knit 11 (12, 13) sts along heel flap; k6 (7, 8) heel sts from Needle 1; mark beginning of rnd—54 (60, 68) sts arranged 17-20-17 (19-22-19, 21-26-21).

Rnd 1: Needle 1: Knit to last 3 sts, k2tog, k1; Needle 2: knit; Needle 3: k1, ssk, knit to end—52 (58, 66) sts.

Rnd 2: Knit around.

Rep [Rnds 1 and 2] 6 (7, 7) more times—40 (44, 52) sts rem.

FOOT

Knit all rnds until foot measures 6 (7¼, 8)" [15 (18.5, 20.5) cm] or 2" [5cm] less than the desired total foot length.

TOE

Rnd 1: Needle 1: Knit to last 3 sts, k2tog, k1; Needle 2: k1, ssk, knit to last 3 sts, k2tog, k1; Needle 3: k1, ssk, knit to end—36 (40, 48) sts.

Rnd 2: Knit around.

Rep [Rnds 1 and 2] 4 (5, 5) more times—20 (20, 28) sts rem.

Rep [Rnd 1] twice, then use Needle 3 to knit across Needle 1—12 sts rem with 6 sts on Needles 2 and 3.

Kitchener Stitch

The Kitchener stitch is a sewing method that grafts stitches together in an invisible seam that's perfect for areas where seams can be irritating to the garment wearer, such as on sock toes.

Instructions

Wrong sides of the sock should be together and needles parallel. **TIP:** When sewing up the stitches on the back needle, don't flip the sock around. Instead, pick up the stitches from inside the back fabric.

Set Up Stitches for the Grafting Sewing

Pass the tapestry needle through first stitch in the front needle as if to purl. Pull up the yarn to gently tighten, but leave the stitch on the knitting needle.

Holding the yarn under the front needle, pass the tapestry needle through the first stitch on the back needle as if to knit and pull up the yarn to gently tighten, but leave the stitch on the back knitting needle.

Grafting

1. Pass the tapestry needle through the first stitch on the front needle as if to knit, slipping the stitch off the knitting needle.
2. Pull the tapestry needle through the second stitch on the front needle as if to purl, leaving the stitch on the knitting needle. Pull up the yarn to gently tighten.
3. Pull the tapestry needle through the first stitch on the back needle as if to purl, slipping the stitch off the needle. Pull up the yarn to gently tighten.
4. Pull the tapestry needle through the second stitch on the back needle as if to knit, leaving the stitch on the knitting needle. Pull up the yarn to gently tighten.

Repeat Steps 1 through 4 until one stitch remains on each needle. To finish, pull the yarn through the front needle stitch as if to knit and through the back needle stitch as if to purl. Pull the end to the inside of the sock and weave in the end.

GRAFT TOE

Cut yarn, leaving a 10" [25 cm] tail.

Holding the needles parallel with working yarn coming from the back needle, graft the toe closed using Kitchener st (see sidebar).

Weave in ends.

Details from Hanna Spinning and Dyeing

SPIN

Fiber type: Wool (from Hanna—Border Leicester mix, see page 118)

Fiber source: Woolen Meadow Farm

Fiber preparation: Scoured fleece, combed and made into top; dyed after spinning

Weight after preparation: 3.7 oz [106 g]

Wheel and whorl used (singles and ply): Lendrum wheel; singles whorl: 10:1, ply whorl: 8:1

Spin method: Worsted, from top preparation

Singles details

  spin direction: Z

  wpi: 23

Ply details

  number of plies: 2

  spin direction: S

  tpi: 6

  wpi: 14

  twist angle: 35°

Final yarn weight / length: 3.6 oz [103g] / 187 yd [171m]

Finishing techniques: Soaked in warm, soapy water; spun out excess water in washing machine and hung with light tension to dry. Yarn dyed with acid dyes (see below).

After the Spin Workshop reflections: A combed, worsted preparation was ideal for this fleece. It removed all the short cuts in the fleece and highlighted the luster of the wool. The sock would have had a smoother surface had I spun it as a 3- or 4-ply yarn at a smaller wpi, and that would have also further emphasized the luster of the wool.

DYE

Dye type/brand: Acid dye/Jacquardline brand

Color: #62 on the color pyramid chart, see page 181 (purple with 40 percent blue and 60 percent red)

Quantity of Dye: 0.5 percent DOS—Total of 0.52 g [0.02 oz] of dye: 0.21 g [0.007 oz] BrilliantBlue (#623) and 0.31 g [0.01 oz] Fire Red (#618) (considered "cool primary" colors in the Jacquardline)

Dye process followed: Kettle immersion method (see page 110 for process)

After the Dye Workshop reflections: The smooth, worsted preparation created a yarn that dyed beautifully with even tones.

See the Natural Dye Workshop, page 92, and Acid Dye Workshop, page 100, to follow the possible dye methods for wool (protein) fiber.

Sami:
A Lovikka-Style Mitten

Sami is also a product of Knit Workshop's wool fleece provider, Hanna. The project wool was hand carded and spun woolen to encourage more air pockets of warmth in the final yarn, then dyed in a woodland color of the region in which the original Lovikka mitten was first designed. I named it "Sami" to honor the Sami tribes of northern Sweden who played a role in the success of the original Lovikka mitten design (see History sidebar).

Project Note

The Lovikka mitten is considered a trademarked knitting design. This "Sami" mitten pattern has been influenced by Lovikka design, but is not a copy. To pay homage to the knitting design yet still honor the trademark, I have designed this mitten in a contemporary style with a button-embellished cuff and nonnatural color. Trademarked and true Lovikka mittens are knit with natural, undyed wool; feature a braided tassel; and are embroidered with geometric patterns typically in the colors of blue, yellow, and red. They are sold with a certification tag to authenticate their origin and are timelessly beautiful.

Pattern Notes

- To figure out proper size, measure hand around the knuckles and include the tip of the thumb. The extra thumb measurement gives the ease needed to cover the modest shrinkage that occurs during the light fulling process. Traditional Lovikka mittens fit quite loosely, but I designed this pattern to fit a bit more snugly and therefore be more functional for driving or other active use. If you prefer a larger mitten, pick a size larger than your hand measurement.
- The slight fulling does not substantially change the knitted measurements.
- The pattern is written to be worked on three double-pointed needles, but can also be worked using two circular needles.
- The instructions are identical for the left and right mittens. Shape left and right mittens while fulling and drying.

SKILL LEVEL

Easy ●■□□

SIZES

Child 5–8 yrs (child 8 yrs/woman's small, woman's medium, woman's large/man's small, man's medium, man's large)

Instructions are given for smallest size, with larger sizes in parentheses. When only 1 number is given, it applies to all sizes.

To fit hand circumference: 7½ (8, 8½, 9, 9¾, 10¼)" [19 (20.5, 21.5, 23, 25, 26) cm] (see Pattern Notes)

FINISHED MEASUREMENTS

Circumference: Same as hand circumference above.
Length: 8½ (9¼, 10¼, 11, 11½, 12)" [21.5 (23.5, 26, 28, 29, 30.526) cm]

MATERIALS

 Bulky low-twist singles wool yarn: 102 (128, 160, 192, 230, 276) yd [93 (117, 146, 176, 210, 252) m]/ 2.9 (3.7, 4.6, 5.5, 6.6, 7.9) oz [83 (104, 130, 156, 187, 224) g]

- Commercial yarn alternative: bulky singles wool
- Size 9 [5.5 mm] double-pointed needles (set of 5) or size needed to obtain gauge
- Stitch holder
- Tapestry needle to finish ends and embroider pattern in cuff

Optional

- Buttons or beads for the embroidered cuff (with a hole size that will fit the yarn or thread)
- 2-ply fingering-weight wool yarn for embroidery: 6 yd [5.5m] for each color, depending on embroidery pattern used or if the yarn is used as a carrier for beadwork

GAUGE

14 sts and 20 rnds = 4" [10 cm] in ST st.
Adjust needle size as necessary to obtain correct gauge.

Instructions

CUFF

Using long-tail method, CO 26 (28, 30, 32, 34, 36) sts. Divide sts among 3 dpns, mark beg of rnd and join, taking care not to twist sts.

Purl 2 rnds.

Knit 7 (9, 11, 13, 15, 17) rnds.

Cuff-turn ridge: Turn work inside out so the purl side is facing you. Knit 1 rnd. Turn work right-side out again and continue working in the original direction. *Note:* A small hole will be created where you turned the work, but it will close up during fulling.

The History behind the Original Lovikka Design

Erika Aittamaa of Lovikka, Sweden, designed the first Lovikka mitten by chance in 1892. Erika spun and knit for the wealthy people in her region of northern Sweden to supplement her young family's income during depressed economic times. One of her customers wanted especially hard-wearing mittens, but the pair that Erica spun and knit with singles yarn was so thick and hard that the recipient said she had "ruined" the wool! So Erika reworked the mitten by washing and brushing it, and it became such a great success that she started to receive orders from the Sami tribes that lived close by. To make the mittens more attractive to the Sami customers, Erika started embroidering geometric patterns on the cuffs in bright, traditional Sami colors of blue, yellow, and red. The design was also practical since the embroidery served an additional purpose of slightly firming up the loose cuff and tassels allowed the mitten to hang for drying.

One key aspect of the Lovikka style is that the yarn is spun as a bulky-weight single and, after knitting, the mittens are only slightly fulled. When dry, the knitted surface is brushed to bring out a halo of fibers, then embroidered—or in the case of this "Sami" mitten, embellished with buttons or beads.

MITTEN BODY

Knit 21 (23, 25, 27, 29, 31) rnds.

Next rnd: K15 (16, 17, 18, 19, 20); put next 6 (6, 7, 7, 8, 8) sts on a small holder or waste yarn; using backward-loop method, CO 6 (6, 7, 7, 8, 8) sts; k0 (0, 1, 2, 2, 3).

Knit 13 (15, 17, 19, 21, 23) rnds or until the mitten reaches the top of the little finger.

Distribute sts onto 4 dpn as follows: 7-7-6-6 (7-7-7-7, 8-8-7-7, 8-8-8-8, 9-9-8-8, 9-9-9-9).

Dec rnd: Dec at end of each dpn as follows: knit to last 2 sts, ssk—22 (24, 26, 28, 30, 32) sts.

Rep Dec rnd until 8 sts rem.

Cut yarn, leaving a 6" [15 cm] tail.

Using tapestry needle, thread tail through rem sts, and pull tight.

Weave in tail on WS.

THUMB

Transfer the 6 (6, 7, 7, 8, 8) thumb sts from the stitch holder to a dpn.

Pick-up rnd: Join yarn and knit across thumb sts; using free dpns, pick up and knit 1 st at side of thumb opening, 6 (6, 7, 7, 8, 8) sts along CO edge and 1 st at other side of thumb opening, mark beg of rnd—14 (14, 16, 16, 18, 18) sts.

Divide these sts onto 3 dpns as follows: 4-5-5 (4-5-5, 4-6-6, 4-6-6, 4-7-7, 4-7-7) and pm at halfway point of rnd.

Dec rnd: [Knit to 2 sts before marker, ssk] twice—12 (12, 14, 14, 16, 16) sts.

Remove 2nd marker.

Knit 8 (9, 10, 11, 12, 13) rnds or until fabric reaches the base of the thumbnail.

Final rnds: *K2, ssk; rep from * around until 8 sts rem. If desired for ease of decreasing, divide sts on 2 dpns for final decs.

Cut yarn, leaving a 5" [12.5 cm] tail.

Using tapestry needle, thread tail through rem sts, and pull tight.

Weave in all ends.

BRAIDED TASSEL (OPTIONAL)

Cut six 12–18" [30.5–45.5cm] lengths of the remaining mitten yarn. Use tapestry needle to pull them individually through two loops at the cast-on edge of cuff below where pinkie will be (Figure A); ends of strands should be hanging in equal lengths on both sides of the cuff edge. Separate the 12 strands into 3 groups of 4, making sure that you keep both ends of the same strand in a single group. (Figure B). Braid the 3 groups until the braid is the length you desire or at least the length of the cuff (Figure C). Holding all ends together, tie a single square knot at the end of the braided strands. To lock the knot in place, take one of the longest strand ends coming out of the knot and wrap it around the base of the knot and, with a tapestry

Sewing and braiding the tassel:

Figure A

Figure B

needle, sew this end into the knot, cutting off the yarn at the knot surface to bury the end. Trim the remaining tassel ends to the length you desire.

FULLING (SLIGHTLY FELT)

Using a dishpan, place the mittens into about an inch (2.5 cm) of hot, soapy water and vigorously push on the fabric until it just begins to tighten. Be careful to not agitate the mittens for too long, or they will overshrink. This is *not* a typical fulling process in which the fabric becomes dense, with little stitch definition. The stitches should still be clearly seen when properly fulled. Also be careful with the tassel ends so they don't clump together in the fulling.

Rinse the mittens in clear hot water and lay flat to dry with thumbs at opposite sides for left and right mittens.

BRUSH

When dry, using a hand carder or hairbrush, gently brush the surface of the mittens until they have an even, furry appearance.

CUFF EMBELLISHMENT

Fold the cuff open before adding embellishments. I sewed ornamental buttons on the pictured mitten cuff, using the remaining spun singles as thread. But any embellishment can be used, such as beads individually strung onto the singles yarn (or a lace-weight spun yarn) and stitched into the cuff fabric, freeform embroidery, or even traditional simple lines or geometric zigzags. With a needle to fit the

Figure C

yarn and embellishment used, sew the yarn through the knitted surface. If embroidering, just pick up the knitting stitches on the RS rather than sewing through the sts to the WS. Sketch out a pattern in advance if that helps you to visualize your final design. For all methods of sewing, at the beginning of the sewing and at the end, hide the embroidery ends in the back of the cuff fabric by weaving the ends back and forth to lock them in the fiber. Trim the ends close to the surface.

Details from Sami Spinning and Dyeing

SPIN

Fiber type: Wool (from Hanna—Border Leicester mix, see page 118)

Fiber source: Woolen Meadow Farm

Fiber preparation: Scoured fleece, hand carded with ro-lags pulled slightly into a roving form for a more evenly spun singles yarn and dyed after spinning

Weight after preparation: 5.5 oz [156 g]

Wheel and whorl used (singles and ply): Lendrum wheel; singles whorl: 5:1, ply whorl: NA

Spin method: Semi-woolen

Singles details

   spin direction: S

   wpi: 8

Ply details: NA

Final yarn weight / length: 4.9 oz [140 g] / 172 yd [157 m]

Finishing techniques: Soaked in warm, soapy water; spun out excess water in washing machine and hung with heavier tension to dry. Yarn was dyed later with acid dyes (see below).

After the Spin Workshop reflections: Short cuts in the Hanna fiber created occasional lumps in the hand-carded prep, but by pulling the hand-carded rolags through a diz, the fiber preparation became more even in diameter and kept the diameter of the singles yarn more uniform when spun.

Optional yarn

For embroidery yarn, you could spin the same fiber used for the mitten, and spin it as a 2-ply fingering weight yarn. Dye it in different colors using the low-water immersion (LWI) microwave technique (see page 90 for process).

DYE

Dye type/brand: Acid dye/Jacquard brand

Color: #7 on the color pyramid chart, see page 181 (green with 30 percent blue and 70 percent yellow)

Quantity of Dye: 1 percent DOS—total of 1.4 g [0.05 oz] of dye: 0.42 g [0.02 oz] Brilliant Blue (#623) and 0.98 g [0.03 oz] Fire Red (#618) (considered "cool primary" colors in the Jacquard line)

Dye process followed: Kettle immersion method (see page 110 for process)

After the Dye Workshop reflections: The final dyed yarn needed to be dried under heavier tension to maintain the integrity of the singles twist.

See the Natural Dye Workshop, page 92, and Acid Dye Workshop, page 100, to follow the possible dye methods for wool (protein) fiber.

Gabriel:
A Boating Hat to Crown the Spiritual Spinner

This hat is designed to fit the head of a man or woman of any age. The design was inspired by the internal structure of a Gothic cathedral ceiling, which mimics the internal structure of a wooden boat. The simple slipped-stitch cable technique moves color from the previous row into the active row, creating the illusion of vertical shaping simply by the manipulation of color. The more contrasting the colors are in the pattern, the greater the effect. The yarn was spun from a commercial Corriedale roving preparation.

SKILL LEVEL

Intermediate ▬▬▬▭

SIZES

Newborn (toddler, 4 years–teen/ adult small, adult medium, adult large). Instructions are given for smallest size, with larger sizes in parentheses. When only one number is given, it applies to all sizes.

FINISHED MEASUREMENTS

Circumference: 14 (16, 18, 20, 22)" [35.5 (40.5, 45.5, 51, 56) cm]

MATERIALS

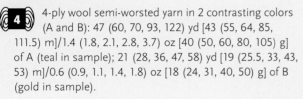 4-ply wool semi-worsted yarn in 2 contrasting colors (A and B): 47 (60, 70, 93, 122) yd [43 (55, 64, 85, 111.5) m]/1.4 (1.8, 2.1, 2.8, 3.7) oz [40 (50, 60, 80, 105) g] of A (teal in sample); 21 (28, 36, 47, 58) yd [19 (25.5, 33, 43, 53) m]/0.6 (0.9, 1.1, 1.4, 1.8) oz [18 (24, 31, 40, 50) g] of B (gold in sample).

- Commercial yarn equivalent: Aran/heavy worsted weight
- Size 8 [5mm] double-pointed needles (set of 4) and 16-inch circular needle or size needed to obtain gauge
- Cable needle
- Tapestry needle
- Stitch markers

GAUGE

16 sts and 24 rnds = 4" [10 cm] in ST st.
18 sts and 28 rnds = 4" [10 cm] in pat st.
Adjust needle size as necessary to obtain correct gauge.

SPECIAL ABBREVIATIONS

S1R (Slip 1 Right): Sl 1 to cn and hold in back, sl 1, k1 from cn.

S1L (Slip 1 Left): Sl 1 to cn and hold in front, k1, sl 1 from cn.

Make 1 (M1): Insert LH needle from front to back under the running thread between the last st worked and next st on LH. With RH needle, knit into the back of this loop.

Pattern Stitch (multiple of 9 sts)

Rnd 1: With B, *k2, S1R, S1L, k3; rep from * around.
Rnd 2: *K2, sl 1, k2, sl 1, k3; rep from * around.
Rnd 3 and 4: With A, rep Rnds 1 and 2.
Rep Rnds 1–4 for pat.

Pattern Notes

- This pattern is worked in the round on circular and/or double-pointed needles.
- For a tighter join, see note in Hanna pattern, page 125, about how to join first cast-on round.
- For a tighter rib, work the cuff with needle one size smaller than the main needle.
- Change to double-pointed needles when stitches no longer fit comfortably on circular needle.

Instructions

CUFF

With A and using long-tail method and smaller needle if you want a tighter rib, CO 60 (72, 80, 88, 96) sts. Mark beg of rnd and join, taking care not to twist sts.

Work K2, P2 rib for ½ (¾, 1, 1¼, 1½)" [1.25 (2, 2.5, 3, 4) cm].

BODY

If working rib on smaller needle, change to larger needle.

Rnd 1 (inc): Knit and inc 3 (0, 1, 2, 3) sts evenly around using M1 inc—63 (72, 81, 90, 99) sts.

Rnd 2: Knit around.

Work 4-rnd pat st until piece measures 4¾ (5, 6½, 7, 7½)" [12 (12.5, 16.5, 17, 19) cm] or desired length to crown.

Cut B, leaving a 5" [12.5 cm] tail.

Next rnd: Knit and dec 3 (0, 1, 2, 3) sts evenly around— 60 (72, 80, 88, 96) sts.

Purl 1 rnd.

SHAPE CROWN

Rnd 1: Knit.

Rnd 2 (dec): *K2, k2tog; rep from * around—45 (54, 60, 66, 72) sts.

Rnds 3–5: Knit.

Rnd 6 (dec): *K1, k2tog; rep from * around—30 (36, 40, 44, 48) sts.

Rnds 7–9: Knit.

Rnd 10 (dec): *K2tog; rep from * around—15 (18, 20, 22, 24) sts.

Rnds 11–13: Knit.

Rnd 14 (dec): Rep Rnd 10—8 (9, 10, 11, 12) sts.

Rnd 15 (dec): Rep Rnd 10—4 (5, 5, 6, 6) sts.

Cut A, leaving an 8" [20.5 cm] tail.

Using tapestry needle, thread tail through rem sts and pull tight.

Weave in all ends on WS.

Details from Gabriel Spinning and Dyeing

SPIN

Fiber type: Wool (commercially prepared Corriedale roving)

Fiber source: Ashland Bay Trading, c/o Saga Hill Designs

Fiber preparation: The roving was dyed and predrafted prior to spinning

Weight after preparation: Teal (A): 3.4 oz [95 g]; gold (B): 3.2 oz [90 g]

Wheel and whorl used (singles and ply): Lendrum wheel; singles whorl: 6:1, ply whorl: 3:1

Spin method: Semi-woolen from commercial prep (roving was slightly twisted with multidirectional, crimpy fibers)

Singles details

    spin direction: Z

    wpi: 20

Ply details

    number of plies: 4

    spin direction: S

    tpi: 2

    wpi: 10

    twist angle: 30°

Final yarn weight / length: Teal (A): 3.4 oz [95 g]; gold (B): 3.2 oz [90 g] / Teal (A): 109 yd [100 m]; gold (B): 82 yd [75 m] (enough to make the adult medium hat)

Finishing techniques: Soaked in warm, soapy water; rinsed with vinegar and clear water; spun out excess water in washing machine and hung with light tension to dry.

After the Spin Workshop reflections: The 4-ply yarn was ideal for this pattern since the greater number of plies created a yarn with a more even appearance and allowed the color pattern to stand out. A 3-ply yarn may also be effective for this pattern although the singles would need to be spun slightly heavier to achieve the same heavy worsted/Aran-weight yarn.

DYE

Dye type/brand: Acid dye/Jacquard brand

Color: Teal (A): #47 on the color pyramid chart, see page 181 (80 percent Blue, 10 percent yellow, and 10 percent red).

Gold (B): #9 on the color pyramid chart, see page 181 (70 percent yellow, 20 percent red, and 10 percent blue).

(These colors are considered "warm primaries" in the Jacquard line and are "split complementary" colors.)

Quantity of Dye: For dyeing 100 g [3.5 oz] of each color

Teal (A): 2 percent DOS—Total of 2 g [0.08 oz] of dye: 1.6 g [0.06 oz] Turquoise Blue (#624), 0.2 g [0.007 oz] Yellow Sun (#601), and 0.2 g [0.007 oz] Cherry Red (#617).

Gold (B): 1 percent DOS—Total of 1 g [0.04 oz] of dye: 0.7 g [0.02 oz] Yellow Sun (#601), 0.2g [0.007 oz] Cherry Red (#617), and 0.1 g [0.004 oz] Turquoise Blue (#624).

Dye process followed: Kettle immersion method (see page 110 for process)

After the Dye Workshop reflections: I placed the roving inside lingerie bags during the dye process to keep it from being over-manipulated and felting in the dye bath.

See the Natural Dye Workshop, page 92, and Acid Dye Workshop, page 100, to follow the possible dye methods for wool (protein) fiber.

Róisín:
Wrist/Ankle Warmer

Róisín is an Irish name meaning "little rose." I think the cable structure on this wristlet is reminiscent of a trellis that might be found a quaint old Irish rose garden. The cable pattern is very basic and would be an excellent first cable project. I chose an alpaca fleece for the project fiber. The cable pattern supports the inherently inelastic alpaca fiber in a soft yet stable fabric form and the buttons make the wristers easily adjustable. As the wrist/ankle warmers are worn, the alpaca will bloom to a lovely softness, but will maintain the deep cable pattern.

Project Note

If you use cochineal to dye your fiber as I did for this project, you can create matching buttons by dyeing unfinished wooden buttons in a small amount of the remaining cochineal dye bath. To do this, soak the buttons in the cooled dye bath for at least 4 hours, let them dry, and spray them with a coat or two of matte lacquer. (Buttons and spray lacquer may be found at craft stores.)

Pattern Note

The length of the wrist/ankle warmer can be adjusted by working more or fewer cable pattern repeats. If you want a wider piece, cast on more stitches and work more edge stitches in garter stitch.

SKILL LEVEL
Easy ◖■◻◻◗

SIZE
To fit 7" [17.8 cm] wrist circumference.

FINISHED MEASUREMENTS
Width: 3½" [9 cm]
Length: 10" [25.5 cm] or desired length.

MATERIALS
 3-ply alpaca yarn: 80 yd [73 m]/3 oz [85 g]
Singles alpaca yarn: approx 1 yd [1 m] for sewing buttons
- Commercial yarn equivalent for main yarn: worsted weight
- Size 7 [4.5 mm] knitting needles or size needed to obtain gauge
- Cable needle
- Tapestry needle
- Set of 4 buttons with approx 1" [2.5 cm] diameter

GAUGE
16 sts and 28 rows = 4" [10 cm] in ST st.
One 16-st, 6 row cable panel = 2½ × 1¼" [3.2 × 6.5 cm].
Adjust needle size as necessary to obtain correct gauge.

SPECIAL ABBREVIATIONS
2 over 2 Left Cross (2/2 LC): Slip next 2 sts to a cable needle and hold the cable needle to the front of the work without knitting the sts. Knit the next 2 sts on the working needle, and then knit the 2 sts held on the cable needle. This turns the cable to the left.

2 over 2 Right Cross (2/2 RC): Slip next 2 sts to a cable needle and hold the cable needle to the back of the work without knitting the sts. Knit the next 2 sts on the working needle, and then knit the 2 sts held on the cable needle. This turns the cable to the right.

Pattern Stitch

CABLE PANEL (16-ST PANEL)

A chart is provided for those preferring to work from charts.

Row 1 (RS): *K2, 2/2 LC, k4, 2/2 RC, k2.

Row 2: K2, p12, k2.

Row 3: K4, 2/2 LC, 2/2 RC, k4.

Row 4: K2, p12, k2.

Row 5: K6, 2/2 RC, k6.

Row 6: K2, p12, k2.

Rep Rows 1–6 for pat, stopping the pat after row 4 before beginning the button band.

Instructions

BUTTON BAND

Using long-tail method, CO 16 sts.

Rows 1–3: Knit.

Rows 4, 6, and 8: K2, p12, k2.

Rows 5 and 7: Knit.

Work 6-row Cable Panel 6 times or until piece measures 2" [5 cm] shorter than desired size, then work Rows 1–5 once more.

BUTTONHOLE BAND

The first row creates 2 buttonholes. The 1-stitch decrease sets up even spacing for the buttonholes on the band and reduces the flare created by the previous cable pattern.

Buttonhole row 1 (RS): K3, BO 2, k3 (including st on RH needle following BO), k2tog, BO 2, k4—11 sts.

Buttonhole row 2: K2, p2; using backward-loop method, CO 2 sts; p4, CO 2, p1, k2—15 sts.

Next 3 rows: Knit.

BO kwise.

Finishing

Cut yarn, leaving a tail of about 6" [15 cm].

Weave in all tail ends on WS and cut off remaining yarn close to fabric.

Details from Róisín Spinning and Dyeing

SPIN

Fiber type: Alpaca (fleece blanket from Amari, a yearling Huacaya alpaca)

Fiber source: Tier One Alpacas

Fiber preparation: Scoured, dyed, and carded fleece with fine, cotton carders prior to spinning

Weight after preparation: 4.6 oz [130 g]

Wheel and whorl used (singles and ply): Lendrum wheel; singles whorl: 8:1, ply whorl: 6:1

Spin method: Woolen, from rolags

Singles details

  spin direction: Z

  wpi: 20

Ply details

  number of plies: 3

  spin direction: S

  tpi: 3

  wpi: 8

  twist angle: 40° (Spun at a higher twist angle than would typically be used for alpaca's inherent qualities. The higher twist angle created a nice defined cable stitch that's appropriate for the fabric of this project.)

Final yarn weight / length: 4.6 oz [130 g] / 100 yd [91 m]

Finishing techniques: Soaked in warm, soapy water; rinse with vinegar and clear water; spun out excess water in washing machine. Before hanging with light tension to dry, I slapped the yarn against a hard edge to enhance the fiber bloom and slightly full it.

After the Spin Workshop reflections: The 3-ply yarn was perfect for this cable pattern. The ply count allowed for stitch definition yet maintained a soft hand that will become even softer with wear.

DYE

Dye type/brand: Cochineal, natural dye (see pages 93–95 for dye details and process)

Color: Natural rose tone

Quantity of Dye: 40 g [1.4 oz] dried cochineal bugs

Dye process followed: Kettle immersion method; with 3½-hour cochineal soak, followed by a boiling time of 15 minutes to extract dye liquor. Yarn was cooked in the strained dye liquor for 1½ hours.

After the Dye Workshop reflections: The fleece was placed inside lingerie bags for the dye process, and that was critical to keep the very fine locks in order. The cochineal dyed the fiber a lovely wild rose color that was perfect for the theme of the pattern.

See the Natural Dye Workshop, page 92, and Acid Dye Workshop, page 100, to follow the possible dye methods for alpaca (protein) fiber.

Dominique:
Fisherman Rib Scarf

The fisherman rib pattern in Dominique creates a soft and warm knitted fabric that makes a small neck scarf, perfect for drinking café au lait in a little French café. It also creates an ideal, lofty fabric for the fluffy merino/angora fiber blend resulting from the Creative Fiber Blending Workshop (page 38). To continue the "blending" theme, I chose to use two different depths of shade of the same color. This gives a softer color effect, perfect for this soft fiber blend, and demonstrates that DOS is a great way to simplify color choices.

SKILL LEVEL

Easy ■■□□

FINISHED MEASUREMENTS

Width: 4" [10 cm]
Length: 34" [86 cm]

MATERIALS

5 3-ply 80% merino/20% angora-blend yarn: 95 yd [87 m]/5.6 oz [158 g] each of lighter color (A) and darker color (B).

- Commercial yarn equivalent: bulky weight
- Size 10 [6 mm] knitting needles or size needed to obtain gauge
- Tapestry needle

GAUGE

12 sts and 16 rows = 4" [10cm] in St st.
13 sts and 11 rows = 4" [10cm] in Fisherman Rib.
Correct gauge is not critical for this project.

The color-band pattern is based on a modified Fibonacci pattern sequence —a series of numerical repeats commonly found in nature and innately appealing to the eye. (Fibonacci repeats are derived by adding the two previous numbers. Example: 0, 1, 1, 2, 3, 5, 8, 13, 21, and so on. But I chose to start with the number 2 and repeat sequentially to 10 and reverse back to 2. See Color Sequence Options.)

Pattern Stitch

Fisherman Rib (odd number of sts)

All rows: P1, *knit into center of st in row below next st [2 sts will rest on the new st], p1; rep from * to end.

Color Sequence Options

Imperial Measurements (shown): Work 2" [5 cm] with B; 4" [10 cm] with A; 6" [15 cm] with B; 10" [25.5] with A; 6" [15 cm] with B; 4" [10 cm] with A; 2" [5 cm] with B. Total 34" [85.5 cm].

Metric Measurements: Work 3 cm with B; 6 cm with A; 9cm with B; 15 cm with A; 24 cm with B; 15 cm with A; 9 cm with B, 6 cm with A; 3 cm with B. Total 90 cm.

Pattern Notes

- If you want a wider scarf, cast on more stitches, making sure that you have an odd number of stitches.

- If you want a longer scarf, just start with a different starting measurement number for the color banding, double the first measurement for the second number, then continue with a Fibonocci sequence. An odd number of color sequences allows the scarf to start and end with the same color.

- Adjust yarn amounts for each color as necessary based on chosen color sequence.

- Since it's difficult to invisibly weave in ends in the reversible Fisherman's rib, and since the merino/angora blend will felt easily, spit-splice the ends when changing colors. To do this, break (don't cut) the working yarn. Unply the first few inches of yarn and fray the singles, thinning out the fibers if you wish. Do the same to the end of the new color. Spit in your hand or on the yarn, then overlap the ends of the yarns and vigorously rub them together between your hands to felt them together. (If you find spitting distasteful, use water in your hand instead.)

Instructions

With B, CO 13 sts.
Purl 1 row.
Work in Fisherman Rib and follow the Color Sequence.
Bind off in pat.
Cut yarn, leaving a 6" [15 cm] tail.

Merino and angora fiber prior to blending

Details from Dominique Spinning and Dyeing

SPIN

Fiber type: Blend of 80 percent raw Merino fleece wool and 20 percent raw angora (plucked rabbit) fiber. Blend goal: to create an incredibly soft, thick scarf that will bloom over time with a lovely halo. (Angora rabbit fiber from Penny, a copper satin angora rabbit. Wool from an unidentified Merino fleece.)

Fiber source: Angora—Oldhaus Fibers. Merino fleece—International Fleeces

Fiber preparation: Scoured Merino and shook out debris in angora; first blended fiber together with hands and then carded the hand-blended fiber into rolags using fine cotton carders. The fiber was dyed after preparation but before spinning.

Weight after preparation: 6 oz [170 g]

Wheel and whorl used (singles and ply): Singles: Lendrum wheel, whorl: 8:1; plying: Louet wheel, whorl: 5.5:1

Spin method: Woolen, from rolags

Singles details
    spin direction: Z
    wpi: 15

Ply details
    number of plies: 3
    spin direction: S
    tpi: 2
    wpi: 6
    twist angle: 15°

Final yarn weight / length: 5.6 oz [158 g] for each color / 95 yd [87 m] for each color

Finishing techniques: After dyeing and spinning, I used a fulling process to finish the yarn, by first washing the yarn in hot, soapy water; rinsing in cold water; rinsing again in hot water; rinsing in cold, clear water with vinegar; and finally rinsing in cold water, no vinegar. After I spun out excess water in a washing machine, I whacked the yarn a few times on the edge of a counter to allow the angora to bloom from the yarn. The skeins were hung with light tension to dry.

After the Spin Workshop reflections: A very light hand was needed while spinning the fiber, and a firm brake provided a quick draw-on.

DYE

Dye type/brand: Jacquard Acid dyes (see page 100 for dye details and process)

Color: Brilliant Blue (#623) in 0.5 percent DOS and 2 percent DOS to achieve the two colors

Quantity of Dye: *Color A* (0.5 percent DOS): 0.8g [0.03 oz]; *Color B* (2 percent DOS): 3.2 g [0.1 oz]

Dye process followed: Kettle immersion

After the Dye Workshop reflections: I chose the kettle immersion dye method to guarantee more even colors in this Merino/angora blended fiber. Both Merino and angora lack a medulla (a central supporting canal in the fiber shaft) and, as a result, have a tendency to dye with less saturated colors and therefore benefit from the longest dye-cooking method. But I needed to watch the dye bath temperature very carefully to ensure the bath didn't boil and felt the fine, delicate fibers. A lingerie bag was used to contain the prepared fibers through the dye process.

See the Natural Dye Workshop, page 92, and Acid Dye Workshop, page 100, to follow the possible dye methods for angora/wool (protein) fibers.

Sylph:
Parachute Cowl

Sylphs are invisible mythical creatures that are considered fairies of the air—much like our fiber subject, silk. This sylph will embrace your neck and reach up to touch your head when you wish to become sylphlike and fly off with airy, silken wings. I chose a pattern stitch that has great elasticity to allow the cowl to either caress the neck or be used as a head wrap. Knit to the optional length of 18 inches (46 cm), Sylph would be a soothing chemotherapy headcover. I call this a "parachute" cowl since it has the qualities of parachute silk—the ability to be condensed into a tight structure and dramatically open up into a larger form.

SKILL LEVEL

Easy ◖■◻▯

SIZE

Average adult

FINISHED MEASUREMENTS

Circumference: 24" [16 cm] or as desired
Length: 10" [25.5 cm] (shown), 18" [45.5 cm] or as desired

MATERIALS

 3-ply silk yarn: 200 yd [183 m]/3.5 oz [100 g].
Commercial yarn equivalent: DK weight yarn

- Size 4 [3.5 mm] 16" [40 cm] circular needle or size needed to obtain gauge
- Tapestry needle
- Stitch marker

GAUGE

20 sts and 32 rnds = 4" [10 cm] in St st.
18 sts and 32 rnds = 4" [10 cm] in pat st.
Adjust needle size as necessary to obtain correct gauge.

Pattern Stitch (multiple of 4 sts)

All rnds: *K2, yo, p2tog; rep from * around.

Pattern Notes

- The cowl is worked in the round.
- Make the circumference smaller/bigger by casting on fewer/more stitches in multiples of 4.

Instructions

CO 108 sts; mark beg of rnd and join, taking care not to twist sts.

Work pat st until piece measures 10" [25 cm], 18" [45.5 cm], or to desired length.

BO kwise, knitting into back of all YOs to close them up.

Cut yarn, leaving a 6" [15 cm] tail.

Weave in all ends on WS and cut off remaining yarn close to fabric.

Wash and block to finished measurements.

Details from Sylph Spinning and Dyeing
SPIN

Fiber type: Cultivated silk hanky bundle (a compilation of approximately 150 cultivated silk cocoons that were stretched into a square format by a silk supplier in China)

Fiber source: Saga Hill Designs

Fiber preparation: Hand painted in advance of spinning. To spin, the hankies were individually separated from the bundle and predrafted into thin roving for spinning.

Weight after preparation: 3.5 oz [100 g]

Wheel and whorl used (singles and ply): Majacraft Little Gem wheel—singles whorl: 8.6:1

Lendrum wheel—ply whorl: 6:1

Spin method: Semi-worsted with a long drafting zone and tight twist

Singles details
  spin direction: Z
  wpi: 25

Ply details
  number of plies: 3
  spin direction: S
  tpi: 6
  wpi: 13
  twist angle: 35°

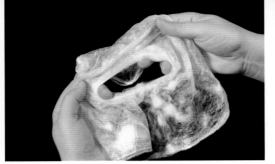

Preparing silk hankies for spinning.
1) Separating hanky layers.

2) Opening up the hanky from the center to
start stretching it open into roving.

3) Silk hanky roving.

Final yarn weight / length: 3.5 oz [100 g] / 200 yd [183 m]

Finishing techniques: Soaked in lukewarm, soapy water, and rinsed in warm water (no vinegar). (A teaspoon [5 ml] of fabric softener could be added if the silk gets stiff after washing. But don't use fabric softener if you're going to dye the silk since the dye may not fix to the fiber.) Excess water was removed by spinning it in a washing machine and then it was hung with light tension to dry.

After the Spin Workshop reflections: The hanky bundles contain very thin squares of silk that need to be separated for spinning. Each one is as thin as a spider's web. Even if you think you've peeled off a single hanky, chances are you've picked up more than one! Hankies are easiest to spin when opened up at the center and gradually stretched into a roving size that approximates the ultimate spinning thickness. Silk fiber is best spun as a fine weight single. To achieve the DK yarn weight for this Sylph pattern, 3 plies were needed. If finer singles had been spun, more plies may have been needed.

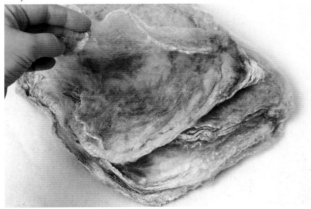

Dyed silk hankies ready to be prepared
for spinning the yarn for Sylph.

DYE

Dye type/brand: Acid dyes/Jacquard (see page 100 for dye details and process)

Color: Hand painted by randomly squirting and dabbing prepared blue and yellow dye solutions onto the hankies to achieve an impressionistic effect with blue and green tones. (The green was created by the merging of the blue and yellow dyes as they were applied on the fiber.)

Quantity of Dye: 1 percent DOS, 5 g [0.18 oz] of each color in solution dilution as follows: 500 ml [17 fl oz] Brilliant Blue (#623) and 500 ml [17 fl oz] Yellow Sun (#601) at 100 percent, 50 percent, and 25 percent dilutions

Dye process followed: Hand-painted with low water immersion; cooked with microwave method for 9 minutes total (3 periods of 3 minutes at 70 percent power)

After the Dye Workshop reflections: Silk takes dye beautifully, although colors will appear lighter due to the reflective nature of the fiber. To avoid wasting dye, don't oversaturate the fiber with dye because it doesn't take much solution to achieve full dye absorption. Open up the hanky in layers to add dye to internal layers and wait at least 15 minutes for the dye to soak through the fiber before proceeding to cook. To better control the fiber, place the hanky bundle into a lingerie bag when pre-soaking, after hand painting and cooking, and before washing the dyed fiber.

See the Natural Dye Workshop, page 92, Acid Dye Workshop, page 100, and Fiber-Reactive Workshop, page 103, to follow the possible dye methods for silk fiber.

Bene:
Skinny Scarf or Tie

If you're bored with garter stitch, try this woven stitch. It's really easy and quick to knit. When blocked (or steam ironed), the fabric lies flat with an interesting texture on both sides. The fabric may also be wrapped around and seamed in the back for a sturdy, double-sided, super-skinny tie. The indigo-dyed cotton gives the project a 1960s hippie vibe, with the color fading through time like a pair of good blue jeans. (Beware: If tied around a light-colored fabric, indigo may leave a stain. With repeated washings, there should be less of a tendency for the indigo color to transfer.) It's reminiscent of a necktie that a voguish character might wear in a vintage Italian film. This is good knitting, so I've named it Bene (Italian for "well done"). *Salute!*

SKILL LEVEL

Easy ◧■□▭

SIZES

As suits the knitter

FINISHED MEASUREMENTS
PER PATTERN & BY TRADITIONAL SIZING

Width: Single-sided: 2" [5 cm]; Double-sided: 1" [2.5 cm]
Recommended lengths: Traditional adult necktie, skinny scarf, or "gypsy" waist belt: 52" [1.3 m]; traditional youth necktie, scarf, belt, or "hippie" headband: 45" [1.1 m]; short bolo-style necktie, traditional headband, or scarf: 30–36" [76–91 cm]

MATERIALS

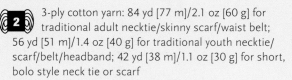 3-ply cotton yarn: 84 yd [77 m]/2.1 oz [60 g] for traditional adult necktie/skinny scarf/waist belt; 56 yd [51 m]/1.4 oz [40 g] for traditional youth necktie/ scarf/belt/headband; 42 yd [38 m]/1.1 oz [30 g] for short, bolo style neck tie or scarf

- Commercial yarn equivalent: sport weight
- Size 3 [3.25 mm] knitting needles or size needed to obtain gauge
- Tapestry needle

GAUGE

22 sts and 32 rows = 4" [10 cm] in ST st.
22 sts and 34 rows = 4" [10 cm] in Woven Pat (blocked).
Adjust needle size as necessary to obtain correct gauge.

Pattern Stitch

Woven Pattern (odd number of sts)
Row 1 (RS): K1, *sl 1 wyif, k1; rep from * to end of row.
Row 2: Purl.
Row 3: K2, *sl 1 wyif, k1; rep from * to last st, k1.
Row 4: Purl.
Rep Rows 1–4 for pat.

Pattern Note

Instructions are for the tie shown in the photograph. To make tie wider or narrower, cast on more or fewer stitches, making sure that you are casting on an odd number of stitches.

Instructions

CO 11 sts.
Work 4-row Woven pat until piece measures desired length for tie, scarf, belt, or headband, ending with a RS row.
BO pwise.

FINISHING

Single-sided tie: Cut yarn, leaving a 4" [10 cm] tail. Weave in all ends on WS, cutting off remaining yarn close to fabric; block the fabric so the tie lies completely flat.

Double-sided tie: Cut working yarn, leaving a tail that is at least 1½ times the length of the tie. Weave in all ends on WS, cutting off remaining yarn close to fabric. With RS facing, use tail to sew edges together using mattress st, forming a tube. Seam ends, then run tail through to interior of tube. Block tie so that tube lies flat.

Cotton roving ready for the dye process

Details from Bene Spinning and Dyeing

SPIN

Fiber type: Pima cotton *Gossypium barbadense*, commercially prepared into top

Fiber source: Mielke Fiber Arts

Fiber preparation: Predyed with indigo natural-dye method, with dyed top slightly predrafted by tugging to open the slightly compressed fibers resulting from the dye process

Weight after preparation: 7 oz [200g] (No more than 3 oz [85 g] was needed for Bene. See * below)

Wheel and whorl used (singles and ply): Majacraft Little Gem wheel; singles whorl: 8.6:1, ply whorl: 5.9:1

Spin method: Semi-worsted, with a tight twist

Singles details

    spin direction: Z

    wpi: 34

Ply details

    number of plies: 3

    spin direction: S

    tpi: 6

    wpi: 14

    twist angle: 35°

Final yarn weight / length: 2.9 oz [83 g] / 185 yd [169 m]

Finishing techniques: After plying, I rewrapped the plied yarn onto CPVC skein blockers and boiled the fiber on the blockers for 45 minutes in a soapy, soda ash bath, rinsed, and let the yarn dry on the skein blockers.

After the Spin Workshop reflections: The short fibers spin best with a relaxed hand that allows the twist to enter with minimal predrafting. See After the Dye Workshop reflections below for comments on dyeing cotton before spinning.

DYE

Dye type/brand: Indigo, natural dye (see page 97 for dye details and process)

Color: Natural indigo blue

Quantity of Dye: 40 g [1.4 oz] *(20 g [0.7 oz] of indigo would have been sufficient for the Bene project but to take advantage of the vat, I chose to dye more fiber than needed.)

Dye process followed: Vat method, dipped twice

After the Dye Workshop reflections: Cotton compresses very easily when manipulated. I chose to predye the roving to achieve a variegated, worn jeans look in the final yarn. This choice made the spinning more difficult because the cotton was slightly compressed from the dye process. First-time cotton spinners might want to spin the cotton before dyeing.

See the Natural Dye Workshop—Indigo, page 97, and Fiber-Reactive Dye Workshop, page 103, to follow the possible dye methods for cotton (cellulose) fiber.

Liv:
Linen Towel

Flax (linen) is not typically a fiber used by knitters, since it spins best at a very fine gauge that is more suitable for weaving. But there are some projects that lend themselves very well to linen yarn—towels, for instance! The inspiration for the surface pattern came from a traditional Swedish image of the Tree of Life, which can be seen in many Swedish designs, from tapestries to grave markers. It symbolizes the family tree, with outreaching branches. Since linen comes from flax, an ancient fiber with a long "family tree," it seemed appropriate to use this fiber for the basis of this Knit Workshop project. The more the towel is washed in hot water, the softer it will become—although it will also shrink, so take care when washing and expect the final cloth to become quite a bit smaller (perhaps one-third smaller) over time. I added a button loop closure as a means of hanging the towel more creatively.

SKILL LEVEL

Easy ◼◼◻◻

FINISHED MEASUREMENTS

After knitting: 11" [28 cm] wide × 7" [18 cm] long
After first washing: 9½" [24 cm] wide × 6½" [17 cm] long

MATERIALS

3 3-ply linen yarn: 87 yd [80 m] /2.6 oz [75 g]
Commercial yarn equivalent: DK weight

- Size 2 [2.75 mm] knitting needles or size needed to obtain gauge

- Tapestry needle
- Three ⅞" [2 cm] post-style buttons (the buttons shown in the sample came from the author's personal collection)

GAUGE

20 sts and 25 rows = 4" [10cm] in St st.
Adjust needle size as necessary to obtain correct gauge.

SPECIAL TECHNIQUE

2-st I-cord: *K2, do not turn, slip sts back to LH needle; rep from * until cord is desired length. Bind off.

Stitch Key

☐ Knit
⊟ Purl

Instructions

CO 53 sts.

Work 58-row chart.

Bind off kwise to last 2 sts, leaving last 2 sts on needle.

I-CORD LOOPS

First loop: Work 2-st I-cord for 6" [15 cm] or twice the desired loop length. Cut yarn leaving a 6" [15 cm] tail. With WS facing, sew end of I-cord securely to top of fabric just left of the beginning of I-cord to form a loop. Weave in tail.

2nd loop: With WS facing, pick up and knit 2 sts in center top of fabric. Work as for first loop.

3rd loop: Work as for 2nd loop, picking up sts in remaining top corner.

With RS facing, sew decorative buttons directly below the I-cord loops.

Weave in rem tails.

FINISHING

Before using the towel, wash it in hot, soapy water and rinse in hot, clear water. This will tighten and soften the fabric, making it more comfortable for use. The towel will shrink during this first washing.

Details from Liv Spinning and Dyeing

SPIN

Fiber type: Flax (*Linum usitatissimum*) unbleached and commercially prepared as line top

Fiber source: Apple Hollow Fiber Arts

Fiber preparation: Chemically processed for spinning by a fiber processor in Belgium, I only needed to separate and open the top for ease of drafting. The yarn was dyed after spinning.

Weight after preparation: 3.9 oz [110 g]

Wheel and whorl used (singles and ply): Majacraft Little Gem wheel; singles whorl: 8.6:1, ply whorl: 4.9:1

Spin method: I used a worsted wet-spin technique, laying a towel across my lap and dipping my fingers into a bowl of water about every three to four treadles to smooth the fibers as they were spun. I only dipped the fingers of the hand that controlled the twist—the front hand. (A sponge may be used if the water bowl method is too messy.) I drew the fibers out of the top preparation with my back (drafting) hand and used light tension to facilitate the twist.

Singles details

    spin direction: S

    wpi: 28

Ply details

    number of plies: 3

    spin direction: Z

    tpi: 4

    wpi: 14

    twist angle: 25°

top for the Liv project.

Spun flax, now "linen", ready to be dyed

Final yarn weight / length: 3.9 oz [110 g] / 113 yd [103 m]
Finishing techniques: The yarn was boiled for 30 minutes in neutral pH soapy water, rinsed, spun out in a washing machine, pounded with a wooden mallet to soften the fibers for dyeing and knitting, and hung to dry with a light tension. No vinegar was used.

After the Spin Workshop reflections: The wet-spin method used for both the singles and plying was preferable for a smoother yarn. A low angle of twist in the plying reduced the overall coarse feeling of the yarn.

DYE

Dye type/brand: Fiber-reactive Procion MX (see page 103 for dye details and process)
Color: Sun Yellow (#108) at 4 percent DOS
Quantity of Dye: 4 g [0.1 oz] dye powder
Dye process followed: Pail immersion

After the Dye Workshop reflections: The dark natural color of unbleached flax makes an interesting overdye effect. Brighter colors should be chosen to enhance the natural color because dark colors will become even darker on unbleached flax. I added an additional 45 minutes to the final dye bath soak time (total: 1½ hrs) to ensure that the dye would soak through the dense, 3-ply yarn.

See the Natural Dye Workshop, page 92, and Acid Dye Workshop, page 100, to follow the possible dye methods for flax (cellulose) fiber.

Catherine:
Small Notions Bag

Named after the patron saint of spinners, St. Catherine, this bag will stand watch over your spinning days and nights. The pattern stitch is easy and creates a very firm, double-sided fabric—ideal for a bag that needs some density to properly hold tools like oil bottles, plying disks, and orifice hooks or knitting notions. The synthetic fiber is also great for a project that might see quite a lot of use and perhaps abuse (if only from the oil bottle). The nylon fiber used is considered a "blending" nylon and is usually blended with other fibers when making socks and other garments that need strength. But of course, it can also be spun totally on its own, as I've done in this project. The brilliant red is regal—as is dear Catherine as she watches over our noble work. May this project enrich your spinning!

Pattern Stitch

2-Faced Double-Knitting (odd number of sts)

Row 1 (RS): K1, *sl 1 wyib, k1; rep from * to end of row.

Row 2: K1, p1, *sl 1 wyib, p1; rep from * to last st, k1.

Rep Rows 1 and 2 for pat.

Pattern Notes

- The fabric created is double-knit (two layers) with knit stitches showing on one side and purl stitches on the other—but only half the stitches show on each side. The edge stitches are worked in garter stitch for easier seaming. The two layers ensure that your spinning tools are cushioned within the bag and that they won't fall out.

- The bag can be made wider by adjusting the number of stitches cast on—just make sure that you have an odd number of stitches.

Instructions

Leaving a 14" [35.5 cm] tail, using cable cast-on method and MC, CO 25 sts.

Work pat st until piece measures 10" [25.5 cm] or to twice desired bag length, ending with a RS row.

Last row (WS): P2tog across and *at the same time*, BO very loosely, ending p1, BO last st.

Cut yarn, leaving a 14" [35.5 cm] tail.

Using the CO tail, sew one side seam; using the BO tail, sew the other side seam.

Weave in all ends, cutting remaining yarn close to fabric.

I-CORD HANDLE

Leaving a 14" [35.5 cm] tail and using CC, work 4-st I-Cord for 12" [30.5 cm]. Cut yarn, leaving a 14" [35.5 cm] tail. Using the tails, invisibly sew the ends of the I-Cord along the side seams of the bag, just catching the sts along either side of the seam to cover the seam.

SKILL LEVEL

Easy

FINISHED MEASUREMENTS

Width: 4" [10 cm]
Length: 5" [12.7 cm] (not including handle)

MATERIALS

- 4-ply blending nylon yarn: 70 yd [64 m]/2.1 oz [60 g] in MC for bag; 17 yd [16 m]/0.5 oz [15 g] in CC for handle
- Commercial yarn equivalent: worsted or Aran weight
- Size 6 [4mm] knitting needles or size needed to obtain gauge
- Tapestry needle

GAUGE

16 sts and 24 rows = 4" [10 cm] in ST st.
24 sts and 22 rows = 4" [10 cm] in double-knit pat st.
Note: Only 12 sts will show on RS.
Adjust needle size as necessary to obtain correct gauge.

SPECIAL TECHNIQUE

4-st I-cord: CO 4 sts. *K4, do not turn, slip sts back to LH needle; rep from * until cord is desired length. Bind off.

Undyed nylon fiber

Details from Catherine Spinning and Dyeing

SPIN

Fiber type: Blending nylon top (a fiber that's often blended with other fibers to strengthen them for garments such as socks)

Fiber source: Ashland Bay Trading, c/o Saga Hill Designs

Fiber preparation: Predrafted top. The yarn was dyed after spinning.

Weight after preparation: 3.7 oz [106 g]

Wheel and whorl used (singles and ply): Lendrum wheel—singles whorl: 8:1; Louet wheel—ply whorl: 5.5:1

Spin method: Worsted

Singles details

   spin direction: Z

   wpi: 21

Ply details

   number of plies: 4

   spin direction: S

   tpi: 2

   wpi: 8

   twist angle: 25°

Final yarn weight / length: 2.9 oz [83 g] of bag yarn; 0.8 oz [23 g] of handle yarn / 95 yd [87 m] of bag yarn (for MC); 26 yd [24 m] of handle yarn (for CC)

Finishing techniques: Soaked in a warm, soapy citric acid bath to prepare for dyeing

After the Spin Workshop reflections: The synthetic fiber easily over twisted, so I tightened the brake band to draw the fiber onto the wheel faster than normally required when spinning a natural fiber with similar characteristics. I found that a short forward worsted draw was the best method of spinning the slippery fiber. I used a larger plying whorl than usual to help relax the singles and make a softer-feeling plied yarn.

DYE

Dye type/brand: Jacquard Acid dye (see page 100 for dye details and process)

Color: 1 percent DOS in warm primary colors

Bag body (MC)—warm red: #65 on the color pyramid chart, see page 181 (90 percent red, 10 percent blue)

Bag handle (CC)—warm green: #12 on the color pyramid chart, see page 181 (60 percent yellow, 30 percent blue, 10 percent red)

Quantity of Dye: 5g [0.18 oz] of each blend in a 500ml solution

Bag body (MC)—90 percent Cherry Red (#617), 10 percent Turquoise (#624)

Bag handle (CC) —60 percent Yellow Sun (#601), 30 percent Turquoise (#624), 10 percent Cherry Red (#617)

Dye process followed: A combination of low immersion and hand painting of 50 percent and 100 percent solutions and microwave cooking method

After the Dye Workshop reflections: The low-immersion microwave technique is quick and perfect for small projects like this bag. But the inherent lack of control over microwave cooking temperature and the synthetic base of this particular fiber produced an unexpected result in the final color of the handle yarn. The dye bath reached too high a temperature for the nylon fiber and overcooked, resulting in mostly brown tones rather than the intended greens for the handle. In this case, the brown worked well with the bag, so I decided to use it as an example of the kind of surprises that can happen when hand painting using the microwave cooking technique. Keeping your expectations open is a part of the mystery and excitement of dyeing your own yarn!

See the Natural Dye Workshop, page 92, and Acid Dye Workshop, page 100, to follow the possible dye methods for nylon (protein-mimicking) fiber.

Resources and Supplies

Here are a few ideas on where and how to find spinning and dyeing resources and supplies.

FIBERS AND OTHER SPINNING SUPPLIES

Vendors at seasonal fiber fairs sell a wide variety of fibers, both raw and processed. Some large cities have spinning shops, but if your area isn't so blessed, some enlightened yarn shops may also carry fibers and equipment. Other venues for purchasing supplies locally may be a spinning guild or fiber arts center. At the very least, they will know the spinning retailers in your area. Find local centers and guilds through an online search. The website for the national Handweavers Guild of America, www.weavespindye.org, has a list of spinning guilds across the United States, Australia, Canada, Denmark, New Zealand, Switzerland, and the United Kingdom.

Don't forget your local fiber producers, where you can buy directly from the source. Fiber fairs are a great place to meet fiber producers in your area. If you have a sheep growers' organization in your state or province, they may have a list of local sheep farmers arranged by sheep breed. Some fiber producers sell their wares throughout the year, and some sell out at shearing time, so it may take a few calls to locate a farm that has the fiber you want at the time of year you'd like it.

If you are unable to connect to any local sources of fiber and supplies, don't worry. Pretty much any fiber or supply can be found online. Of course, you can't touch the fibers or personally see the equipment online—at least not without incurring a shipping charge. But some online stores will send samples of their fibers for a fee. Even if they don't mention the option on their site, it never hurts to ask if you can purchase a sample pack. You may also find fibers at online auction sites, but take caution if you buy at those sites. Be sure the fibers come from a smoke-free environment (unless you don't care) and isolate the fibers when they arrive to be sure they are pest free. (See FA-8: Fiber Storage and Pests (page 170) for details on how to keep your fibers safe from pests.)

Wheel dealers may be found online and through catalogs, but know that you're taking a chance when you buy a wheel without trying it first. If you don't live near a spinning wheel dealer, look for the nearest fiber festival, as they often have vendors selling wheels. Festivals may take place any time of year, depending on where you live, but the majority are in the spring, just after shearing time.

THE "BEST" WHEEL

My students always ask me, "What's the best wheel?" I have no definitive answer. It seems that everyone with an engineering bent has at one time or another tried to build a "better" wheel. Even Leonardo da Vinci got into the act when he designed what may have been the first version of the spinning wheel flyer. I'm going to say something that sounds like a cop-out, but it's the truth: The best wheel is the wheel that is the most comfortable for you and suits the kind of spinning you want to do. My advice for beginners is to look for a wheel with a drive ratio spread of slow to moderately fast, since that will let you experience a wide variety of fibers and a broad assortment of types of yarn—from chunky to lace.

I must admit, until I tried several wheels at my local fiber shop, I didn't "get" the subtleties between wheels and how they truly do operate differently. Some sing with fine silk and some with bulky wool. Some are annoying and fussy and others are pleasing. It's a very personal thing. So now I understand why every serious spinner that I know has multiple wheels. They are all unique. So take your time when selecting a wheel. Try different fibers on different wheels. See if you can rent the one you like from the seller first or ask for a "rent to buy" option. But don't deal with a seller who won't let you sit at the wheel for a few hours or acts annoyed when you keep changing your mind about which wheel you like the best. I can't emphasize this enough: Try a variety of wheels before buying.

A wheel can be a substantial monetary investment, but, when kept in good shape, it gives nearly a full return if you choose to sell or trade it. But beware! One wheel leads to another, and leads to another …

Dye Supplies

Secondhand sales are great places to look for pots and other dye tools. Remember to look for stainless steel and glass that can withstand boiling temperatures. Most wholesale restaurant supply dealers sell to the general public, and they may have both new and used equipment for a bargain.

For health reasons, gloves, safety glasses, and dust/fume masks must be purchased new. You can find these items at hardware and paint stores.

Dyes and Assistants

These are sold locally in some art and craft stores. But the biggest variety of dyestuff is found online from specialty companies. These companies may have either natural or synthetic dyes, and some carry both. A simple online search will lead you to a source.

The vinegar used in the acid process can be purchased at any grocery store, and citric acid crystals may be found in the bulk foods section of some groceries or food cooperatives.

Natural dyestuff may be found in your own yard or grocery. It's best to grow your own dye plants or purchase them from a grower rather than take them from the wild. The more "exotic" natural dyes, such as indigo and cochineal, may be purchased from specialty companies.

Some fiber fair vendors sell dyes, and they might also have samples of actual fiber that was dyed with the dye. A dyed fiber sample is truer than a printed chart, although your own dyeing situation and fiber is a strong factor in the final dyed result.

Retail Supply Sources Used or Mentioned in *Yarn Works*

The following is a list of retailers and wholesalers where you can find many of the supplies and fibers mentioned and/or used in *Yarn Works*.

FIBERS

Apple Hollow Fiber Arts—www.applehollow.com
Ashland Bay—www.ashlandbay.com (wholesale only)
Oldhaus Fibers—www.oldhaus.net
Saga Hill Designs—www.sagahill.com
Tier One Alpacas—Cornell, Wisconsin
The Cottonman—www.cottonman.com
Woolen Meadow Farm—Delano, Minnesota

SPINNING TOOLS AND FIBERS

Detta's Spindle—www.dettasspindle.net
Howard Brush—www.howardbrush.com
Mielke's Fiber Arts—www.mielkesfiberarts.com

DYE TOOLS AND DYES

Dharma Trading Co.—www.dharmatrading.com
PRO Chemical & Dye—www.prochemicalanddye.com

Bibliography

Don't be afraid to use old spinning books for basic reference. Most are as up-to-date as recently published books. After all, spinning is an ancient art! The best dyeing references are from more recently published books, since dyeing is an ever-changing art.

MAGAZINES

Spin-Off magazine and online magazine, Interweave Press
Wild Fibers, Linda N. Cortright
The Wheel, Ashford Handicrafts Ltd.

BOOKS

Amos, Alden. *The Alden Amos Big Book of Handspinning.* Loveland, CO: Interweave Press, 2001.
Baines, Patricia. *Flax and Linen.* Buckinghamshire, England: Shire, 1998.
Dean, Jenny. *Colours from Nature: A Dyer's Handbook.* Kent, England: Search Press, 2010.
De Boer, Janet. *Dyeing for Fibres and Fabrics.* Australia: Kangaroo Press, 1987.
Field, Anne. *The Ashford Book of Spinning.* Christchurch, New Zealand: Shoal Bay Press, 1999.

Field, Anne. *Spinning Wool: Beyond the Basics.* Christchurch, New Zealand: Shoal Bay Press, 1997.

Fournier, Nola, and Jane Fournier. *In Sheep's Clothing: A Handspinner's Guide to Wool.* Loveland, CO: Interweave Press, 1995.

Franquemont, Abby. *Respect the Spindle: Spin Infinite Yarns with One Amazing Tool.* Loveland, CO: Interweave Press, 2009.

Garfield, Simon. *Mauve: How One Man Invented a Color That Changed the World.* New York: W.W. Norton & Company, 2000.

Hochberg, Bette, and Bernard Hochberg. *Fibre Facts.* Santa Cruz, CA: Bette and Bernard Hochberg, 1981.

King, Amy. *Spin Control: Techniques for Spinning the Yarn You Want.* Loveland, CO: Interweave Press, 2009.

Klos, Dagmar. *The Dyer's Companion.* Loveland, CO: Interweave Press, 2004.

Kluger, Marilyn. *The Joy of Spinning.* New York: Simon and Schuster, 1971.

Knutson, Linda. Synthetic Dyes for Natural Fibers. Loveland, CO: Interweave Press, 1986.

Kolander, Cheryl. *A Silk Worker's Notebook.* Loveland, CO: Interweave Press, 1985.

Leadbeater, Eliza. *Spinning and Spinning Wheels.* Oxford: Shire, 2008.

Linder, Olive, and Harry Linder. *Handspinning Cotton.* Phoenix, AZ: Cotton Squares, 1977.

Linder, Olive, and Harry Linder. *Handspinning Flax.* Phoenix, AZ: Bizarre Butterfly Publishing, 1986.

Lynne, Erica. *Angora: A Handbook for Spinners.* Loveland, CO: Interweave Press, 1992.

Macdonald, Anne L. *No Idle Hands: The Social History of American Knitting.* New York: Ballantine Books, 1988.

MacKenzie McCuin, Judith. *The Intentional Spinner: A Holistic Approach to Making Yarn.* Loveland, CO: Interweave Press, 2009.

MacKenzie McCuin, Judith. *Teach Yourself Visually Handspinning.* Hoboken, NJ: Wiley Publishing, Inc., 2007.

Menz, Deb. *Color in Spinning.* Loveland, CO: Interweave Press, 2005.

Milner, Ann. *The Ashford Book of Dyeing.* Ashburton, New Zealand: Ashford Handicrafts Ltd., 2007.

Parkes, Clara. *The Knitter's Book of Wool: The Ultimate Guide to Understanding, Using, and Loving This Most Fabulous Fiber.* New York: Potter Craft, 2009.

Parkes, Clara. *The Knitter's Book of Yarn: The Ultimate Guide to Choosing, Using, and Enjoying Yarn.* New York: Potter Craft, 2007.

Parry, Barbara. *Teach Yourself Visually Hand-Dyeing.* Hoboken, NJ: Wiley Publishing, Inc., 2009.

Raven, Lee. *Spin It: Making Yarn from Scratch.* Loveland, CO: Interweave Press, 2003.

Reeve, Jo. *The Ashford Book of Carding: A Handspinners Guide to Fibre Preparation.* Ashburton, New Zealand: Willson Scott Publishing Limited, 2007.

Robson, Deborah, and Carol Ekarius. *The Fleece & Fiber Sourcebook: More than 200 Fibers from Animal to Spun Yarn.* North Adams, MA: Storey Publishing, 2011.

Ross, Mabel. *The Essentials of Handspinning.* South Yorkshire, England: Wingham Wool Work, 1999.

Rutt, Richard. *A History of Hand Knitting.* Loveland, CO: Interweave Press, 1987.

Sandberg, Gösta. *Indigo Textiles: Technique and History.* Asheville, NC: Lark Books, 1989.

Singer, Amy R. *No Sheep for You: Knit Happy with Cotton, Silk, Linen, Hemp, Bamboo & Other Delights.* Loveland, CO: Interweave Press, 2007.

Taylor, Kathleen. *Yarns to Dye For: Creating Self-Patterning Yarns for Knitting.* Loveland, CO: Interweave Press, 2005.

Teal, Peter. *Hand Woolcombing and Spinning: A Guide to Worsteds From the Spinning-Wheel.* Dorset, England: Blandford Press, 1979.

Varney, Diane. *Spinning Designer Yarns.* Loveland, CO: Interweave Press, 2003.

Walsh, Penny. *The Yarn Book.* Philadelphia: University of Pennsylvania Press, 2006.

Wayland Barber, Elizabeth. *Women's Work: The First 20,000 Years.* New York: W.W. Norton & Co., 1994.

Books That Provide Patterns for Making Traditional Wooden Spinning Tools and/or Wheels

Amos, Alden. *The Alden Amos Big Book of Handspinning.* Loveland, CO: Interweave Press, 2001.

Schneider, Richard, and Myrna Schneider. *A No-Lathe Saxony-Style Spinning Wheel Construction Manual.* Stevens Point, WI: R. Schneider Publishers, 1984.

Appendix

Fiber Appendices (FA)

FA-1: Fiber Measurement System
(See Spin Methods, page 57, for more about woolen and worsted spinning methods.)

Micron Count
Micron count measures the diameter of a single fiber of wool by using scientific instruments that measure micrometers (one millionth of a meter). The smaller the number, the finer the wool. In general, small micron counts (fine wools) are suited for fine, lace weight yarns; medium micron counts (medium wools) for DK and worsted weights; and large micron counts (coarse wools) for chunkier, rough-wearing yarns.

Bradford Count
Bradford count is a visual measurement referring to how many 560-yd skeins can be produced from 1 lb of combed wool top. It was created in England as a measurement before there were instruments to accurately count the fineness. Even though the micron count system is a more accurate measure, some wools are still being measured by Bradford counts. The Bradford count system uses a reverse numbering system from the micron count. In the Bradford count, the larger the number, the finer the wool. The "s" behind the number means the count was based on a skein spun as a single.

Staple Length
Staple length is measured from an unstretched fiber. The length of a fiber's staple helps determine the best spinning method: woolen or worsted, or a combination of the two. A long staple (more than 5 in. [12 cm] long) is often spun worsted, to highlight the long fiber structure. Medium staple fibers (3–5 in. 7.5–12 cm] long) can be spun well as woolen or worsted.

A short staple (less than 3 in. [7.5 cm] long) is often spun woolen, since shorter staples are easier to catch and control in the woolen spinning method. Protein fibers are variable, depending on the type/breed, and cellulose fibers can be very short, as in the case of cotton, or very long, as in the case of flax and hemp. Many books and online resources are available to help you select a fiber based on staple length. See Resources and Supplies, page 159.

NOTE: The finer the diameter of the fiber, the shorter the staple length tends to be. Fine fibers with long staple lengths are often delicate and must be handled with care to avoid breakage.

Crimp and CPI (Crimps Per Inch)
Crimp is also measured from an unstretched fiber. By knowing the crimps per inch (2.5 cm), or CPI, the whorl and spinning style can be more accurately gauged to suit the fiber. For example, a staple with a larger CPI is often best spun with a higher speed whorl (smaller whorl) to get more twists per inch (2.5 cm). This means the number of twists in the final yarn will more closely match the fiber's natural crimp and make a more suitable yarn with the fiber.

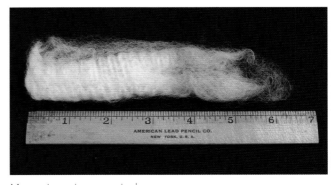

Measuring crimps per inch

FA-2: General Wool Types

(See Spin Methods, page 57, for more about woolen and worsted spinning methods.)

The characteristics of sheep wool vary as much as the breeds of sheep—more than 200 at current count. But for purposes of narrowing down the selection for spinning, there are five general types of wool:

1. Fine (28 or fewer microns)

This group is the softest of the wool types. Fine wools spin well into fine yarns for knitting. They are wonderful for garments that are worn against the skin and for baby clothing. Fine wools blend well, adding elasticity and loft to fine nonwool fibers, such as alpaca, angora, and silk. They are appropriate for woolen or worsted spinning, depending on the specific fiber characteristics and preparation method. Merino is an example of fine wool.

2. Medium (28–34 microns)

These wools are the best for beginning hand spinners. They are good all-purpose wools, with a medium staple length and well-defined crimp. They spin well into medium or bulky yarns for knitted garments such as socks, scarves, sweaters, mittens, and hats. They are best spun with a woolen spin, but may also be spun worsted or semi-worsted. Corriedale is an example of medium wool.

3. Down (24–34 microns)

Down wool has lots of wavy crimp, often has a short staple, and gives great bulk to yarns. It spins a nice medium or bulky yarn for knitted garments such as scarves, mittens, and hats. It's spun best with a woolen spin. The undercoat of the Clun Forest breed is an example of down wool.

4. Long (31–40 microns)

Long wools have a long staple, have a larger diameter, and make strong, lustrous yarns for knitted garments such as socks and long-wearing sweaters. They are spun best with a worsted or semi-worsted spin. Border Leicester is an example of long wool.

5. Primitive (micron count variable)

These are sheep whose breeding has remained unchanged through the centuries. Primitives have variable coats, depending on the particular breed characteristics. An example of this type of wool is Icelandic, which has at least five to seven different structures of wool fiber in its coat under the main categories of *thel* (downy fiber) and *tog* (long, coarse fiber). Icelandic wool is often separated through a combing preparation to facilitate easier spinning—with the thel spun woolen and the tog spun worsted. The spinning methods of other primitive wools depend on their unique fiber characteristics.

FA-3: How to Clean Raw Fleece

SUPPLIES NEEDED

- A top-loading clothes washing machine, laundry tub, or large pail for soaking. Front-loading machines will not work. Don't overhandle the wool if using the tub or pail method. Overhandling leads to felting!

- Very hot water—100–140°F (38–60°C). The grease in wool dissolves at 100–110°F (38–49°C).

- Neutral pH soap or detergent. Wool is damaged by alkaline. Most hair shampoos, horse shampoos, and grease-removing dishwashing liquids (such as Dawn liquid dish soap) work well for washing wool. My favorite soap is Orvus Paste, sold in bulk quantities at farm supply stores. I've found it doesn't strip the wool as severely as other grease-cutting soaps.

- Regular household white vinegar. This neutralizes alkalinity in the bath.

- Lingerie or mesh bag—preferably with a zipper closure.

- Towels or sweater rack for drying.

Washing Steps
(using clothes washing machine)

If using a tub or pail, follow the same basic steps below. A towel or colander can be used instead of the washing machine spin cycle.

1. Fill the washer with the hottest water available and then turn off the machine.

2. Prepare ⅛ to ½ c (30–118 ml) of a neutral pH detergent. Pour this into the hot water. If the fleece is exceptionally greasy or dirty, don't be afraid to add more soap. The water should feel slippery.

3. Place up to 1 lb (454 g) of fleece into this hot, soapy water. (Lingerie bags will keep the fibers in order, but don't overstuff them.) Gently push the wool into the water. *Do not agitate or push the fiber down more than once!* Give the wool plenty of room to "float" in the water. Never let water run directly onto wool, since that will cause felting.

4. Let the wool sit in this soapy water for at least one hour. (There is no real time limit for soaking, but maximum cleaning will occur when the water is more than 100°F (38°C). If the water becomes cold, the grease may resolidify onto the wool fibers.) *Be sure the machine is shut off and no agitation occurs or the wool will felt!*

5. Set the washer to the spin cycle and spin the water out. Gently remove the wool and refill the tub with hot water and half the amount of soap used in the first wash. Turn off the washer and put the wool in again for at least thirty more minutes. No more soap should be needed in subsequent baths.

NOTE: Keep the new bath water at the same temperature or slightly hotter than the previous water, or any remaining grease particles in the water may redeposit onto the wool. If the first bath was around 140°F (60°C), the washing baths may end at about 110°F (49°C). But don't worry about whether the temperature holds to a specific number. I have never had wool felt just by going from a warm water bath to a hot water bath. I *have* had it felt by going abruptly from hot to cold and definitely when it's been agitated in the process. Repeat these steps (without soap) until the spinoff water runs clear. Put 1 C (237 ml) of white vinegar into the second-to-last wash bath to help remove or neutralize any lurking alkaline soap residue. Then rinse one more time to remove the vinegar from the fiber. (Wool is more resistant to acid (vinegar) than alkaline (soap), but if acid is allowed to sit too long on the fiber, it will degrade it.)

Air dry on towels or a sweater rack. The wool can only be air dried and must be completely dry before storing.

Step 3

Step 4

Left: unwashed fiber. Right: washed fiber

FA-4: Raw Fiber Preparation Options

If you don't want to do the processing yourself, you can send raw or washed fiber to a commercial mill. There are a few small mills in the United States and Canada that are accustomed to processing small batches of wool for home spinners. If you want the mill to wash the fleece, send them only skirted fleece that has been well picked of VG. Some mills only take prewashed wool to process into roving, so be sure to ask what services they provide before shipping it.

Mills may prefer to combine your fleece with others if they are processing several of a similar fiber. If you want the same fiber returned to you, be sure to ask in advance about their procedure. Also tell them what type of wool you are sending. Some mills can't handle very fine wool, but they may try to process it anyway, ending up with a matted mess. Or, they might combine the fine wool with a medium wool just to get the job done, and you'll have a final product that wasn't at all what you were expecting.

Most small mills make roving as their final product, and spinners can request the roving size they want. "Pencil roving" is a very common size—about the diameter of a No. 2 pencil—and makes a worsted weight or thinner yarn single. But a thick single can't be made from a thin roving, so seriously consider the weight of yarn you want to make before selecting the roving size.

A few mills with dyeing capabilities can also dye your wool. Their color charts are usually based on their own yarn lines, so don't expect that they will create a new color just for you.

Search online for mills or ask spinning guilds, fiber shops, and vendors and farmers at fiber fairs for help in the search.

FA-5: Pre-Prepared Fibers and Their Typical Spinning Methods

(See Spin Methods, page 57, for more about woolen and worsted spinning methods.)

The language of pre-prepared fibers can be daunting. Use this list to guide you when selecting the type of preparation that will be best for your unique spinning needs.

Wool

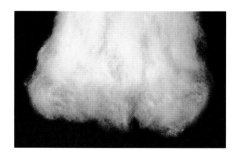

Batts. Thick, carded fibers processed by a drum carder or other carding machine. Split them into small sections. Spin woolen.

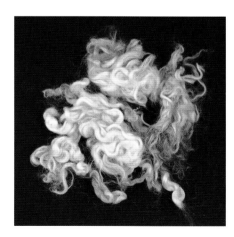

Locks. Fiber locks in which no preparation has occurred except perhaps washing. Lincoln locks are an example of a sheep breed with long, wavy fleece that is often sold in lock formation. Locks can be used in novelty spinning as a textural element. Spin woolen, worsted, or semi-worsted.

Plate. Stout rolls of unspun roving. Spin woolen

(FA-5: Continues on page 166.)

Puni. Small rolag (see "rolag" below), usually made from cotton fibers. Spin woolen

Make Your Own Puni

NOTE: Many fine-diameter fibers spin well from this puni preparation method.

A puni is a pencil-size rolag that makes the spinning of short fibers much easier.

- Use a cotton carder to card the fibers.

- Pick up the horizontal edge of the carded fiber and, using a wooden dowel or a size 11 (8 mm) or similar straight knitting needle, firmly roll the fiber around the dowel until it looks like a fat pencil.

- Push the fiber off the dowel, twisting it slightly, and you have a puni. Spin from the point for a long draw, woolen-spun yarn.

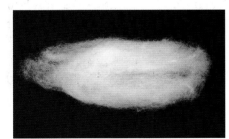

Rolag. A "cigar" of fiber made with hand carders. Spin woolen.

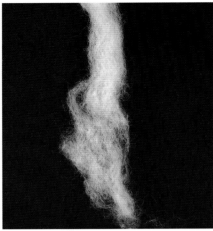

Roving. Sometimes confused with top and sliver (see below) since, like top and sliver, it is processed into a long, ropelike form. Roving is made from carded or combed fiber and, unlike top or sliver, is slightly stretched and twisted in the processing. It can be processed in many thicknesses, depending on the fiber and the final purpose. A little predrafting is probably needed. Spin woolen.

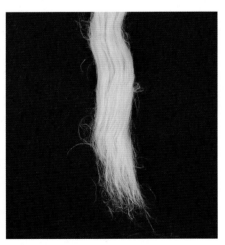

Sliver. A continuous ropelike form of fiber preparation. Sometimes the term is used interchangeably with roving or top. It's either carded or combed and may not need predrafting. Spin as woolen or worsted depending on the fiber preparation.

Strick. A twisted preparation of the long fibers of flax, hemp, or other bast fibers. A strick is untwisted and placed on a distaff, which is attached or suspended from a spinning wheel, and the fibers are pulled from that for spinning. Spin worsted.

Top. Combed fiber with no twist and all short fibers removed. Minimally predraft top before spinning by gently pulling the fiber lengthwise just until it releases tension or giving it a good shake to loosen it up for spinning. Tug on the pulled sections to help put them back in parallel alignment. The parallel fiber direction must be kept intact for worsted spinning. Top can be spun from the fold to give the yarn more loft. It can be split into staple lengths and carded with other fibers to create a blend. Without modification: spin worsted. If blended with another fiber: spin woolen or semi-worsted.

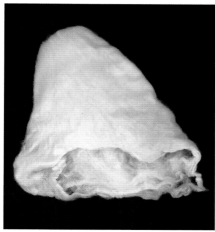

Silk

Cap/bell. A single cocoon that has been stretched into a bell shape for spinning. Spin semi-worsted.

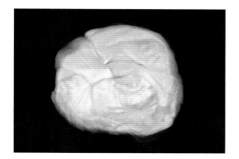

Brick. This is a compacted mass of combed silk top. Open it up and strip it down for spinning. Spin worsted.

Carrier rods. A waste product from commercial silk spinning. It contains sericin and must be degummed before use. Spin semi-woolen.

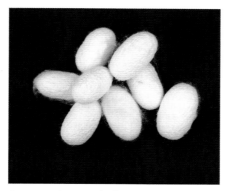

Cocoon. The actual silkworm cocoon. The cocoon must be prepared for spinning through a boiling process that removes the gluelike sericin from the fiber. Spin semi-woolen.

Cocoon strippings. This is the shorter first silk extruded by the silkworm. Strippings make a smooth, matte yarn. Spin worsted or woolen, depending on your final purpose.

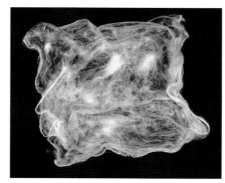

Hanky. A single cocoon that has been stretched into a square shape for spinning. Hankies are often sold in large bundles that contain about seventy-five cocoons per 2 oz (56g) bundle. Spin semi-woolen.

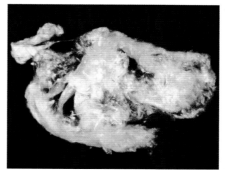

Noil. Short odds and ends from the "bassinette" fibers (the last fibers the silk worm spun) at the center of a cocoon along with some remnants from the cocoon processing. To card them in preparation, use fine cotton carders. They make fun additions for creative spinning.

Oblongs or laps. These are large batts of carded silk that have been prepared like drum-carded wool. They are most often used in silk fusion or felting but, with great patience, can be spun. Spin semi-woolen.

Sari silk. This is the waste from the pre-dyed warp threads of sari weaving. It's sometimes called recycled sari silk, although it's never been used in a garment. Sari silk is another interesting addition to creative spinning.

Throwster's silk. Another "recycled" by-product of the silk industry, this longer silk comes from the machine waste of the commercial silk spinning process. Spin worsted or semi-worsted.

FA-6: Be Your Own Fiber Chemist: How to Blend Fibers

The ability to blend unique fiber combinations is one of the great benefits of spinning your own yarn. This Fiber Appendix will guide you through the process.

TOOLS

- Digital kitchen scale (with the ability to measure at least 0.01 oz [1g]). All spinners should have a quality kitchen scale, reading ounces and grams, as part of their spinning arsenal. Use a deep bowl to help weigh large quantities of fibers.
- Carders (hand or drum), combs, or a hackle.

NOTE: Percentages of fiber blends are measured by weight, not by physical volume. Be aware that even if a fiber *appears* to be 25 percent of one fiber quality and 75 percent of another, the actual weights of those blends may be more like a 10 percent to 90 percent mix, depending on the fiber density.

Blending Practice Workshop

For your first attempt at blending, have several ounces of the blend fibers on hand to sacrifice to the test.

1. Put the fibers you wish to blend into separate piles labeled A and B. Weigh each pile by grams. (Grams can be substituted with ounces or pounds if you wish, although the metric system is easier to use in formulas.)

2. Which fiber has the most volume? (Again, this is physical size, not weight.) Is that the fiber you want to dominate in your fiber blend? If not, you will need substantially more of the other smaller volume fiber to achieve its dominance.

3. Take small amounts out of each pile.

4. Blend the fibers in your hands, and when you like the look and feel of the blend, card fiber A with fiber B (or comb if you are doing a worsted prep). How does this blend look and feel after the prep? Do a test spin, then set the twist of the sample using hot water. After setting the twist, the blend may look very different from the spun yarn.

5. When you're happy with the blend, weigh the remaining piles and subtract that from the original pile weights to find the amounts taken out and proceed to figure the percentages.

Example: Let's say the blend totals taken out weigh the following:

Fiber A: 18 g
Fiber B: 7 g
Total: 25 g

Fiber A: 18 ÷ 25 = Wpercent
Fiber B: 7 ÷ 25 = 0.28, or 28 percent

Your blend is 72 percent of fiber A and 28 percent of fiber B.

If more of this fiber blend is needed, continue to use these percentages as a guide in weighing fiber A and fiber B. For example, to make one more gram of the blended fiber, weigh as follows: 72 percent of one gram is 0.72 on a digital scale and 28 percent of one gram is 0.28 on the scale. (Two grams would be figured as 0.72 × 2 (1.44) and 0.28 × 2 (.56); 1.44 + 0.56 = 2 g.)

Now do you see the advantage of a digital scale?

Mixing the Blend

To blend top or roving with other top or roving, pull the top or roving into staple length sections and card the different fibers together. If blending a top or roving and a loose staple fiber, just pull the top or roving into staple length pieces and combine those with the loose staples from the other fiber. A spritz of water containing a drop or two of essential oil will settle down any flyaway fibers.

Remember to keep blends to three fibers or less!

FA-7: Determining Fiber Quantities for a Project

Ah, the spinner's age-old question. How much fiber do I need to make that? Here are a few different techniques for estimating yarn amounts.

NOTE: A digital scale is an essential tool for this Fiber Appendix.

Yarn Weight by Scale

Use the scale weight of the yarn that is typically required for a similar project by looking at an existing pattern or referring to these general guidelines:

General Projects and Typical Scale Weights of Finished Yarn

These numbers are loosely based on the scale weight of the yarn required for generic wool projects in these categories:

- Adult hat, adult socks, adult mittens: 2 oz (57 g) – 4 oz (113 g)
- Baby sweater, adult scarf, lace shawl: 8 oz (227 g – 12 oz (340 g)
- Child's sweater, adult vest: 12 oz (340 g) – 1 lb (454 g)
- Woman's medium sweater, man's medium vest: 1 lb (454 g) – 1.5 lb (680 g)
- Woman's large sweater, man's large vest: 2 lb (907 g) – 2.5 lb (1.1 kg)

Digital scale

Of course, these estimates work best if spinning a yarn that closely approximates the project's recommended yarn.

Getting More Specific

Weigh 1 oz (28 g) of the fiber and spin a test yarn, including plies. Measure how many yards (meters) are in the test yarn. Weigh the remaining fiber and multiply the total remaining weight of the fiber in ounces (grams) by the number of yards (meters) the test yarn made. This will give an approximate count of the yards (meters) in the fiber. Then compare that number with the amount of yardage (meters) needed for the project, and add a bit of "spinner's luck" for insurance by increasing the final number by about ¼ to have enough to get through the project.

Example:

Let's say 1 oz (28.4 g) of fiber = 26 yd (23.8 m) of spun and plied yarn and 1.2 lb (19.2 oz/544.3 g) of fiber remains.

19.2 oz × 26 yd = 499.2 yd
(544.3 g × 23.8 m = 12,954.3 ÷ 28.4 g = 456 m)

By rounding down to get an even number, there are 499 yd (456 m) in the remaining fiber.

NOTE: If working with a raw fleece, consider the final "yield" (cleaned weight). Grease and other matter can add as much as 50 percent to the weight, depending on the sheep breed. Fiber preparation will also affect the final yield. Be sure to wash and prepare the fleece before finalizing the numbers. It's easier and more accurate to measure the quantity needed if working from an already prepared fiber like top or roving.

Knit a Swatch

Finally, knit a swatch from the test yarn just to be sure it knits up the way you anticipate. (See Knit Workshop, page 119, for suggestions on how to pick the right needle for a swatch.) Wash the swatch before spinning the entire weight of fiber. Some fibers can bloom (fluff out) considerably after a wash and look very different when finished. No surprises are good in the final product when you're spending so much time making your own yarn!

FA-8: Fiber Storage and Pests

Fiber needs to be protected from bugs, animals, and moisture. The prime bug enemies are clothes moths and carpet beetles, although other bugs may add fibers to their menu if the fibers contain any other edible matter, such as urine or skin secretions. Some of the other troublesome bugs are silverfish, which may attack cellulose, and crickets, which may eat wool or cellulose.

Fiber-eating bugs can come from anywhere—they can hitch rides on just about anything you bring into the house, from flowers to fiber itself—and set up housekeeping if the environment is favorable. I am sorry to say that keeping a clean house is the first step to discouraging the little buggers. A favorable environment is one where cleaning is seldom done, so they are undisturbed and free to do their nasty deeds.

Know Your Enemy: The Clothes Moth

Let's dispel a myth right from the start. Clothes moths actually aren't the ones doing the eating of the fiber. In fact, the moth itself doesn't eat at all during the course of its one-month life. It exists merely to lay eggs that become larvae and grow to be caterpillars. The larvae/caterpillars are our true enemy. As larvae, they are very difficult to see, especially when they are in an out-of-the-way corner or embedded in a lovely bit of fiber, dining on their wooly smorgasbord. Their only purpose in life (which can be quite long—more than two years!) is to eat. The larva offspring of a pair of clothes moths can eat fifty pounds of wool in one year! Clothes moth larvae can also be found in other areas of the house since they like all forms of protein, including food in our kitchen. They will not eat cellulose fibers, and they aren't that fond of silk but will eat it if that's the only offering.

There are two types of clothes moths:

- *Tineola bisselliella* (a lovely Latin name for a horrible creature) —the webbing clothes moth. It leaves its eggs in a silky web over the cloth or fiber that the soon-to-emerge larva/caterpillar likes to eat. When the caterpillar is fully grown and spins a cocoon in preparation for its moth stage, it actually attaches bits of food and debris to the cocoon as camouflage!

- *Tinea pellionella* (a name best left to something less sinister) —this moth's larva/caterpillar form makes a case out of the excreted fibers that it's eaten and then carries the case so it can move in safety from location to location. (You've got to admit—this bug could teach the military a few things about camouflage.)

Even though the moths don't directly do the destruction, they are the "soccer moms" that move the bad guys (eggs) around. If you see a moth, you are either dealing with an early stage of infestation (if you're really lucky) or a late stage (adios to your fiber).

Physical Description

Clothes moths have a wingspan of about ½ in. (1.3 cm) and are tan in color. They look a bit like an Indian meal moth (most of us have probably had those in our pantries) and have the speed and cunning that would test the best digital gamer. But killing a flying moth is probably not going to be terribly effective in eradicating the problem anyway, since the flying moths are usually just males looking for a female. The females are more cunning and are busy hiding to protect their eggs from predators. You could almost respect their tenacity if it didn't involve your precious fiber.

The adult moths live just long enough to mate—about one to three weeks after they emerge from the cocoon. The female lays 100 to 150 eggs at one time, gluing them in a food source like wool so they are not easily dislodged. The larvae grow into caterpillars and continue their lifetime at the fiber banquet table, crawling on their own to any good food establishment nearby. They can eat for six weeks to two years or more, depending on the temperature (their metabolism increases in warm, humid weather). When they are fully grown (at birth they are 1/50 in. [0.5 mm] long and, at full size, 3/8 in. [9.5 mm] long), they spin a cocoon and about two-and-a-half weeks later emerge as an adult moth.

The Other Enemy: The Carpet Beetle

Like the clothes moth, the carpet beetle (*anthrenus scrophulariae*) isn't the main culprit in the demise of fibers. Their larvae are the ones responsible. There are a few different colors and types of carpet beetles. They may be white and orange-red; white and yellow; white, brown, and yellow; dark brown; or black. They are about 1/10 to 1/8 in. [2.5 to 3 mm] long and round to oval in shape. Their larvae range from about 1/8 to 1/4 in. [3 mm to 6 mm] long and they crawl rapidly. The adult beetles fly around in the late spring. They can come into the house by hitchhiking onto just about anything, including cut flowers from the garden. Like most moths, the beetles are attracted to light. The larvae prefer the dark. Larvae may live for sixty days to a year or more while enjoying their fiber feast, as long as the temperature is favorable to them. Their life cycle is shorter in cold environments.

What to Do If You Have a Bug Infestation

If you can bear to part with the fiber, the first choice is to toss it in the garbage or the compost. If it holds sentimental value or cost a dear amount of money, then clean, clean, and clean—both the fiber and the space the fiber was in. Then put the fiber in the sun to dry and store it in an airtight container that allows light to infiltrate (see notes on storage below). You can also try a freezing method to kill any possible remaining bugs (see below), but that's not always effective. The best bet is to toss the fiber and take measures to prevent such infestations in the future. Consider it a lesson learned the hard way.

How to Prevent Infestation of All Bugs

Isolation is the key! Always isolate new fibers and examine them thoroughly in a neutral zone, away from other (assumedly) parasite-free fibers. Some spinners put new fibers into cold storage (a deep freezer at 0°F for at least seventy-two hours), but that practice doesn't guarantee pest-free fibers. Bugs can go into hibernation when exposed to cold and come back to life when their environment warms up—in other words, when you store them with your other fibers. Another thing to keep in mind is that if there's any air in the freezer package, the deep freezer's low temperature might damage the fiber. If you use the deep freeze method, the fiber must be taken from a warm environment and abruptly put in the deep freeze. It's the shock of the cold that will kill the bugs and not the cold itself.

Some have success in killing the bugs by alternately freezing the fibers, cleaning them, and exposing them to sun. Herbal sachets and cedar can repel moths. In fact, any product that makes fiber smell less like protein may help. The chemical in classic mothballs (para-dichlorobenzene) actually kills moths, eggs, and larvae/caterpillars, but it will also affect your health (it's a possible carcinogen) and make your fibers smell awful. Mothballs aren't as effective for carpet beetles. There are also pheromone traps that use chemical scents to attract certain bugs. They work like flypaper, sticking the bugs to the traps. Some insecticides work on bugs other than clothes moths, but large infestations are best left to a professional pest controller.

The best deterrent is keeping up on housekeeping skills. Vacuum all the cubbies where eggs and larvae may hide. Occasionally put your fibers in the sun. Don't let them sit for years on end without inspection. Check your entire wool stash at least once a year (open the containers in isolation just in case you find some "visitors" inside). Put some herbal or cedar sachets with the fibers. Keep the fiber in an environment with humidity levels of less than 30 percent, since clothes moths cannot survive in low humidity. When you get a raw, unprocessed fiber, wash it right away. Clothes moth larvae are not able to develop as well on completely clean wool, since they need vitamin B and some salts as essential nutrients, and these are not present in completely clean wool.

Moths have no life span in my house. In fact, I show no compassion to any bugs that are around my fibers, as I assume they are looking for a free meal. (However, I may show mercy to spiders. They aren't a serious danger to fibers, and they consider moth larvae, moths, and carpet beetles to be a tasty meal. Besides, with their experience in web making, they "get" the whole spinning thing. That's worth some compassion.)

Fiber Storage Options

Some spinners and knitters only store their fibers in cardboard boxes or paper bags because they think the fibers breathe better in that environment. Every one of the bug infestations I've heard about came from fibers in cardboard box or paper bag storage. (Some of those people also ended up entertaining mice that decided to turn their fiber into a maternity ward.)

Although many spinning resources will tell you never to store fibers in plastic containers, since the fibers will "sweat" and that encourages mold, I've stored my fibers in plastic for up to ten years (throwing in an herbal or cedar sachet for extra ammunition) and have never had the fibers sweat or develop mildew—and better yet, I've never had a bug or mouse infestation problem (knock on wood—or maybe I should say "plastic"). So I can't honestly say that you should use plastic. In my opinion, I'd rather have an isolated problem with mildew and have to destroy one lot of fiber than have an infestation of bugs or a mouse hotel and have to destroy my entire stash.

When using plastic for storage, the fibers must be dry and at room temperature. Throw in some sort of herbal concoction to confuse the bugs passing by. Store the fibers loosely so some air can circulate around them. Store fine, delicate fibers between layers of tissue paper so they are less susceptible to compression. (Compression in storage can be an enemy of fine fibers such as angora. Their delicate, open-cell structure may be damaged when compressed.) I like the clear plastic option since I can see what's in the container. Just being able to see that pretty fiber is incentive enough for me to want to work with it, further discouraging bugs that might consider taking up residence there.

Spin Appendices (SA)

SA-1: Wheel Maintenance—Become Your Wheel's Grease Monkey

Knowing how to oil a spinning wheel is essential to being a spinner. The better the wheel is lubricated, the better it operates. I've heard of spinners who were convinced there was something terribly wrong with their wheel so they sold it, only to find out later that they hadn't maintained it properly. For just a few drops of oil, they gave up a perfectly fine wheel worth hundreds of dollars!

My theory about oiling is this: Oil anywhere two parts slide or spin past one another. Don't worry about overoiling a wheel (unless it's creating an oil spill in your living room). The more a wheel is oiled, the happier it hums along.

NOTE: Use mineral oil, 30-weight oil, or lightweight machine oil (like the type used for sewing machines). The oil needs to drip into the wheel parts, so use a container that has a needle end rather than a spray nozzle.

Before oiling a part that slides around or is inside another part, clean the area with a dry cloth or a cotton-tipped swab to remove old oil, fibers, and other residue. If the old oil is really nasty, carefully clean the area with mineral spirits before applying fresh oil.

Double-check the condition of the drive band. Replace it if it's frayed or too loose to adjust. Never oil a drive band or it will slip. Use beeswax to smooth areas of linen or cotton bands that have become rough. Sometimes beeswax can also cure odd squeaky sounds where parts are rubbing against each other and where it's inappropriate to use oil that might discolor the wood. Leather parts can be conditioned with leather oil.

Wheels should operate silently or nearly silently. If your wheel has developed a noise, assume there's something wrong. Wheels don't just develop noises over time. Put on your detective hat!

Keep the wheel clean. Tighten loose parts. To help keep the wood from cracking, apply a little furniture polish or wood oil from time to time. Never use glue on any parts of a wheel. Spinning wheels are finely tuned instruments and are designed to hold together without glue. Someday you might want to ship your wheel, and then you'll regret having glued any parts. If there's a loose or cracked part, find a reputable wheel repair person to fix or rebuild it. Don't expose a wheel to extreme temperatures or direct sunlight. Your wheel is a valuable handcrafted object. Treat it with care, and it will serve you well.

SA-2: Fiber Prep and Spinning Tools on a Budget

We are all looking for ways to trim our budgets, and as spinners, we have many alternative options to get our spinning fix without breaking the bank.

Alternative Fiber Processing and Finishing Tools

Carders. Use square or rectangular dog brushes. They come in different sizes, and some have a feature that pushes the fiber off the brushes—making them even more useful than regular spinning carders! Get two brushes with quite rigid tines. They are sold at most pet supply stores and large discount stores.

Used carders may be found at secondhand or antique stores. If the cloth isn't in good shape, Howard Brush can recondition them. See Resources and Supplies, page 159, for contact information.

Combs. Dog combs work well and come in a variety of tine lengths and widths. Get two combs and set them up in a similar configuration to a comb setup or just hold them in your hands. The best dog combs are the ones with two rows of staggered teeth or an undercoat rake. They are designed to pull out short, downy hairs, and that's exactly what you are doing when creating a worsted preparation. They are found where dog-grooming supplies are sold.

A hand carder or hackle and a dog comb can also mimic combs. The carder or hackle is the stationary fiber holder, and the dog comb acts as the working comb.

Distaff. To create your own distaff, use a dowel with a dowel cap glued to one end. Use a ribbon to tie the strick to the cap and dowel, letting a few strands hang low for spinning.

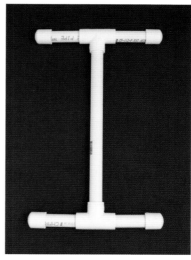

Niddy noddy.
Use PVC pipe to make this great tool for wet-setting the twist.

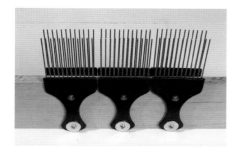

Hackle. A row of long pick-style hair combs with metal tines works better in situations where more combing torque is needed, but plastic versions are quite adequate for blending prepared top into a worsted configuration. Attach the combs to a wood strip by drilling holes into the comb bases and screwing them in place. C-clamps can be used to hold the comb onto a table during use.

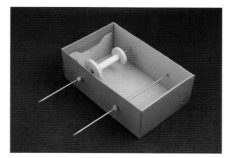

Lazy Kate. Use a shoebox and straight knitting needles. Punch holes on both sides of the shoebox, slide the pointed end of a long knitting needle into one hole, slide a bobbin onto the knitting needle, and put the needle through the other hole. Hold the pointed end of the needle in place with a rubber band.

SUPPLIES

A total of 36 in. (0.9 m) of ½-in. (12.7 mm) PVC pipe, cut to the following dimensions:

- Two ½-in. (12.7 mm) T-shaped PVC pipe connectors (no threads—smooth inside)
- One 12-in. (30 cm) length (This is the stem of the niddy noddy)
- Four 6-in. (15 cm) lengths (These are the arms of the niddy noddy)
- Four ½-in. (12.7 mm) closed end caps (no threads)

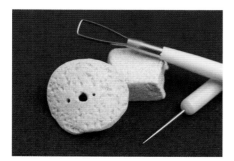

Diz. An alternative diz can range from a seashell with a hole in the center to a large button with sewing holes. But if you're in the mood to do something creative, make a diz out of polymer clay. Roll the clay to about ¼-in (6mm) thickness. Cut the clay into a shape that can be easily held, bend it into an arch by placing the diz around a narrow glass jar or a soda can, and punch different size holes. Then cook the clay according to the directions.

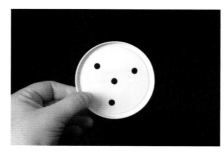

Plying disk. This is a very easy tool to make. Take a piece of flat, rigid plastic and punch multiple holes in the material with a paper punch or drill bit. Sand the holes to a smooth surface. I used a lid cover to create the plying disk shown here.

DIRECTIONS

Push the base of the T-shaped connectors onto each end of the 12-in. (30 cm) PVC pipe (stem) and the four 6-in. (15 cm) lengths (arms) into the sides of the T connectors. Push the end caps onto the four arm ends, and you're done! The end caps can be removed when taking the skein off after wrapping.

(SA-1: Continues on page 174.)

SA-2: *(Continued from page 173.)*

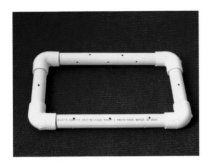

Skein blocker.

Use CPVC pipe for this blocker. It's great for fibers that need strong tension while setting the twist through a cooking method (such as cotton).

NOTE: PVC material can release heavy metals when put in boiling water. The CPVC (chlorinated poly-vinyl chloride) pipe used in this skein blocker is a nontoxic, thermoplastic material that is not affected by boiling temperatures. CPVC is easily identifiable by its almond color (PVC pipe is white).

SUPPLIES

A total of 24 in. (61 cm) of ½-in. (61 cm) (12.7 mm) CPVC pipe, cut to the following dimensions:

- Two 8-in. (20.3 cm) lengths (long sides of blocker)
- Two 4-in. (10.2 cm) lengths (short sides of blocker)
- Four ½-in. (12.7 mm) 90-degree angle CPVC connectors (no threads)

DIRECTIONS

Push the two 8-in. (20.3 cm) and two 4-in. (10.2 cm) straight pipe ends into the 90-degree angle connectors to form a rectangle. Then drill random ¼-in. (6 mm) holes into all sides of the straight pipes so the blocker will sink when set in water. When the yarn is dry, pull one side of the blocker apart to remove the yarn.

Alternative Spindles and Wheels

Drop spindle. Make your own with a ⅜-in (9mm) wooden dowel, ⅜-in (9mm) rubber grommet, a small brass cup hook, and a couple of CDs, a wooden toy wheel, or handmade polymer clay whorl. A search on the Internet will bring up several sites with instructions. But "real" drop spindles are fairly inexpensive, too.

Wheels. Wheels are a little trickier to find on a low budget, and if you do find one, it may have something wrong with it that will cost you in the end. Beware of online auctions or any sales venue where you can't personally try the wheel. A photo may not show that a wheel is warped, and it certainly cannot show the squeaks and creaks. Trade or barter wheels may be found on a local online shopping site. An online search of used spinning equipment may also turn up some sellers in your area. Or check out "for sale" notices on bulletin boards at your local fiber or yarn shop. Be sure to first have some spinning experience under your belt or take an experienced spinning friend along to check out the wheel. Then befriend a spinning wheel repair person, as most old wheels have seen a hard life and will require initial repair.

Well-maintained used wheels can be found at reputable spinning wheel dealers.

Check with local yarn shops or ask spinning friends for a good shop. See Resources and Supplies, page 159, for more on how to buy a wheel.

The ultimate budget wheel is one you make yourself. There are patterns for both wood and PVC wheels in books (see Bibliography, page 160), and a few may be found online.

SA-3: **Yarn Measurement Systems: WPI, TPI, Ply Angle, SPI, and YPP**

Yarn measuring systems are invaluable for maintaining a desired spin and creating the type of yarn we need for a project. Here's the nitty-gritty behind how to use them.

Measuring Wraps Per Inch (WPI)

Measuring wraps per inch (2.5 cm) first occurs when spinning a single. You will need a ruler or a WPI tool. Find an area of the yarn that is the most evenly spun. This is usually a few yards into the yarn—

the point when your body started getting comfortable with the fiber and wheel, and began spinning more mindlessly. Wrap the yarn around the ruler or tool so each strand just touches the next one. Be careful to not add any additional twist when wrapping.

NOTE: If measuring an S-twist yarn, wrap the single in a counterclockwise direction. For Z-twist yarns, wrap in a clockwise direction. This wrapping method will help keep the original twist in the yarn.

WPI for Knitting

WPI is also used during plying to help determine the knitting weight of the spun yarn and shows how the spun yarn compares with a specific yarn in a knitting pattern. The chart below shows how WPI also relates to stitches per inch (2.5 cm), or SPI.

How to Measure Twists Per Inch (TPI)

It can be difficult to see the twists in a singles yarn, but the effect of too much or too little twist in a single is obvious when

it corkscrews back or if the yarn can't hold together. Since keeping a consistent number of twists per inch (2.5 cm), or TPI, in a single makes a more even yarn, it's important to keep the twist count consistent when spinning singles. The easiest way to keep a consistent twist is to compare the number of treadles needed to spin a given length of yarn and maintain that pace throughout the spinning.

Twists are much easier to see and are a more informative measurement in the plying stage. To count the number of twists in a ply, count the twist "bumps" in 1 in. (2.5 cm) and divide that by the number of singles in the ply. See the chart below for a general comparison of TPI to yarn types.

NOTE: Plying releases about half of the twist in the singles, as it twists the yarn in the opposite direction. Therefore, to keep a "balanced" yarn (a yarn that has an even twist and doesn't corkscrew around itself when hung in a skein), ply at about half the TPI of the singles. Caveat: There are some circumstances when you might want the TPI to be different from the norm. For instance, in yarn for a sock, more twist in the ply will make a firmer, longer-lasting yarn. In yarn for a scarf, less twist than normal in the ply will make a softer yarn.

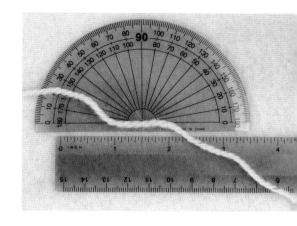

Ply Angle

Ply angle affects the final feel of the yarn and is a side effect of the ply TPI measurement. Soft-ply yarns have ply angles from 5 to 20 degrees (fewer TPI) and a more delicate fabric; medium-ply yarns have ply angles of 20 to 30 degrees and create a moderately durable fabric; and hard-ply yarns have ply angles of 30 to 45 degrees or more (the most TPI) and create a longer-wearing fabric.

General Yarn Measurement Comparisons

This chart is a general guide for selecting a good twist angle when plying yarn. Caveat: This chart doesn't take into account the effects fiber quality and spin method have on the twist angle. For example, a soft-feeling ply can be spun at 45 degrees if the fiber and spin method enhance that quality.

NOTE: The YPP on this chart represents wool fiber. Other fibers may have different qualities that affect their YPP. For instance, cotton is a heavy fiber and has about one-third less YPP than wool.

These chart numbers aren't a truly scientific measure, and they will vary somewhat according to the type of fiber that's being spun, but the chart gives a general idea of the numbers to aim for when trying to spin compatible yarn.

Singles WPI	2-Ply WPI	2-Ply TPI	Ply Angle	SPI (sts per in)	Knitting Weight	YPP (yards per pound)
13 or less	8 or less	1–2	5°–10°	3 or less	chunky	400 or less–600
17	10	2–4	10°–15°	3.5	bulky	600–800
19	11	4–5	15°–20°	4	aran	800–900
21	12	5–10	20°–25°	4–5	worsted	900–1100
25	14	10–12	25°–30°	5.5	DK	1100–1300
29	16	12–14	30°–35°	6	sport	1300–1800
33	18	14–17	35°–40°	7	fingering	1800–2400
37 or more	20 or more	17–20	40°–45°	8 or more	lace	2500 or more

SA-4: Tips for Matching Commercial Yarn: A "CSI" Examination

1. Check the label content to see what fiber was used. If there isn't a label on the yarn, do a burn test, (see page 24).

2. Look at how many plies the yarn has and note the direction of the twist (S or Z). Do a WPI count on the ply singles and WPI and TPI counts on the plied yarn. The WPI on the singles may not be an entirely accurate measurement for matching, since the singles may have changed after the spin was set, but it will be close to the true number. Do the fibers look woolen or worsted spun? Measure the ply angle.

3. Note the yarn weight (diameter and pounds/grams), yardage, and SPI.

Use the General Yarn Measurement Comparison's, chart in SA-3, page 175, to compare spin measurements to yarn categories.

When you have all the information to recreate the yarn, do a test spin with the fiber, and then finish the yarn by setting the twist. It may take a lot of steps to get a matching yarn, but what a feeling of accomplishment you will have in the process! Plus, you will know that your hand-spun yarn will work well for the knit project.

SA-5: How to Adjust Your Spinning Method

Use the following techniques to adjust your spinning method.

Making Adjustments to the Worsted Spin

Worsted is more dependent on the wheel to modify the spin, so many of these methods are wheel based.

Scotch Tension Wheels

To achieve a thicker, less twisted yarn, increase tension on the draw-in by tightening the brake band. This will draw the fiber onto the wheel faster and, if your hands remain in their traditional drafting position, result in a thicker yarn.

To achieve a thinner, more twisted yarn, decrease tension on the draw-in by loosening the brake band. This will draw the fiber onto the wheel more slowly and give you time to draft it into a thinner yarn.

Wheels without Scotch Tension

To make a thicker yarn, adjust the drive band so it's tighter. To make a thinner yarn, adjust the drive band so it's looser. The adjustment in the drive band changes the speed of the flyer and wheel, acting like a brake tension in the spin.

If changing the tension doesn't do enough, change the whorl size. As the whorl size changes, the tension placed on the draw-in also changes. A larger whorl places more tension on the draw-in and results in a thicker yarn. A smaller whorl places less tension on the draw-in and results in a thinner yarn.

Are you seeing a pattern here?

More tension + faster draw-in + less twist = thicker yarn.
Less tension + slower draw-in + more twist = thinner yarn.

Make that your mantra!

NOTE: If you want to spin really fine yarn and the wheel doesn't adjust enough to achieve this, wrap the just-spun yarn across your bobbin hooks to further decrease tension on the draw.

Making Adjustments to the Woolen Spin

Woolen is more dependent on the spinner to adjust the draw and the wheel to modify the spin. The woolen spin can be adjusted by allowing more or less fiber into the drafting zone. Some wheel modifications are helpful, such as changing the whorl size, but the main adjustment in woolen spinning lies in the fiber drafting.

For a thicker, less twisted yarn, your hands need to work faster so the fiber moves to the bobbin with fewer twists. Also slow down your treadling speed so the flyer makes less twist in the yarn.

For a thinner, more twisted yarn, your hands need to work slower to allow more twist in the yarn. Speed up your treadling to increase the number of twists the flyer makes.

Adjusting Yarn While Plying

Minor unevenness and tight twist can be corrected while plying.

SA-6: How to Spin and Finish Fine, Medium, and Bulky Weight Yarns

(See Spin Methods, page 57, for details on spinning methods.)

Here's a list of the principal techniques for spinning yarns with fine, medium, or bulky weights.

Fine Yarns

Spin and finish lace and fingering weight yarns as follows.

PREPARATION

- If spun worsted, use a combed preparation.
- If the fiber is appropriate for woolen spinning, hand card or drum card with a fine carder cloth.
- If static electricity is a problem, lightly spritz the fiber with water or an essential oil.

SPINNING

- Spin with a small whorl to increase the TPI. If you don't have a small enough whorl, approximately one whorl size can be dropped by wrapping the yarn across the hooks on both sides of the flyer before it wraps onto the bobbin.
- Use a light, even tension.
- Increase the size of the bobbin shaft by covering it with a foam wrap or an empty paper towel roll to help create a lighter tension for the spin and increase the TPI.
- Use a short draw for a worsted spin and a long draw for a woolen spin.

- Open up the drafting zone fibers until they are translucent.
- Try controlling the diameter of the yarn by the width and length of the draft.
- On Saxony-style wheels, tighten the drive band further than normally allowed by placing a shim under the drive band screw.

PLYING

- The bobbins need to spin freely.
- If the Lazy Kate has a braking system, use it so the bobbins don't spin faster than the plying speed.
- Don't stretch the fibers while plying.

FINISHING

- To avoid tangling the yarn while washing (and dyeing), tie the skeins in at least eight places. Or use just two arms of the niddy noddy to wrap the yarn into a smaller skein.
- After washing, snap the skeins by stretching them between two hands and snapping your hands apart. This will further align the twist and help to soften the fiber. If worsted spun, hang with a light tension. If woolen spun, lay out flat to dry or hang with very little tension.

Medium Yarns

Spin and finish sport, DK, and worsted weight yarns as follows.

PREPARATION

- Use either a combed or carded preparation, depending on the qualities desired in the yarn.
- If spun woolen, use a standard hand carder or drum carder cloth.

SPINNING

- Spin with a medium whorl.

- Use a normal tension.
- Use a long, short, or "from the fold" draw, as appropriate to the preparation.
- Spin with an ordinary woolen or worsted spin.

PLYING

- Standard plying methods work well.

FINISHING

- Standard finishing methods are appropriate.
- Fulling may be desired, depending on the fiber.

Bulky Yarns

Spin and finish chunky, bulky weight yarns as follows.

PREPARATION

- Spin with a worsted or woolen method, depending on the fiber and final yarn desired. (Bulky yarn is most often spun woolen.)
- Card the fiber thoroughly, since the quick-drafting method required will highlight any irregularities in your wool.

SPINNING

- Spin with a large whorl.
- You may also need a larger orifice on the wheel. (Not all wheel brands offer larger orifice sizes in their flyer heads. You might need to purchase, rent, or borrow a different wheel if you're spinning bulky yarn.)
- Use a heavy tension/brake.
- Move the fiber quickly onto the bobbin so fewer twists occur.
- Use a quick draw.

PLYING

- Keep a loose hand on the singles, allowing the ply to be open and with few twists.
- Ply fairly slowly.

FINISHING

Ordinary finishing methods are appropriate, although bulky plied yarns are best when laid flat to dry. Fulling may be desired, depending on the fiber.

SA-7: Troubleshooting Your Wheel and Spin Technique

This is the ultimate guide to solving spinning problems and as close as I can get to holding your hand when spinning is getting difficult. First, take a deep breath, and then find your situation below and follow the suggested resolution.

Wheel Issues

- The wheel walks away: The chair may be too low or the treadle is being pushed outward rather than downward.

- The wheel doesn't treadle easily: Loosen tension on the drive band and/or the brake band. Check the wheel alignment to see that everything is lined up. Remember to regularly grease the wheel!

Bobbin Take-Up Issues

If the yarn doesn't feed onto the bobbin, it may be caught around one of the bobbin hooks or on another area of the wheel, there may be tension issues (see below), the wheel may be set up incorrectly, or the drive band(s) is in the wrong position(s).

Drafting and Spin Issues

- Fiber breaks before it's spun: Put more fiber into the draft, loosen the wheel tension, and/or go to a smaller whorl.

- Fiber becomes a big swirly mass and doesn't feed onto the bobbin: Put less fiber into the draft, maybe tighten the wheel/brake tension, and/or go to a larger whorl.

- Twist is "bleeding" into the draft in worsted spinning: The forehand pinch isn't being held tightly enough. Stop and roll the twist out of the draft by rolling it in the opposite direction. Readjust the drafting zone and resume spinning.

- Singles have unintentional slubs: Keep an even draft, allowing the twist to enter all fibers. Too much unspun fiber may be in the forehand pinch, so adjust the pinch. Also see if your fiber needs more preparation (carding or combing) prior to spinning.

Break Repairs

- A singles break: Back up the spun yarn and make a drafting triangle that's about the length of the fiber staple. Place an equal staple length of fibers from the fiber supply in a triangle on top of the other drafted triangle. Start up the wheel and draft and spin the triangles together. (This procedure will be familiar to knitters who know the "spit splice" method of fixing yarn breaks in knitting. The spinning version just doesn't need the spit!)

- A ply break: Overlap the broken single into the ply and continue plying, knot the broken singles together and continue to ply, or do the knitters' spit splice to connect the broken singles together and continue to ply.

- The yarn end has disappeared on the bobbin: With a toothbrush, lightly brush across the bobbin in the opposite direction of the wind-on, and the end should pop up.

Repairing a singles break

Repairing a ply break

Tension Issues

- Yarn winds on the bobbin too quickly with little twist: Loosen the wheel tension and/or go to a smaller whorl.

- Yarn winds on the bobbin too slowly and the twist is coiling up: Tighten the wheel tension and/or go to a larger whorl.

- Singles are twisted too tightly: Make more room in the drafting zone or draft and feed faster, tighten the wheel tension, and try to treadle a bit more slowly.

- Singles are twisted too loosely: Draft slower, loosen the wheel tension, feed slower, and try to treadle a bit faster.

Plying Issues

- Yarn is unintentionally uneven with slubs after plying: The singles were unevenly spun. Perhaps too much unspun fiber was held in the singles pinch. Learn from it and move on.

- Yarn has tight and loosely plied areas: The plying was done at different angles or two hands were used to ply. The angle should be kept consistent and try spinning the ply with only one hand.

Twist Issues after the Spin

Too much twist is in the yarn after spinning: Of course, this should be corrected at the time of spinning, but sometimes a spun yarn with too much twist can be resuscitated by taking twist out later. Attach the single or plied yarn to a wheel bobbin, tighten the brake so the yarn will pull onto the bobbin quickly, and spin the spun yarn onto the bobbin in the opposite direction of the problem twist. There's one caveat: When yarn is plied or spun in a tight twist, a condition called "nip" occurs. That's the inherent grabbing of fibers between the plies/fibers. Some yarn fibers may still grab each other when the yarns are untwisted and try to pull themselves back together into the original configuration. This effect is more pronounced in a really grippy wool fiber like mohair or Icelandic wool, in which it can be quite tricky to change the original twist.

Yarn Issues after the Spin

- Fibers are leaking out of the spun yarn: This may happen with fine fibers that haven't been fulled to finish the twist. Fulling (see Finishing Act: Wrapping Up the Spin, page 65) tightens up fine fibers and makes them less likely to pill or fly away in the final product.

- Yarn consistency can be improved by getting all of the fiber for a project from a single source and preparing all of the fiber at the same time.

SA-8: Record Keeping for Spinning

Keeping records of your techniques will help you duplicate yarns and keep your spinning consistent.

Control Cards

These cards are a record of the fiber you used for the spin. They can hold a length of the spun single, a WPI wrap as a yarn thickness guide, a length of the spun single twisted back on itself (your "control" yarn) if you are planning to ply the singles, a record of the TPI, and any other pertinent notes. Refer to your control card to keep your yarn true. When the spinning is done, keep the card as a reference for future projects or to help you recreate the yarn later. I make cards out of large shipping tags and hang them from my wheel for easy reference. When the project is done, I keep the control cards in a three-ring binder for future reference. (Keep the cards in a plastic bag with a tight seal to help keep bugs out. Those critters will even infest your samples if you let them! FA-8: Fiber Storage and Pests, page 170 for more information on how to deal with fiber predators.)

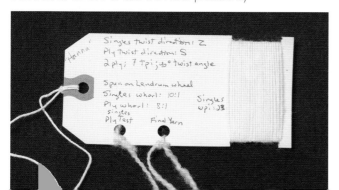

Spin Journal: Record of a Spun Fiber

Include a snippet of the fiber along with a sample of the final spun yarn and a knitted swatch, or another final test sample, if appropriate. Then record these details before you forget them:

Fiber type:

Source of fiber:

Fiber preparation required (washing, carding method, etc.):

Weight after preparation:

Wheel and whorl(s) used:

Spinning method (worsted, woolen, or other—with details):

Singles WPI:

Ply details (single, multiple; with WPI, TPI, and angle of final ply):

Final weight and yarn length:

Finishing technique (washing, setting twist, fulling, etc.):

Dyeing technique used:

Final use of yarn (knitting, crocheting, weaving, other):

Other notes (problems encountered, discoveries, etc.):

Dye Appendices (DA)

DA-1: Dye Workshop Definitions

Adjective dyes. Natural dyes that require mordants to fix the dye to the fiber.

Chemical assistants. Chemicals that alter the dye bath to allow the dye to chemically react or bond to the fiber. In acid dyes, the main assistant is vinegar or citric acid (lowers the pH of the bath). In fiber-reactive dye baths, the main assistant is soda ash (raises the pH of the bath). In natural dye baths, assistants may be mordants, leveling agents, reducing agents, and fixatives.

Dye sites. Molecular areas on a fiber that are structurally suitable for dyestuff to bond with or absorbed into through positive and negative charges. Every fiber has different dye site characteristics, which determine the fiber's suitability for dyeing.

Dye liquor. The dye bath water when it contains dye.

Exhausted dye bath. When all the dye has moved from the dye bath liquor and attached itself to the fiber, leaving a clear dye bath.

Fast. When a dye remains unfaded or otherwise unaltered by light and washing.

Fixatives. Chemicals that specifically help to bind the dye to the fiber. Vinegar or citric acid is the fix for acid dyeing, and soda ash is the fix for fiber-reactive dyeing.

Leveling agent. A chemical that evenly distributes dye to the surface of a fiber. Glauber's salt (decahydrated sodium sulfate—a more efficient leveling agent than table salt) is a leveling agent.

Liquor ratio. The proportion of water to the fiber weight in a dye bath.

LWI. Low water immersion dyeing. A microwave or steam method that uses very little water in the processing.

Mordant. Mordants are metals such as alum, tin, copper, iron, and chromium that are used to prepare fiber to accept natural dyestuff. They chemically bind dye to a fiber surface through their metallic salt chemistry.

Reducing agent. A chemical that removes oxygen from a dye bath, facilitating hydrogen molecules to form bonds between the dye and the fiber. Indigo is a plant dye that needs a reducing agent to bind to fiber.

Stock solution. A concentrated solution created, for example, from dye powder or dyestuff.

Substantive dyes. Natural dyes that can dye fiber without needing a mordant assist.

Vat dyes. Natural dyes requiring fermentation of the dyestuff to make the dye soluble and viable for dyeing.

DA-2: Color Wheel and Dyeing

Most people are familiar with color wheels from school days. This color wheel shows the primary (yellow, red, blue), secondary (orange, violet, green), and tertiary (yellow-green, yellow-orange, red-orange, red-violet, blue-violet, blue-green) colors.

The dye industry has additional color wheel systems to reflect the complexities of mixing color for dye. One simplified system is represented by a triangular color chart using three primary colors in percentage blends. (See DA-3: Guide for Mixing Custom Dye Colors, page 181.)

Dyeing uses the subtractive primary system of color.

- There is a black dye but no white.
- Tints are created by using less dye rather than by adding white.

- Dye manufacturers have their own primary blends that lean toward different directions of the color wheel.
- Primary colors, when mixed equally, become black, but not a pure black, since they carry tones from the colors in the blend.
- Secondary colors are mixes of two primaries, but not equal mixes. For instance, green is not an equal mix of yellow and blue, but rather a mix that has more yellow than blue.

P = Primary Colors
S = Secondary Colors
T = Tertiary Colors

- Tertiary colors are a mix of a primary and a secondary, but also not in equal amounts.
- Brown is orange plus a diluted mix of the three primaries (a gray), but it can also be created with an unequal mixture of the three primaries.

Color by Definition

To help communicate in color, here's a brief list of color terms commonly used by dyers.

Hue: The color name.
Saturation or intensity: The amount of pure color in a hue.
Shade: A hue with black added.
Tone: A hue mixed with its complement or gray.
Value: The lightness or darkness of a hue compared to a gray scale.

DA-3: Guide for Mixing Custom Dye Colors

This pyramid chart represents one method of mixing custom dye colors by percentage. Mixing tones of each color on the chart (by adding percentages of black to the colors) and creating hues (diluting the colors with water) will create entirely different color choices, leading to a huge range of colors from just the three primaries.

NOTE: Grays can be created by mixing in the main color's complementary color—the color across from it on the color wheel.

Dye Colors Cover a Wide Palette

With this chart as a visual guide, you can see that secondary colors can be mixed using different percentages of the primary bases, resulting in up to nine different colors within each secondary range (if using 10 percent intervals), making a total of twenty-seven different secondary hues. The six tertiary colors can also be mixed into nine different colors, making a total of fifty-four different tertiary hues. And of course, each of these colors can be diluted into ten different shades by adding black and tones by adding ranges of grays, making the total color palette choices number in the thousands.

NOTE: Consider switching one of the primary colors in your mix for your own unique colorway. Just changing one of the primaries can change the whole palette of color choices. But if you use colors other than primaries for a base, the colors will be duller, since the manufacturer's mixed dyes already contain a blend of primary colors. Only pure primaries will give pure mixes.

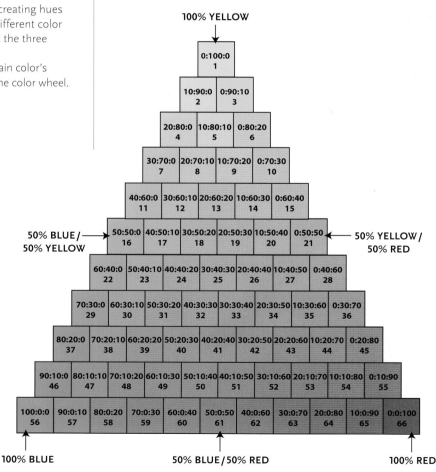

Chart concept adapted from *The Ashford Book of Dyeing* by Ann Milner

DA-4: Measuring Dye Powder Using the Standard DOS (Depth of Shade) Formula

In dyeing, the word *shade* in "depth of shade" doesn't follow the more common color definition of "a color with dark tones added," but is rather the intensity of the pure color. Here is a universal formula to discover how much dye powder to use to achieve standard depths of shade in acid and fiber-reactive dyeing:

Fiber weight (dry) × depth of shade percentage (DOS %) = weight of dye powder needed.

Standard DOS percentages can range from 0.1 percent (very light) to 6 percent (very dark), depending on the color and dyestuff. Some colors dye to different shade depths within the same dye brand. The dye manufacturer can provide a color chart to help determine which DOS to use, or you can create your own through experimentation. In general, acid dyes are based on 1 percent DOS for a medium shade, and fiber-reactive dyes are based on 2 percent DOS to achieve a medium shade.

NOTE: Natural dyestuff quantities to achieve DOS vary greatly among the different natural dye materials. Specialized books on natural dyeing have dye charts that suggest how much natural dyestuff to use for various shades. The ratio for a medium DOS can be as high as 100 percent or more of the dyestuff to the weight of the fiber. If the dyestuff is cooked or allowed to soak longer, the DOS will often become darker. In general, natural dyeing isn't an exact dyeing method, so its DOS is less mathematical and based more on the appearance of the dyed fiber.

Fibers dyed in a DOS range of .1 percent, 1.0 percent, and 2.0 percent

Dye Quantities Based on Depth of Shade (DOS)

It's easiest to use the metric measuring system to determine the percentages. Avoid rounding numbers up or down, as that will affect the accuracy of the color. Unless you use a calculator with a percentage function, remember to move the decimal point two points to the left when multiplying by percentages. These percentages are based on 100 g/3.5 oz of fiber.

Intensity	DOS Percentage	Dye Powder
Pale	0.1%	0.1 g
Medium (acid)/light (fiber-reactive)	1.0%	1.0 g
Dark (acid)/medium (fiber-reactive)	2.0%	2.0 g
Very dark (acid)/dark (fiber-reactive)	4.0%	4.0 g
Very dark (fiber-reactive)	6.0%	6.0 g

Example: 2% DOS × 250g of fiber = 5g of dye powder.

Formula for Mixing Dye Powder for Custom Colors

Mixing colors by percentage is the best way to make consistent color blends. You first need to know the total amount of your dye quantity based on the fiber weight that you've calculated through the previous formula. With that information, follow this formula to calculate your dye quantities:

Weight of dye × % of one color = amount (weight) of dye for one color in blend.

Example for dye quantities based on 5 g of dye for a color blend that's 30 percent cyan and 70 percent red:

5 × 30% cyan = 1.5 g cyan   5 × 70% red = 3.5 g red

DA-5: Recipe for Concentrated Dye Stock Solutions

Follow standard safety precautions when mixing all dyes. Safety information is found on page 85.

The concentrated dye stock solution percentage system is similar to the dye powder DOS numbers discussed in DA-4: Measuring Dye Powder Using the Standard DOS (Depth of Shade) Formula, but for stock solutions, the dye is first turned into liquid form, and the liquid stock is used in a formula relating to the fiber weight.

You can prepare concentrated stock solutions for acid, fiber-reactive, and natural dyes, but they are most useful for acid and fiber-reactive powdered dyestuff, so those are the only dyes used in this workshop. In general, well-stored acid dye stock solutions have a shelf life of up to six months (perhaps more), but fiber-reactive stocks may only last one to two weeks, since they lose their ability to bind with fibers after sitting over time in liquid form. Storage in glass is more stable than plastic. Store the bottles in a cool location out of light. Refrigeration is not necessary.

Stock Solution Recipe

Measure the dye according to the DOS desired and the stock solution (see the chart below). Add 30ml (2 tbsp) of boiling water to the measured dye and mix to create a paste. Mix until smooth, adding more water until you have the percentage you need for the stock solution quantity. Stir until all dye particles have dissolved or there will be "surprise" colors showing up in your fiber or yarn. Mark the bottle with the brand, color, creation date, and dye stock percentage number, and keep it in your inventory for future dyeing.

Milliliters (ml) of water	100	500	1000
0.1% dye stock solution:			
Dye powder	0.1 g	0.5 g	1.0 g

NOTE: many digital scales don't measure less than 1g.

	100	500	1000
1% dye stock solution:			
Dye powder	1 g	5 g	10 g
2% dye stock solution:			
Dye powder	2 g	10 g	20 g
2% dye stock solution:			
Dye powder	4 g	20 g	40 g
6% dye stock solution:			
Dye powder	6 g	30 g	60 g

Formula for Calculating Dye Quantity from Stock Solutions

This may start to get confusing if you're math challenged, like me. The DOS and the strength of dye stock solution are two separate things. The DOS percentage is just the shade, and the strength of dye stock solution refers to the solution percentage that was mixed in the water quantity chosen above. Trust the formula. The examples below have calculations using the far ends of the DOS and dye stock solution percentages and should help you understand the concept.

(Dry weight of fiber × DOS percentage) ÷ strength of dye stock solution = amount of dye solution needed in processing.

Examples:

100 g fiber, 0.1% DOS, 6% dye stock solution:

100 g (3.5 oz) of fiber × 0.1% DOS = 0.1 g
0.1 g ÷ 6% dye stock (g/ml) = 1.67 ml of 6% dye stock needed

100 g fiber, 6% DOS, 0.1% dye stock solution:

100 g (3.5 oz) of fiber × 6% DOS = 6 g
6 g ÷ 0.1% dye stock (g/ml) = 6,000 ml of 0.1% dye stock needed

As you can see, for the same amount of fiber, you need very little of the 6% dye stock solution to reach a 0.1% DOS and quite a lot of the 0.1% dye stock solution to reach a 6% DOS.

The dye stock solution is either put into a dye bath according to the dye method instructions or put into glass bottles for hand painting or future dyeing. Remember to label the bottles with the date, stock solution percentages, and colors.

Formula for Mixing Dye Stock Solutions for Custom Colors

The best way to mix colors is by percentages, but you first need to know the volume of your dye stock solution based on the fiber weight that you've calculated through the previous stock solution formulas. The following formula will work only if the dye stock solutions being mixed have the same DOS concentration.

Follow this formula to calculate your dye stock solution quantities:

Volume of dye stock × % of color A = volume of stock solution for color A in blend.

Example: Using the dye stock example from the previous formula (for a color that requires 20 percent magenta and 80 percent yellow):

For 100g of fiber with a stock solution volume of 6000 ml:

6,000 ml × 20% magenta = 1,200 ml magenta
6,000 ml × 80% yellow = 4,800 ml yellow

DA-6: "Painting" with Fleece

Hand carders, drum carders, and hackles make great tools for blending primary colors into new colors for spinning.

The Color Wheel in Dyed Fiber

Six Basic Color Blending Schemes

These guides will help you pick harmonious colors when blending fibers.

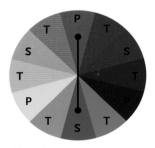

1. Complementary

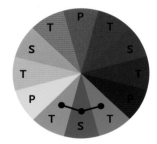

2. Analogous

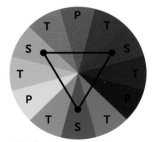

3. Triadic

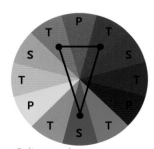

4. Split-complementary

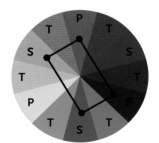

5. Rectangle/tetradic

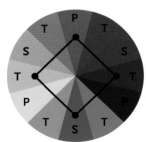

6. Square

DA-7: Record Keeping for Dyeing: A Dye Journal

As with spinning, it's good to note details about your dyeing process, especially if you hope to some day recreate the color. Fill in all applicable information below and include a sample of the dyed fiber in your journal record.

Date:

Fiber type and name:

Fiber preparation:

If yarn, type of spin, ply, etc.:

Dry weight:

Presoak method:

Dye brand or natural dyestuff used:

Dye colors used:

DOS %, all colors:

Quantity of dye stock used (powder), all colors:

Quantity of dye stock used (solution), all colors:

Dye bath volume:

Mordants used, quantity, soak time:

Chemical assists used and quantity:
Vinegar: Citric acid crystals: Glauber's salt:
Soda ash: Other:

Cooking method used:
Immersion   Hand-paint   Other

Cooking process:
Kettle   Slow cooker   Microwave
Steam   Other

Times for individual processes (if applicable):

Dye bath temperature:

Total fiber cooking time:

If hand painted, painting method used:

Quantity of dye stock solution(s):

Adjustments to dye stock solution(s):

Additional materials used and their weights/volumes:

Other notes (problems encountered, discoveries, etc.):

DA-8: Worksheet for Jacquard Acid Dye Immersion Dyeing

DA-4 and DA-5 contain instructions for measuring dye quantity based on fiber weight.

Photocopy or scan this worksheet and enter your fiber weight and other particulars in the spaces provided. Place the worksheet in your spin/dye journal so you know how to reproduce the color later.

Fiber	Wool and Other Animal Fibers	Silk	Nylon
Dry fiber weight:	_____g	_____g	_____g
Dye powder or dye solution:	_____g or _____ml	_____g or _____ml	_____g or _____ml
Max cooking temp:	212°F (100°C)	185°F (85°C)	194°F (90°C)
Dye Liquor* (water) 3 L (3.2 qt) to 100 g (3.5 oz) of fiber	_____L	_____L	_____L
Acid quantity: Vinegar – 44 ml (3 tbsp) per 100 g (3.5 oz) fiber:	_____ml	_____ml	_____ml
OR citric acid crystals (dissolve in 236 ml/1 c hot water) 4.5 g (1 tsp) per 100 g (3.5 oz) fiber:	_____g	_____g	_____g
Cooking time:	30 min	30 min	45-60 min

*Dye liquor (dye bath) volume includes the dye solution volume if a dye stock solution was used. The acid solution is in addition to the dye liquor volume.

DA-9: Worksheet for Fiber-Reactive Procion MX Dye (for cotton & bast fibers)

DA-4 and DA-5 contain instructions for measuring dye quantity based on fiber weight.

Photocopy or scan this worksheet and enter your fiber weight and other specific details in the spaces provided. Place the worksheet in your spin/dye journal so you know how to reproduce the color later.

Dry fiber weight: _____ g

Dye powder or
 dye solution: _____ g or _____ ml

Max cooking temp: 86°F (30°C)

Dye liquor* (water):
 3 L (3.2 qt) to 100 g (3.5 oz) of fiber _____ L

Glauber's salt**: _____ g

Soda ash***: _____ g or _____ ml

Dye time: 1½ hours

Dye liquor (dye bath) volume includes the dye solution volume (if a dye stock solution was used) and the volume of water used to dissolve the salt and soda ash.

**Salt quantity is determined by the weight of the fiber and DOS. Follow this chart and multiply the percentage of salt (see DOS and Salt Percentage Equivalent chart below) by the fiber weight. (For example: 100 g of fiber and a DOS of 2 percent: 0.90 × 100 g = 90 g)*

DOS and Salt Percentage Equivalent Chart

DOS	% of Salt (× Fiber Weight)
Up to 0.5%	20%
0.5 to 2%	50%
2% to 4%	90%
4%	110%

***12 g (4 tsp) per 100g (3.5 oz) of fiber. Or make a soda ash stock solution by mixing 45g (5 tbsp) of soda ash in 500 ml (2 C) of water. Use 125 ml (½ C) of the stock for every 100 g (3.5 oz) of fiber. (Refer to DA-5, page 183 for storage information.)*

General Appendices

Measurements for Spinners, Dyers, and Knitters

Abbreviations

in.	inch	mm	millimeter
yd	yard	m	meter
tsp	teaspoon	kg	kilogram
tbsp	tablespoon	g	gram
C	cup	L	liter
pt	pint	ml	milliliter
qt	quart	dl	deciliter
gal	gallon	F	Fahrenheit
oz	ounce	C	Celsius
cm	centimeter		

U.S. Volume Comparison Measures

1 gal = 4 qt = 8 pt = 16 C = 128 fl oz
1 qt = 2 pt = 4 C = 32 fl oz
1 pt = 2 C = 16 fl oz
1 C = 8 fl oz = 16 tbsp
½ C = 4 fl oz = 8 tbsp
1 fl oz = 2 tbsp
1 tbsp = ½ fl oz = 3 tsp

Length—U.S. to Metric

U.S. Measurement	Metric Measurement (metric equivalents are rounded)
1 in.	2.5 cm
4 in.	10.0 cm
1 ft/12 in.	30.5 cm
1 yd/36 in./3 ft	0.9 m
1.1 yd/39.4 in.	1.0 m

Volume—U.S. to Metric

U.S. Measurement	Metric Measurement (metric equivalents are rounded)
1 tsp	5 ml
1 tbsp	15 ml
1 fl oz/2 tbsp	30 ml
2 fl oz/¼ C	60 ml
8 fl oz/1 C	240 ml
16 fl oz/2 C/1 pt	480 ml
32 fl oz/2 pt/1 qt	950 ml
1.06 qt	1 L
128 fl oz/4 qt/1 gal	3.8 L

Weight—U.S. to Metric

U.S. Measurement	Metric Measurement (metric equivalents are rounded)
.03 oz	1 g
¼ oz	8 g
½ oz	15 g
1 oz	30 g
4 oz	115 g
8 oz/½ lb	225 g
16 oz/1 lb	450 g
2.2 lb	1 kg

Conversion Formulas

To convert ounces to grams: multiply ounces × 28.35

To convert pounds to grams: multiply pounds × 453.59

To convert Fahrenheit degrees (F) to Celsius degrees (C):
°C = (°F−32) × 0.56

To convert Celsius degrees (C) to Fahrenheit degrees:
°F = (°C × 1.8) + 32

Knitting Abbreviations

beg	begin, beginning, begins
BO	bind off
CC	contrast color
cm	centimeter(s)
CO	cast on
cont	continue, continuing
dec(s)	decrease, decreasing, decreases
dpn	double-pointed needle(s)
est	establish, established
foll	follow(s), following
inc(s)	increase(s), increasing
k	knit
k1f&b	knit into front then back of same st (increase)
k1f,b,&f	knitting into front, back, then front again of same st (increase 2 sts)
k1-tbl	knit 1 st through back loop
k2tog	knit 2 sts together (decrease)
k2tog-tbl	knit 2 sts together through back loops
kwise	knitwise (as if to knit)
LH	left-hand
m(s)	marker(s)
MC	main color
mm	millimeter(s)
M1	make 1 (increase)
M1k	make 1 knitwise
M1p	make 1 purlwise
pat(s)	pattern(s)
p	purl
p1f&b	purl into front then back of same st (increase)
p1-tbl	purl 1 st through back loop
p2tog	purl 2 sts together (decrease)
pm	place marker
psso	pass slip st(s) over
pwise	purlwise (as if to purl)
rem	remain(s), remaining
rep(s)	repeat(s), repeated, repeating
rnd(s)	round(s)
RH	right-hand
RS	right side (of work)
revsc	reverse single crochet (crab st)
sc	single crochet
sl	slip, slipped, slipping
ssk	[slip 1 stknitwise] twice from left needle to right needle, insert left needle tip into fronts of both slipped sts, knit both sts together from this position (decrease)
ssp	[slip 1 stknitwise] twice from left needle to right needle, return both sts to left needle and purl both together through back loops
st(s)	stitch(es)
St st	stockinette stitch
tbl	through back loop
tog	together
W&T	wrap next stitch then turn work (used in short rows)
WS	wrong side (of work)
wyib	with yarn in back
wyif	with yarn in front
yb	yarn back
yf	yarn forward
yo	yarn over
✢	repeat instructions from ✢
( )	alternate measurements and/or instructions
[ ]	instructions to be worked as a group a specified number of times

Acknowledgments

As with any endeavor of this size and detail, there are many people and organizations to thank. In particular: Ashland Bay Trading Co. (Jill and Jim Laski); Marlene Banttari; The Cottonman (Butch); Elena and Rita Doucet-Beer; Drummond Farms Alpacas (Leslie Peterson); Gale Woods Farm/Three Rivers Park District (Tim Reese, Shari Polzin, and all the staff); Solveig Gustafsson; Susanna Hansson; International Fleeces; Jacquard Dyes (Michael Katz); the Knitters With Attitude (Barb, Colleen, Evelyn, Gerri, and Rebecca); Little Gidding Farm (Margaret Long & Sue Simonton); Mielke's Fiber Arts; Minnesota Textile Center Library (Nanci Mambi); Amanda Naughton; Oldhaus Fibers & Rabbits (Kathi & Joel Huebner); Paradise Fibers; Todd Randall; Karen Searle; Sogn Valley Border Collies (Kathy Flynn); R.S.; The Cat That Walks on Water (Colleen Werdien); Treenway Silks; and Woolen Meadow Farm (Sue Ross). So many people have helped me to open doors and move ahead. If I have forgotten anyone, please forgive me for it wasn't intentional.

A special thank you to my editor, Kari Cornell, who maintained her calm nature when the Spin Workshop section first came in at nearly the number of words the entire book was supposed to be; my sister, Shelley Johnson, for reviewing drafts from an editorial and organic chemistry perspective; Detta Juusola of Detta's Spindle, who loaned me tools and a great photography site for some of the pattern projects, along with her friendship during this arduous task; Charlotte Quiggle, for her brilliance in pattern editing and saving me when my rattled brain could no longer add two and two together; and to the talented design staff at CPI who went above and beyond to make it all come together in the form you see before you.

And finally, thank you to my husband, Jim Gambone, for not only being the photographer when I needed to be in the shot but also for always encouraging my creative endeavors.

About the Author

W. J. Johnson (*a.k.a. Wendy J. Johnson*) has been spinning, dyeing, and knitting for more than thirty years. She has a BA in Fine Arts and Music with additional arts education in Filmmaking, Fiber Arts, Graphic Design, and Architecture. She is a fiber artist, photographer, media and installation artist, and educator in the fiber arts, with an emphasis on spinning, dyeing, felting, weaving, and knitting. Her fiber arts, photography, and fine art work is highlighted in her company Saga Hill Designs, www.SagaHill.com. She is a champion for Swedish textile arts and has facilitated exhibits on Swedish knitting artists (Elsebeth Lavold, Inger Fredholm, and Bohus Stickning—at the American Swedish Institute in Minneapolis, Minn.). Wendy is a principal author, photographer, and designer of the book *Bohus Stickning—Radiant Knits: An Enchanting Obsession*; and has published knitting patterns in the books *Knitting Socks from Around the World*, *Knitting Scarves from Around the World*, and *Baby Knits from Around the World*. She is also the President and Art Director of Points Of View Productions, a multimedia company; and founder of Elder Eye Design, where she is "The Legibility Doctor," advising clients on legibility issues in print, space design, and products for the aging eye. On the side, Wendy visits fleece on the hoof as she and her border collies attempt to "come by" sheep every so often in a dance called "herding." Wendy lives in an area west of Minneapolis with her husband and two crazy border collies in a home she designed using aging-friendly principles.

Index